Mist Over the Meadows

The Columns of
Ron LeHew

Volume One: 1989-1991

MIST OVER THE MEADOWS
THE COLUMNS OF RON LEHEW
VOLUME ONE: 1989-1991
by
Ron LeHew
149 Sherron Avenue
Salem, NJ 08079
856-339-0079
ronlehew@dandy.net

Copyright © 2006

Library of Congress Number: 2006937314
International Standard Book Number: 1-60126-007-5

Front cover photograph: © Jeanne Brandiff LeHew
"Meadow Quietude"

Back cover photograph: © Mary S. Smith

Printed at
Masthof Press
219 Mill Road
Morgantown, PA 19543-9516

CONTENTS

ACKNOWLEDGMENTS

In grateful and heartfelt appreciation for the following people who so unselfishly gave their support and encouragement . . .

Irene and Bill Brown
Jack and Trudi Hathaway
Ralph and Mary Ann Lyford
Bob Johnson,
    Salem City Councilman
Rick Neuroth
Raymond L. Sheppard
Terry and Pat Wright
Elaine Trumbull
George and Ann Tatnall
Ross Levitsky, Esquire
Steve and MaryAnn Hassler
Frank and Carole Green
Jack and Janet Elk
Ron Zarin, CPA
Ralph and Rita Dean
Joe and Mary Jane Hudock
Joe and "Treasure" Lombardo
Ron and Marcia Fann
William and Marian Aldrich
The Wagon Wheel Restaurant
    Paul and Sharon Langley,
    Owners

Al and Betty Giumetti
George and Marcy Lewis
Forrest and Judi Houtz
Ed Sykes,
    Parker Jewelers, Inc.
Norm and Linda Myers
Mad Horse Crab Company
Paul Trumbull, Jr.
Tom and Jodi K'Burg
Joe and Loretta Colanero
A Caring Friend
Susan Clark Hamant
Diana Locuson
Leigh Ingersoll
Rae McDowell
Vic and Pat Major
Bill and Jeanette Mahan
Paul and Bobbi Jo Coblentz
John and Margo Desparrois, Sr.
Dr. Curtis and Linda Lockwood
Sylvia Kimmel
Alfred J. Nicolosi

DEDICATION

This book is lovingly dedicated to my incredible mother,

ANNA MARY LEHEW

. . . who plunked me down in a corner of her kitchen, between the supper table and the drain board, and there built herself an artist, a dreamer, and a horrid Romantic.

And to all those who kept the faith, and always believed—

FOREWORD

This book of columns is the result of a myriad of colliding courses. All of which I find wonderfully exciting, perhaps even *wondrously* exciting.

I always joked and said my column writing career came about because *Today's Sunbeam* editor, John Schoonejongen, tired of publishing my "Letters to the Editor." John, and Bill Long, my hero-mentor who was then editor of *The Gloucester County Times*, came up with the idea of my doing a column.

In the spring of 1989, when the idea of writing a column was presented to me, John believed I should write from my perspective as an artist. In my excitement, I heard incorrectly what the column paid and accepted the assignment at half of what I thought I heard!

Before I even set pen to paper I would learn of two things in life that don't pay: crime and writing columns. Artwork runs a real close second!

Duped as I was, I was in it for the duration. Long before this column, I wistfully would ponder how sweet life would be if I could be an artist the first half, and a writer for the second half.

The column fell into my lap at just about that halfway mark.

And then there was you . . .

Creativity cannot be practiced in a vacuum. It needs nurturing and encouragement. It needs to be admired and appreciated for the force it is. And you give it to me in wonderful, loving measure. I have the letters, phone calls, notes, e-mails, conversations and the sweet memories to prove it.

I hope you enjoy this collection of columns from the first three years. The comment I hear most often is that sometimes the columns make you laugh, and sometimes they make you cry. Just the other day someone said, ". . . and they make me think and ponder, and that's good too!"

In the long, long ago a writer friend first told me that I, ". . . use words to paint beautiful pictures." Thank you for the blessing you are. I hope you like the paintings.

Ron LeHew, Salem County, October 19, 2006

Today's Sunbeam, Salem, N.J., Thursday, May 4, 1989

Beginning this Sunday . . .

A Unique View of Salem County

Ron LeHew, a well-known local artist and resident, has long been an advocate of the inspirational beauty of Salem County. His unique view of the area in which we live has been on display numerous times at several local schools and buildings. He also has lectured to a number of community groups throughout the Delaware Valley.

Now, LeHew will be sharing his thoughts on the county he deeply loves in a column that will appear every other Sunday in *Today's Sunbeam*. His first column will appear this Sunday, May 7.

We welcome LeHew as he extends his artistic endeavors to the world of journalism, and hope our readers will enjoy this new feature.

Ron LeHew

Today's
Sunbeam
Columns

1989

Today's Sunbeam, Salem, N.J., Thursday, May 7, 1989

There's No Better Place than Salem Co. to Call Home

I had been asked by *Today's Sunbeam* if I'd consider doing a column that would consist of impressions and observations on life here in the county as I saw them and as I experienced them. Being a believer in snap decisions, I quickly said, "Yes!"

I am thrilled, flattered, scared and excited over this new opportunity to be creative and to show and share with others the world around them. The world being, in this case, Salem County.

Feelings are premier to the artist. It is what he lives for and exists on, and now I have been given the chance to share my feelings about all those wonderful things that I feel are so worthwhile about this area. I see this column dealing with the spirit of the people who live here, the old-timers and the newcomers; the exciting fun times that can be found here; the beauty of its landscapes; and the history that is pervasive to it all.

What really is scary is that every English teacher I ever had is still alive to see this dawning of a bold new day in journalism!

People around here have been so generous in their support of some of the "Letters to the Editor" that I have written in the past. There are so many folks out there that really do believe that this corner of God's vineyard is one of the sweetest and best of all because it is home . . . it is where the friends of a lifetime live and work.

People do take time to be friendly and neighborly. People do care about each other, and in this day and age, that is a gift that far surpasses worldly wealth.

On trips to Philly or New York, I couldn't help but notice just how isolated and alone people are in jam-packed theater lobbies, subways and museum shops. They know only the person that they are with, if they are lucky enough to be with someone. I couldn't help but wonder if relationships aren't more intense because it's only "you and me" amid all the others.

In Salem County you can travel to any of the towns and attend a Market Street Day, the Woodstown by Candlelight tour, Septemberfest, Crafts on the Delaware, Alloway Halloween Parade, the Elmer Hospital Day or LAC Day and always see someone you went to school with, someone you work with, an old neighbor, a church member, etc.

You get to laugh and joke, or moan and complain, but at least you are among folks you know. You're a part of the festivity. Its success depends on you being there! The events are all the nicer because you get to renew old friendships and create new ones!

I have a deep unabashed love for this area and its people. I am very content with my life here. I hope and pray for good things for this column. There are always going to be folks who stamp and stomp and spit and sputter over the conditions of things in the county. There are just some folks who wouldn't be happy even if you hung them with a new rope! We need all kinds to make this county function.

Artists, by tradition, have always been chroniclers of their times and their locales. Some have used poison pen, others are dreamers and romantics.

It has been said that artists create the world closer to their heart's desire . . . being an artist before I am a writer, I find that it is from this background that I perceive my world and it is from this background that I intend to write.

I am not blind to the problems here in the county, but I do prefer to let others, who are better qualified and of that temperament, deal with them. I see the good of this county far outweighing the problems.

I believe that this area has a wonderful spectrum of concerned, caring, and talented people and that excites me no end! I may have rose-colored bifocals, but I love the view from here!

The late, very beloved Tommy Grieves, former Salem mayor and long-term county clerk, always said that he never left the county for his vacation because what place could be any better than this? I pray that if artists/writers have guardian angels, that Tommy Grieves is looking after me and this column!

Today's Sunbeam, Salem, N.J., Sunday May 21, 1989

A Place of Peace, Beauty

In Flanders Fields the poppies blow
between the crosses, row on row. . .

There is a picture of peace, and of calm, and of a great stillness that these lines bring to me when I read this poem. The poem describes the final resting place of Allied soldiers who died on the battlefields of Belgium during World War I.

In our county, we, too, have a final resting place; a piece of hallowed ground for our war dead that is one of the most serene and tranquil spots anywhere; a place so emblematical of the peace that I find in the words of Capt. John McCrea's poem.

I love to visit Finn's Point Cemetery. On a summer afternoon you can sit under those great tall pines and hear the rush of the wind through their branches. The grass shimmers in sunlit-sparkled waves as the breeze from off the river moves over and around that beautiful area.

Your eyes come to rest on the Confederate Memorial. With quiet, white dignity, it rises upwards to mark the final resting place of more than 2,000 Confederate soldiers. These men died such lonely, tragic deaths on Pea Patch Island during the Civil War, and are buried so far from home and those who loved them.

Over to the side are the graves of 13 German POWs. Here and there are the graves of others who gave their lives, or a portion of such, to the defense of their country and its ideals, ideas and its freedoms that have brought me to this moment and this place.

The beauty and calm of Finn's Point does not allow one to contemplate the politics and the policies of war . . . our emotions are stirred by the fact that these were men that, for most, "twilight came far too early in the day."

After every Memorial Day parade when I was a kid, my mother would hurry me over to the great iron fence on the courthouse lawn and we would view the services for the war dead. For most of the years that I was growing up, I had an older brother who was a professional soldier. To me, he was a hero in the finest tradition of a John Wayne.

Being a kid meant that I would tire of the speaker rather quickly, and so would find myself reading all those names on that huge stone monument. As I would read them, thoughts would come to me that someday my big brother's name could be there along with the others and how awful that would be.

I would dismiss this silly, inane thought because I just knew it could never happen. The John Waynes of this world always came home.

As I read the names, I would try so hard to envision them for the real people that they had been, and wonder all sorts of things about what they had been like. It seemed really important to me to be able to sense that they once lived in this town, this area, this county.

I still attend the services on Memorial Day morning, parade or no parade. It seems that very few people attend the services anymore. As I am told, the other services held elsewhere in the county are not attended in much force either. Why this lack of interest? Can we be this uncaring and forgetful?

We always seem to be talking and lamenting about how the real meaning of our holidays is slipping from us. We have come pretty close to eliminating Christ from Christmas. Thanksgiving has now become a day of feasting to pack in the calories to fortify and sustain us for the next thirty days of maddening shopping. It's probably also our last home-cooked meal till Christmas.

Memorial Day seems to be slipping into this syndrome as well. We read Sleazy Sid's Mattress City is holding a "Memorial Day Madness Sale" using ads decorated with stars and stripes and silhouettes of buglers and rifles. This slipping away and letting go to me is a very sad blow to our moral fiber as Americans. We should feel the need to give a sense of respect, honor and patriotism to the next generation, and not let the meaning of this day slide into oblivion.

We do not need to glorify and romanticize the war. We can leave that to the moviemakers and writers. But, to forget those who died in these wars, worse even, to just not care or not give a moment's thought to them on this day, is as sorry a sin against humanity and country as I can think of.

They were real people. They walked the same streets that we do now. They were behind us or ahead of us in school. They loved the seasons. Holidays excited them. Their deaths forever changed the lives of their families and loved ones. They dreamed dreams of and for all their tomorrows. And now they are gone.

Early on Memorial Day mornings, St. John's churchyard has many quiet, lovely, shaded areas. From any one of them, I can see the sun shining on the flag that marks my brother's grave.

On those mornings an American Legion rifle squad and a bugler arrive. Shots are fired. "Taps" are played. And I am again, for an instant, swept back to 1966: a telegram, a heartbroken mother, a widow with a young family. I know again that I have a real investment in Memorial Day.

I love picnics on Memorial Day. Friends of ours always invite us out to Mannington for one every year. About mid-March I start figuring out picnic attire and I just get all excited about going and seeing all the folks who will be there! That first charred burger or hot dog is to picnic season what throwing out the first ball is to baseball! What a warm, loving, happy time we will all have!

As we leave in the evening, a neighboring farm is silhouetted in the glow of a full moon rising through the trees. Newly-cultivated fields pick up the silver light. So peaceful, so calm, so uniquely American is the scene. As the morning of this day started with thoughts of others, it so ends now. A day in which I hope I lived every moment as a tribute to their sacrifice and their gift of freedom to me and mine.

Capt. John McCrae did not survive the war and someone else penned these lines:

> The fury of the battle hell
> Shall wake you not, for all is well;
> Sleep peacefully for all is well.

Today's Sunbeam, Salem, N.J., Sunday, June 4, 1989

An Affair of the Heart Amid a Mannington Meadow

To the good, quiet and gentle folk of Mannington, I have to inform you of an "affair" that is taking place in your own backyard! It involves a local artist and about eight to ten of your women-folk! A sort of " . . . amour amid a Mannington Meadow!"

This amorous adventure really is another way of describing a weekly reading group that is happening at the Salem County Nursing Home. This group started out early this spring and grew out of a desire to have a Lenten project where I could share a love of reading with others. It ended up snowballing emotionally for me over the next 40 days. What started as an attempt to give to others only seemed to get me deeper in debt! I am now blessed with many new friends that have made my life all the sweeter and richer. I was warned that this could happen. It did and I love it!

The first day I ventured forth armed with five days of "Dear Abby" columns, three books of poetry, the Bible, *Today's Sunbeam* and the latest copy of the *Ladies Home Journal.* I arrived very nervous and filled with trepidation. I promised myself that next year I'd give up chocolate or something a little less committal.

The first people to greet me were Callie Davis and Margaret Sickler. Consider this an open epistle of love to these two wonderful ladies who run the social activities at the home. Whoever coined the phrase "unsung heroes" must have know the two of them!

They both assured me that this whole thing was going to work out just fine. Callie and Margaret brought in about ten ladies who were interested in this reading activity. Over the next few days we all exchanged polite and pleasant bits of conversation. We sort of felt each other out and jockeyed for position.

Rather quickly personalities started to emerge, then gel, then mesh and then the fun began! I feel like Johnny Carson describing an audience. These gals are fabulous!

We joke and laugh and tease and flirt with each other . . . we share quiet misty thoughts at times. It seems that we are all just happy to share each others company for an hour or so.

On Valentine's Day, I brought them flowers and read them love poems. On my birthday they fooled me into a surprise party. Surrounded by 12 lovely women and a chocolate layer cake is a wonderful way to approach mid 40s! Their thoughtfulness was truly a gift in the sweetest sense.

My friend Georgia and her stuffed doll named Butterball always sit right next to me . . . when she laughs her whole body has a good time!

Edie has twinkly eyes and a smile like Fred Sanford. Edie always falls asleep the minute I start to read and will wake up the minute I stop! She then will always tell me how much she enjoyed the story or the article!

And Betty. Without Betty the group lacks a bit of its luster and gaiety. Betty is full of spunk and the devil and she always laughs in all the right places!

Edna adds a real class to the group. She comes with her jewelry and coiffed hair as if she were attending the orchestra or theatre.

Gertrude is 95-years-old and will open the door for me when I retire to the home some years down the line. She looks, thinks, and acts as if she were about 60! She is proof that spending your whole life in Philadelphia could have some health benefits!

Dot never misses a word and is our most intent listener. Teressa is our quietest yet has a smile that can light up half the home!

These six are my steadies. There are four to six others who will attend while alternating between visitors, doctors and their favorite soap opera.

I look forward to my visits with them. As I walk through the main social hall I'd be heartbroken if Georgia didn't call out my name. That's my cue to then offer to push her wheelchair down to our reading room. I think about them, I worry about them . . . they have all become a great source of happiness and friendship for me.

In today's press we see so many articles and newscasts that speak of horrible conditions that are found in some nursing and convalescent homes. I came out to this one and wasn't sure what type of world I'd be entering. We all think of "homes" and shudder and hope we never have to move into one.

If anything shocked me it was the amount of love and affection that I have seen displayed between the patients and staff. It seems to flow so effortlessly from the director, the office staff, the nurses, the orderlies and just everyone who comes in contact with the residents.

Love does exist " . . . amid a Mannington Meadow." It dwells here, it pervades here and this county can be proud and fortunate to have it here in its midst.

The place in not Disney World. It is not a live-in country club. By nature of its role to and in society, it is what it is however your mind wishes to see it. I feel that it could offer some great opportunities spiritually and mentally to anyone who could afford to give an hour or so a week out there.

On weekends, Georgia and Butterball sit out in the lobby and preside over the guest book. They greet all the visitors and are sort of the unofficial hostesses for the home.

I hope the freeholders know and realize the great P.R. job the two of them are doing!

Today's Sunbeam, Salem, N.J., Sunday, June 18, 1989

Salem County: A Diverse Landscape All Can Enjoy

Have you ever noticed that when you are coming home from Delaware to New Jersey, if you stay far over in the right lane as you approach the Twin Bridges, you get a fantastic view of that great expanse of towers and roadways sweeping around in a flowing majestic curve. What a sight!

Modern sculpture usually leaves me uninspired and confused but if there was a creation of beauty made from nuts and bolts, cables and "I" beams, those bridges have my vote! Soon after crossing this wondrous piece of design, you can be passing through the trees and the lovely area of water and marsh reeds near Cedar Crest Manor.

This marvelous contrast in visual delights is but one example of the diversity of the landscape here in our area. Our landscape changes about every 37 feet or close to that at least! We live surrounded by a real visual bounty.

The land around here is a wonderfully rich study in rhythms and textures and variations. We have views and vistas that can be heart-achingly beautiful, sweetly nostalgic, humorous, powerful and delicate.

Last summer while on a trip to the Great Smoky Mountains, I was awed and breathless to see the mountains with each new day. What a thrill to see the flow of blues and grays as mountains overlapped mountains. After a while, I began to realize that all I saw was just mountains.

The trees on the mountains hid everything from view; no open fields, no houses, no farms, an occasional town down in a valley. Very little change to the world around you. How different it is here in Salem County where we have such a variety of delights for the eye!

Here's some woods! Oops! All of a sudden we are now looking at acres of wheat stubble poking up through the snow! Cows! Pigs! Herons! Wild geese! A great huge body of water and foxtails all against a sky set aglow with the colors of a setting sun or winter's sunrise!

A lovely stately Federal period home appears on the horizon out of a Dutch genre painting scenario of wonderful billowy, rolling, tumbling clouds. And then . . . a town.

If you're lucky, you may be coming into Alloway. I always think that the center of Alloway must be the epitome of "crossroads America."

Or, you may be in Hancocks Bridge, where your sense of history and imagination will allow you to see the very meadows that a troop of the Queen's Rangers crept through in the early hours of a

March morning over 200 years ago to massacre those asleep in the Hancock House.

You may even find yourself buying lunch at the little store in Harmersville. It's fun to drive on down to Maskell's Mill and have your lunch and view the beauty and peace of the mill pond, especially on a fall afternoon.

My son and I love to go fishing on the lake in Woodstown which has a beauty and a serenity at almost any hour of the day. It seems so fitting that they call it Memorial Lake.

It is with sweet reverence that I love to describe this area to friends who live in the city. I talk of how you are hardly ever more than a ten-or twenty-minute walk from seeing cows in a field, a patch of woods or a meadow.

On this walk you can pick several varieties of wild flowers, sometimes see a beautiful blue heron gliding over a ribbon of water.

We live surrounded by nature. We are made so aware of its cycles, it seasonal changes. It expresses itself with a look that is only of that season, a set of colors and lines, edges of trees and fields and barns are lost in rainy, foggy, wintry mists as in an oriental watercolor, or pronounced crisp and clean and defined in the morning sun of December.

Loving this county and writing this column is not without its perils and trials and tribulations.

A case in point: in the midst of working on it the other day, a friend called and asked me to join a group of folks for lunch. Off I go just filled to the brim with an "up with nature" attitude only to find myself having lunch with at least three guys from Cherry Hill.

Normally I have no problem with the fine folk of Cherry Hill, after all some of the best friends I have live there, but these three upon hearing of my morning's work and the text of this column, could only start to boo and hiss and hoot and holler over how awful life is here in Salem County!

I leaped to my feet and with pen in hand quickly pointed out that Cherry Hill had 36 million people per square mile, 96 million cars, six squirrels, and only four trees. They quickly agreed and, to a man, expressed a fervent hope that the four trees would soon catch a disease and die so that another convenience store could be erected over their decaying roots!

One of my antagonizers looked at me . . . his eyes glazing over, sighed deeply and whispered low and said, "Ah, yes! There is nothing I love better than the feel of concrete between my toes!"

Their outlook was that any place where it took you more than two minutes to reach a 7-Eleven store, a movie theatre, a mall or the interstate was just not worth living in! Salem County to these guys was New Jersey's answer to the "outback" of Australia!

Perhaps it's this kind of "outlook and mentality that allows contractors to bulldoze acres of fruit orchards and then have the nerve to call it "Peachtree Acre Estates." What of a "Meadowview Mall?"

At least if they have cut it all down and buried it under concrete and plywood, by giving it such quaint names, they have helped to memorialize and forever keep its beauty close to our hearts and minds while robbing it from our sight. Thank goodness for small favors!

"No, Virginia, I have no idea where they ever found such a silly name as Cherry Hill."

G'day mates.

Today's Sunbeam, Salem, N.J., Sunday, July 2, 1989

Parades Help Make a Holiday a Special Day

From early on I have always remembered hearing the phrase "by and by it'll be Fourth of July." Believe it or not, it's now here.

To have a Fourth of July without a parade as part of your day is about as tragic as not having any fireworks, hot dogs or hearing the 1812 Overture at least once, if not preferably 15 times during the day!

Salem County is a real parade-lover's paradise. Pennsville gives us the Septemberfest Parade which is a farewell to summer ritual. No respectable witch, ghost or goblin could celebrate Halloween without marching through Alloway!

Christmas without the Salem Christmas Parade would be like . . . well, it just wouldn't be Christmas! I guarantee there will be more about these parades in future columns!

All of the above parades have grown and expanded in leaps and bounds since their inceptions over the past several years. Many dedicated man-hours throughout the year are involved in their planning and logistics.

The sweet results are a delightful couple of hours of merriment, pageantry and entertainment on a grand scale! All those readers who dislike parades, please turn the page.

Shh . . . (read on in a whisper please). I am now going to share with you my feelings about the neatest little parade around and a big favorite of mine.

This parade is completely unplanned until the morning of the parade when the participants decide to register! Until moments before, the organizers have no idea who or what will be in it! It's a sort of "potluck parade," if you will.

This marvelous morsel of street-fare is the Woodstown Fourth of July Parade! When you talk of all that is American, "Mom, flag and apple pie," you just have to be talking about the charm and fun of this parade.

To best enjoy this parade I have come to realize that it is more than just a visual experience. One needs to enter into a "state of mind."

Your sense of appreciation and the ambiance of the parade change in direct proportion to the architecture around as a backdrop, how many wonderful old trees are shading you, and your curbside companions mean a lot also!

Our vantage point for the parade is from the front yard and the steps of the Hutchison home on South Main Street. They have invited the same basic group of parade aficionados to their home every year. We have, over the years, become quite the experts on parade perusal.

They usually invite a new couple that the others don't know as a sort of "parade opinion control."

It's so much fun to sit among such avid, devoted parade watchers and have coffee, tea and all other creature comforts, and wave and cheer without choking to death or throwing your iced tea in the ear of the person sitting next to you!

As we group our chairs and gather the friends and goodies together, the various squeals and hops and skips of the kids let us know the parade is on its way!

So much of the fun and enjoyment of parades is being able to wave and applaud all the various people who are marching or riding in it. It really makes little difference whether you know them or not. It's just a fun way to participate, to feel a part of it all, to let your body realize it's not watching television!

Your enthusiasm gives the folks in the parade an audience to play to. It's a way of letting them know you appreciate the hours and efforts that they put into a restored antique car, a polished fire engine, creating a costume or decorating a bike.

The Woodstown parade is so much a kids parade. Your feelings of joy and happiness that you derive from it deals, in part, because of all the children who participate in it. The adults, who participate have been caught up in their surroundings and appear with the same glee and exuberance as the young ones.

Children have that magical power to elicit the emotions in all of us. How super it is to watch these kids play out their various roles.

Some of them know they look silly in a certain costume and play out this silliness to everyone's delight. Other walk down Main Street as if they were the very embodiment of an Uncle Sam or a Statue of Liberty.

They bring to their role a dignity and seriousness of purpose that causes one to get a bit teary over the pride they allow the costume to instill in themselves.

When one leans this way or that and can take in the whole panorama of Main Street, we see a scene that comes right from the heart of our heritage and our history. Our eyes and ears and our hearts behold and thrill to all that is best and sweet about small-town America.

Flags, bright and bold against the laciness of Victorian gingerbread.

Wonderful old trees that let sun and shade play in lovely soft-edged patterns. People lining the curbs that are not afraid to talk and laugh and share with each other.

Small-town America, Fourth of July summer, hazy morning, today thy name is Woodstown.

These marvelous, happy children who parade by us today carry the hopes and dreams and aspirations for a future that children from all times have borne for us adults. Here, now, today, it all seems so very possible.

Their sweetness and innocence cause us to lead with our hearts and to know and have faith that our world is not as bad off as we think. These kids will carry on a sense of morals, hope, strength, tradition, and pass it on to their children.

Well, after many bright, shining fire trucks, numerous handsome antique cars, at least 8 million smiling, happy children and child-like adults, lovely teen-age beauty queens and handsome bodybuilders, bedecked bicycles, lawn tractors and wagons, the arrival of the horses and costumed riders signify the end of another parade day in Woodstown.

With sighs of resignation, we gather up our lawn chairs and bid dear friends good-bye with many thanks for a fun-filled morning of delight, laughter, friendship and memories.

The streets, as we leave, are now bare of most traffic and parade watchers. How quiet and calm and peaceful it all seems after all the hubbub of only moments ago.

To feel this calm, this quiet, is to be so grateful for this whole land of peace and freedom that today this lovely little town amid the fields of South Jersey embodies.

My heart aches for those who live in the Middle East, who shed blood on Tiananmen Square, whose creative artistic efforts are done under totalitarian governments. Those whose entire lives have been war, death and destruction.

This day is the Fourth of July in America. This day represents to the whole, wide world everything that is synonymous with individual freedom and human rights.

You and I are the envy of 95 percent of the citizens of this world that we awoke this morning to find ourselves alive and well on this most special day in this most special country.

Every Fourth of July should renew in our souls the appreciation for those wondrous gifts of freedom, liberty and peace. Blessings by the grace of God that are beyond measure and beyond compare.

Today's Sunbeam, Salem, N.J., Sunday, July 16, 1989

Cultural Diversity Is Sign of Growth

Not long ago, someone asked me if I was doing any teaching locally, and I told them that I have had about 70 students over the last year or so. They were taken aback and then went on to say that they didn't think that anybody around here would be that interested in anything "like that!" I guess "like that" implies any creative pursuit or means of expressing yourself beyond grunts and groans and hand gestures.

A wonderful sign of growth in this county is the great diversity and quality of its creative circles over the past 25 years. There is a great gathering together of energies that can, and do, enrich the quality of everyone's life here in the area.

Like anything else, you have to make the effort. They don't put wheels on paintings, plays and pottery. YOU have to come to them to benefit from what they have to offer. Creative acts have to be met half way. The artist does the expressing. You need to come to it to absorb the experience of that which is expressed!

Whenever I go out to talk to the area school children, I love to tell the kids about how they are surrounded by a wealth of creative people in Salem County. Twenty-five years ago I felt truly alone and lost as I tried to get an 18-year-old, small-town mind prepared for going off to the "big city" to study art.

Three centuries from now I hope to be a household name just so the labors of Wendell Smith will not have been in vain!

Mr. Smith worked at the Salem Sherwin-Williams store which had a small selection of art supplies. Mr. Smith treated me like I was the local fresco painter doing a chapel ceiling. He would pour through catalogues and brochures and offer advice, and he just tried to help get me on my way as best he could.

More young people could use a Wendell Smith in their lives.

And Doris Bryant, my high school art teacher. On graduation day morning, she gave me a hug and set of tube watercolors (no doubt sold by Mr. Smith!) and sent me on my way. That hug and beautiful pristine box of paint could not have been any more meaningful if it had been delivered by some gossamerclad goddess on a golden beam of light!

So with the help of these two and some sage advice from Charlie Swope, sign painter, I set off for art school and the creative life I am now part of.

So much has changed since then. There are so many areas for a young person to turn to, to seek advice and inspiration from and so many cultural aspects that are a part of life in this area. There is so much to our credit here in Salem County. It would be too parochial not to mention the wonderful offerings of the area that includes Glassboro, Bridgeton, and Millville. No longer are we to be considered a cultural desert!

I could write 10 columns on the wonderful gift that Oakwood Summer Theatre alone gives to our lives. Regional theater is part of the wave of the future because of the outrageous prices one has to pay for theater in the cities. You had better get your Oakwood season tickets early!

Glassboro College offers some wonderful things in both the performing and the fine arts. They always seem to have something exciting going on over there!

Ahhh . . . Bridgeton Symphony Orchestra. Do you know what a tremendous orchestra they are? I just get so impassioned knowing that I am sitting in the middle of the meadows of South

Jersey, yet hearing a sound every bit as rich and full and exciting as if we were at the Academy of Music in Philadelphia!

Their *Nutcracker* of last Christmas was the most enjoyable one I had ever seen. It snowed on stage and everything!

In late April, hosted by the Salem Community College, an all-day event called the Teen Arts Festival takes place. Under the dedicated and untiring efforts of Judy Marraccini, teenagers of various creative interests can exhibit, perform and be part of a number of creative workshops. It offers them the opportunity to be with working professionals in the visual and performing arts.

Judy has also put together a 38-page directory of artists in Salem County.

Appel Farm Arts and Music Center. How fortunate we are to have this world-renowned, year-round cultural center as part of our artistic resources. Located over by Elmer, it has a wonderful arts and music summer camp and has recently been offering some outstanding music programs all year long.

Salem County Brass Society and the voices of the Salem Community Chorale give such a wonderful start to the local Christmas season. The Brass Society gives other performances throughout the year at a variety of locations.

Salem's Dana Gayner, this year's president of Gallery 50 in Bridgeton, is putting a great deal of effort into merging creative energies between Salem County and Cumberland County artists and craftsmen. Gallery 50 helps to bring many talented local people's work to the fore as well as sending many exhibits out among the communities of these counties.

Dante said that artists are the grandchildren of God. How blessed we are that our lives are so enriched by having all these talented people around us. We have sculptors, photographers, writers, poets, actors and musicians. We have lyric sopranos who sing in Philadelphia.

The first person to sing in Avery Fisher Hall at New York's Lincoln Center was Hallie Nowland, now retired and a voice teacher in Bridgeton. There are others who sing not so far from home but have voices that can break your heart as sweetly as anyone, anywhere.

Close to home, too, were brought the laurels and kudos of Salem poet Victor Tripp who recently had his poetry selected for admission into a new anthology of American poetry.

Actor Bruce Willis of Penns Grove and comedian Ritchie Shydner of Pennsville are showing to all of America that our sense of humor in Salem County is of the best!

Our craftsmen take a back seat to no one. We have decoys from Alloway and LAC, as well as slate and brass and dulcimers from Mannington. Lovely, soft, delicately-dyed woven items from the Three Stars Fiber Guild and one-of-a-kind pottery created in Woodstown are beautiful crafts to caress, to touch and to fall in love with.

Actors on a stage amid lights and scenery help us to transcend and transfer our lives for a while. Clear, lovely, wonderful notes of a French horn echo in a December Sunday twilight.

One can find oils and watercolors that have captured the feelings that have been whispered between an artist and his subject. We can hear a performance of Handel's "Messiah," of a song from "Cabaret" or, perhaps, of "Music Man." There are poems to read and muse over. It's all here, friend. All here for you to sort over, pick from, select, choose, reject . . .

To those young people out there, the ones who feel those wonderful highs and lows of the spirit, do not despair.

They are the ones who know that they see and sense their world a little differently than the others. Maybe they aren't able to quite express it, or maybe they don't even understand it perhaps. Yet, they feel the sweetness.

They feel the pull on the heart-strings. They hear the siren song. The poetry murmurs just beyond the twilight. To those young people I only want to say . . . you are not alone anymore.

Today's Sunbeam, Salem, N.J., Sunday, July 30, 1989

Hudock's: It's Bali Hai with a Takeout Window

In this world of the '80s, things tend to remain the same for about two and a half days and then you better duck because here comes something . . . New! Innovative! Updated!

We all need to know and feel that we can find something in our world that brings to us a sense of the familiar. Something unchanged, something to be trusted. A something that will stroke our heartstrings, soothe our minds, and murmur pleasant memories in our ear.

As I ease the car over the speed bump, I am gloriously assailed as swirls of wonderful aromas rush in to mingle with the mistiness of memories. The symphony on my car radio fades softly into the background, the world moves in slow motion, I have **ARRIVED!**

This could be Brigadoon, Bali Hai, Shangri-La, El Dorado! The pilgrim has come home! I am at **HUDOCK'S CUSTARD STAND!** "The Stand" is located about a mile east of Salem on Route 49, locally known as the Salem-Quinton Road.

Howard Johnson taught a traveling America to recognize his restaurants and 28 flavors of ice cream by looking for the orange roofs. Hudock's has wonderfully bright yellow roofs accompanied by yellow picnic benches and chairs. These bright colors on the highway alert the locals, as well as hundreds of shore travelers, that once again they are back at that neat little place with 9-inch diameter hamburgers called a "belly-buster."

The Stand was most likely the very first place around Salem County to have foot-long hot dogs, too!

The Stand was first opened in the early '50s by a great old character named Jack Oster.

Jack was selling frozen custard to double lines of folks 30 deep on hot summer evenings. He later opened a takeout sandwich area in an identical little building right across the way.

If you remember Jack, you will never forget his tremendous booming voice that always made me think of "Foghorn Leghorn," a rooster in the Warner Bros. Cartoons on Saturday mornings.

It was in 1967 that Joe and Mary Jane Hudock took over and carried on the great local tradition that Jack had started.

So little has changed during the last 35 years at least to the customers point of view. Occasionally a new food item or ice cream treat has been added to the menu over the years. The beauty of it is that all of those great wonderful tastes that one remembers as a kid are still available!

The "foot-longs" with sauerkraut and sauce still have that great taste like when you were 11-years-old. The hot dog is still slightly crisp on the edges, too!

A "Big-Boy" with sauce and cheese still drips all over your body if you have even an iota of passion as you plunge headlong into this marvelous concoction. You really need extra sauce to make it the moral equivalent of manna from heaven.

The frozen custard is still everything that evokes a "Midsummer's Night Dream" of being 8 years old and having some kindly parent pack 100 neighborhood kids into one car for a drive to get a custard! Milk shakes are still thick enough to cause your eyes and ears to invert when you try to slurp them through a straw.

One of the modern additions to the Stand is some sort of pressure-cooker device that enables you to have "broasted chicken!" On most any day I'd trade my first-born for a 12-piece box of this style of chicken.

Last season I miscalculated Hudock's fall closing date by a day and the police found me on my knees pawing at the locked door, crying and begging for just one more 12 piece-box of chicken to get me through the long cold winter. On wintry nights, my son and I sit by the fireplace and reminisce about how good a piece of broasted chicken would taste.

Have you ever noticed that at most of today's fast food franchise places you never get to experience the aroma and sounds of your food being cooked! Boy, at Hudock's you can drive by at 50-60 miles per hour and still be aware that someone has ordered three burgers, fries, a foot-long hot dog and is getting sauce, sauerkraut and fried onions on all of them!

Not only is the food great, but there are some other really neat benefits to eating there.

How many restaurants hype the fact that they are situated by an airport runway or sit atop an airport terminal. For only six times the normal price of food you can watch the planes land and take off!

You have to get all dressed up, drive a goodly distance and, if you're lucky, there won't be 79 people between you and the window! You went to all this trouble and here you could have driven to Hudock's. Situated mere inches from the main runway of Salem Municipal Airport and at no extra cost!

Hey, the pilots even wave! We even have real antique biplanes to look at!

I love to have lunch at Hudock's, and most especially in the fall. I love to sit at a picnic bench in the crisp air of late September and early October.

You can look and gaze at beautiful bright blue skies filled with great white fluffy clouds all sailing over a landscape of trees starting to turn colors, summer corn stalks now a lovely golden tan, all bathed in the brilliance of the noontime sun.

How I love the skies of Salem County. Nothing to block them, lots of farmland or meadows, and huge expanses of sky. The degree of beauty dictated only by the seasons. What a wonderful, gorgeous way to have your lunch!

Part of my fondness for The Stand is because of the Hudock's themselves. As hectic and maddening as things can get out there at times, Mary Jane and Joe can always find a moment or two to offer a greeting and a laugh or a smile!

I shall always remember an incident of a few years ago. This was a time before every yahoo and his brother was out renting stretch limos.

A lovely, classic, black limousine pulled up at the custard stand. A uniformed, gloved chauffeur got out, bought a vanilla custard, returned to the car, very elegantly opened the door, handed the cone to the "madame" and then purred on down the highway leaving all of us peasants a bit agasp!

Well, it sure said something for the quality of frozen custard at Hudock's! That's probably how she got that rich, she could have afforded Haagen-Dazs but saved her money by buying Hudock's instead!

The Stand and I go back a long, long way. Every stop there has a bit of nostalgia to it. It's as much fun today as it ever was, and therein, for me, lies the secret of its success.

Next time you're out there, look for me. I am the one with the sauce all over my body, my head in the clouds and my heart at Hudock's! Would you just please bring me over another 15 napkins?

Today's Sunbeam, Salem, N.J., Sunday, August 13, 1989

Sweet Memories Still Linger from the County Fair

Well, by now you know, the votes are in, the ribbons have been handed out and Aunt Mae's pickles have been declared the very best in Salem County! Succeeding generations of her family will always know that in 1989 they were the best entry in the county fair! Probably the state, too, if you ask me!

"Enoch" the pig was a cinch for a ribbon. If I ever saw a pig with panache, he had it! I knew the minute he smiled and winked, that he was some sort of pig!

Suzie's paintings of the zinnias in a fruit jar and Grandma's cross stitch are now bedecked with ribbons as they go on a permanent one-woman exhibit in the living room at home.

As you read these words, the Salem County Fairgrounds stand empty, windswept and wet. This year's fair has joined our collection of delightful memories of things past. Memories of the fair have to be tinged with the smells of caramel corn, chicken barbecue, cows and hay and sheep. Our mind's eyes sees the lights at night, the familiar faces, the art displays. We feel again the sawdust and straw beneath our feet, the hugs and the handshakes of friendship.

This fair has all the country charm and quaintness of a cross-stitched sampler. American painter Thomas Hart Benton would've set up his easel smack in the middle of a cow barn, or next to a pig stall, and painted for three days and turned the whole scene into a great American theme!

Going to the fair is a real spiritual state-of-mind type of experience. Your degree of fun and entertainment is in direct proportion to how receptive you are to the gleam of shiny new farm equipment, the beauty of cows, the bustle of pigs, old friends, fair queens and funnel cake.

Its charm and uniqueness are allowed to exist due to an obvious lack of gross commercialism, a wise decision on someone's part.

It's a real people-orientated type of social gathering. Most likely 99 percent of the folks come out only "to-see-who-else-came-out-to-see-who-was-here-and-boy-am-I-glad-you-came-out-because-this-is-the-only-time-all-year-I-ever-get-to-see-you-and-the-kids-have-really-gotten-big-and-speaking-of-big-you-kinda-put-on-a-few-pounds-yourself, huh?" (Whew!).

Every day we should be saying a prayer for the farmers of this county and the rough times they have had to deal with. The fair is a visual testament and tribute to the wonderful agrarian lifestyle that permeates throughout this corner of God's vineyard. A lifestyle that is lovely and good and grows out of this tradition of farming and family and friends.

It's so much fun to see the animals so close up and to talk to the 4-H kids who raise them! I love the realization that you know this 11-year-old kid forgot more about raising a 1,600 pound cow than you'll ever know. Up close you can see that cows have gorgeous, liquid, amber-brown eyes. And pigs have long eyelashes and smile when they sleep! Goats have a noble, fragile, delicate quality that makes them such a treat to stroke and caress. A sheep's coat, when you touch it, leaves the wonderful aroma of oily lanolin on your hand – marvelous!

To eat chicken barbecue and corn-on-the-cob any other place but the fair is to not have the same culinary experience! Chicken barbecue is a great common denominator and leveler of society! It is impossible to eat and not talk to your neighbor since you just put your elbow in his cole slaw or you share a spare napkin with the lady whose two-year-old kid just got her attention by tapping her on the shoulder with a chicken leg!

This fair is a patchwork quilt of all the wonderful things that tug at our emotions and our senses and make us feel marvelously human.

It is the sweet sentiment of the crowning of a fair queen. It is a heart-broken 4-H girl whose goat did everything wrong except eat the judge. It's the joy of giggling children petting a rabbit through a wire cage. It is displays decorated with the bounty of a Salem County harvest that become a visual prayer for all the good things of this area. It is the cacophony of moos and bleats and oinks and crowings. Most of all and best of all, it is the sense of "rightness" to the whole scenario.

Salem County has clung to this agricultural heritage through God's grace and the fortitude and determination of the families who work the land and raise the animals.

How magnificent to see acres of tall corn, dark green against the hazy, humid twilight of a summer's evening. To smell the spring rain on a newly plowed field, so receptive to bare feet and seedlings. To see cows gathered in congenial, non-abusive committee meetings in the shade of some old tree. A peach or apple orchard tinting the very atmosphere with the color of its buds one week, its blossoms the next. Whose long, hard day has not been eased by the charm of the baby pigs along the roadside of Sparks' farm in Mannington?

To live and work in Salem County and to not visit and experience the fair is a bit like having the words to a song – but you can't hum the tune.

Just a brief, but heart-sent thank you to all of the wonderful folks who read this column and have sent notes or made a phone call, or stopped me on the street to tell me how much they enjoy it. I love you all for it. You and this column are a marvelous blessing and gift to my life. Don't stop now. I can always use the encouragement!

Today's Sunbeam, Salem, N.J., Sunday, August 27, 1989

Magic on Market Street from Morning Until Night

Yesterday, while commonly known as Saturday to most of the world, was simply called Market Street Day to the folks around here.

As of this writing, Market Street Day is still two weeks away, and you are reading it one day after! What if it rains and yesterday is canceled two weeks from now!?! Thoughts of this special day always fill me with a sense of optimism so I'll dream of good, sunny weather for the day and plod on.

On Market Street Day, I always set up an easel and draw portraits as an excuse to sit in the middle of things and see everyone. Also to let the excitement swirl around me and envelop me in all of it.

I always try to arrive early and get set up for the day. It's so neat to ease back in your lawn chair and watch the world awaken all about you. Regular early morning traffic is still going by and here perched in the middle of the sidewalk is some screwball with a big straw hat, an easel and his coffee cup.

The architecture on Market Street is so beautiful in the light of this early morning hour. Between the rim of my coffee cup and the brim of my straw hat I have a view of the world in a myriad of blues and purples.

Soon the sun ascends just enough and pushes her rays over the courthouse and around the sculptural edges of the Presbyterian Church, and now the old buildings on the western side are bathed in a warm glow of tans and golds.

It's so easy in this suffusion of blue mystical light sparkled with gold and tan to see, if you try, all of those spirits of another century and time. They stand on the steps of the Alexander Grant House, they knock on the door of the Robert Gibbon Johnson House, they gather early to attend church at St. John's.

William Wordsworth said that church steeples are "silent fingers pointing to God."

Is there any lovelier illustration of this phrase than to see the magnificent, towering steeple of the Presbyterian Church, so striking, so white against the rose-blue morning sky?

As my eyes shift and my mind wanders on, my early morning revery is now shattered suddenly by a showroom perfect '57 red Chevy convertible! My passions careen from 18th century ghosts to memories of high school in the early '60s and "checking town" in a car exactly like this!

Look! There is a Plymouth just like my neighbor's had when I was about 9 years old! It was the size of a Sherman tank, but it had white walls and no guns!

Wait! What is this? I'm still a young guy. Aren't I? The cars from my youth are now antiques? Am I really that old?

By now the street is filled with many wonderfully restored cars. So beautiful in their classic appeal and design. How easy to see the transition from a carriage to what was then called a "horseless carriage." How elegant they are.

As I look around me, more and more people have set up their crafts tables and other displays and stands of memorabilia. The food vendors now advertise their arrival by the wonderful aromas that are wafting throughout this carnival-like scene. I am assailed by the smell of chicken barbeque, hot dogs, coffee, caramel corn and peanuts!

Craft folks are shouting greetings to each other as they unload their cars and vans. They are swapping notes on the foibles and follies of other street fairs, but all agree that Salem's Market Street Day is one of the best.

This happy, fun event is entering its 15th year as an institution to show off Salem and provide a fun time for everyone. People come from all over to join in the excitement and spirit of the day. Due to the efforts of the Salem Committee, Market Street Day grows more successful with each passing year.

This festive day is culled from a tradition that goes back to Fenwick's Colony. There was actually a law that stated that two fairs a year were to be held, one in the spring and one in the fall.

The idea of a spring and fall gathering derives from the pagan rites of the Romans.

Well, while not very pagan or declared by law, Market Street Day is still a wonderfully, happy, festive-like day.

By now, early-comers are starting to mill about browsing through some lovely craft items or produce, or just admiring the cars and figuring out what is the street's best bet for lunch!

The day has transpired from empty streets and early quiet to a more crowded, merry bustle of people. There is a happy air of friendliness and relaxation to the atmosphere.

As people are gathered in little islands of laughter and chatter, the various music groups can be heard in the background.

No one is in any hurry to go anywhere. They tend to sit on any available step of curbstone or wall and just observe the life around them. Everyone tends to offer chuckled "hellos" to a special friend or neighbor . . . and "seldom is heard a discouraging word."

To add to my happiness, I get to sit amid it all and draw cute kids with bangs and freckles. A lady wants to know if I'll draw her with one chin and not three!

A teenage girl whose boyfriend is buying the drawing and loves it when I make her as beautiful as he knows she is . . . she blushed to think an artist finds her eyes so lovely. They are.

And then there are all the folks who stop and talk and tease me. We laugh and hug and make big scenes and it gives my day a special happiness and a joy that is beyond compare, measure or worldly wealth.

Special recognition is given to someone whose life and work has made the community a better place by their having been here. This year's recipient is Sr. Marian Hummel, the principal at St. Mary's Regional School. She lives right in my neighborhood, so it makes it extra special for all of us in my area.

As I love to be early for the beginning of this day, so I usually am one of the last to leave. I love the wistfulness of being among the last to leave almost anywhere; theaters, circuses, orchestras, parties.

The romantic in me loves to feel and sense the contrast of the merriment and activity to the quietude and emptiness when an affair is finished. The street is now one of these special times.

As the morning light offered, to our senses, the street in clear, crisp contrasts, now a soft, golden glow of late afternoon suffuses it all together into a visual poem of serenity and timelessness.

Those same spirits of another century that I imagined so well this morning now appear to be standing casually in a door frame, starting to go within, but they seem to pause, to wave a smiling goodbye to me for now.

I laugh to myself and grin and as I pick up my easel and start to walk away, I just have to turn, look back, and wave . . . just in case.

Today's Sunbeam, Salem, N.J., Sunday, September 10, 1989

Feeding the Body and Soul One Night on the River

Returning to live in Salem 15 years ago, I came home to and for many things and reasons. A perfect example was the friendliness of the man who installed my phones. He had lived in LAC all his life and attributed his robust health and full head of hair to eating muskrats and raw oysters whenever possible!

We got into talking about some of the local eating traditions that make up part of the special quality of life here in South Jersey. We extolled the virtues of such wonderful things as lima bean pot pie, fried green tomatoes, and rhubarb pie. He kept trying to add muskrat and raw oysters to the list.

Finally, without any hesitation I admitted to never having liked either one!

After he picked himself up off my studio floor, he thumped my chest and exclaimed that there was no way I could ever lay claim to being a birthright Salem Countian and not eat muskrat and raw oysters!

I couldn't find it in my heart to tell him that I don't like shad either.

My aversion to muskrat does gain me great credibility to my friends in the more metropolitan areas of Delaware Valley where they find the idea appalling.

Don't stop reading! I think I can redeem myself!

One of the great loves of my life is the complete and thorough devastation of a bushel of crabs! It is usually only once or twice a season that I do have them, but when I do, I relish that act as I would a religious experience!

One needs to come to food with their minds prepared for the experience. In this way, the spirit is fed as well as the belly. As words make pictures happen for me as an illustrator, so food makes images for me also.

Certain dishes return me to other times, other places. It reunites me with old friends or loved ones in my memories. It returns me to lands never traveled save in my mind. I imagine those who created the dish, nobleman or peasant? This is how I learned to play games with my food and not get yelled at by my mother.

The eating of crabs for me is so purely and deliciously physical. The only mind games played here are just sheer delight and enjoyment of messy fingers, butter just about everywhere, piles of shells, the tangy bite of cold beer to the sweetness of the crab. Tomatoes! Corn on the cob!

In the midst of all this wondrous mess of things, I always manage to gaze lovingly on my hosts and let my eyes tear up as a way of showing enormous amounts of gratitude for all the trouble they've gone to by inviting us out.

Note that I have said, "Out." This relates to "out on the river."

My most treasured memories of eating crabs were at the invitation of either George and Betty Jean Eby or Jim and Marcy Waddington. I am cruelly conditioned to eating crabs on the front porch of either of these two gracious riverside havens of hospitality.

Front porch crabfests on the river is to have a foretaste of heaven. It is so peaceful and calm on the river at this hour. The beauty of it all is to know that God is smiling down on us and we must be living right.

Dinner always starts in the fading daylight of a summer's evening. It is nature's way of saying grace for our dinner.

By the light of day, call the river whatever disparaging color you wish, but at twilight it lightens to a soft, beautiful blue and the oranges of a setting sun are diamond-sparkled over every ripple on it.

The sky takes on the dusky flavor of rose and orange and blue and the silhouette of the distant Delaware shore starts to twinkle with the advent of various lights being turned on to punctuate the coming darkness. Your line of sight is suddenly blocked as a ship slides by in silent surprise.

Everyone seems to eat and sky-gaze at the same time. As this lovely vesper hour gives way to the night, these folks get into some serious crab eating. The votive candles and the bug lights are lit, and all and everything are cast in the glow of the candlelight.

As shadows sashay around the walls and porch posts, the sounds of several people "pickin'" crabs and oohing and ahhhing and licking fingers become a hymn of comradery, warmth and friendship.

Behind you, always there for your "listening pleasure" is the river lapping against the sea wall. Perhaps a ship's horn somewhere in the dark. Many years ago one could hear bell buoys with their lonely sound to lull you asleep. My soul yearns to hear a bell buoy on the river the same way I wish to tilt my head back and smell Heinz ketchup cooking as I walk home from the third grade on a September afternoon.

One is never quite sure when to stop eating crabs. You keep promising to stop after just one more. I've never figured it out. I just know that in some subconscious state I've made a gesture of saying no to one last crab and a tenth ear of corn.

I am now aware that these artsy old fingers are cut and sore from breaking and dismembering shells all evening. Between the salt from the corn on the cob and the Old Bay spices on the crabs, I do hope that they heal so that I shall be able to hold a brush some time again in this life. This, I am sure, is the crab's way of having revenge.

Now the feast is over and it comes time to help rehabilitate the porch. How is it that one bushel of crabs, a bag of corn and a few pounds of tomatoes can so thoroughly wipe out a house? Again we broach the question of a revenge put upon us by perhaps some Goddess of the Garden, is Neptune angry?

Our wonderful, delicious, fun-filled night "on the river" draws now to a close. The stillness of a starry night on the river shore is only slightly rent by the murmurs and moanings of over-zealous crab-feasters trying to stuff themselves into their cars for the journey homeward.

As the road leads us past the moonlit fields of Elsinboro, we once again sense and feel the closeness of the land. Surrounded as we are by rows of tall corn, acres of tomatoes and peppers, we realize that we are doubly blessed. Blessed by the bounty of a mighty river that fed us so heartily and yet, soothed and lulled our senses all this evening long.

Today's Sunbeam, Salem, N.J., Sunday, September 24, 1989

Autumn: A Time of Year that Can Stir Our Souls

Autumn is that wonderful, magical, haunting time of year. It is a season when the souls and spirits of the poets and romantics that are within seem to be at one with the world of nature that is around us.

Shelley refers to autumn in this way: "The day becomes more solemn and serene when noon is past – there is a harmony in autumn, and a luster in its sky, which through the summer is not heard or seen . . ."

Summer is a season of great contrasts: dark green foliage to clear blue skies, bright garden flowers to wet brown earth, surviving the heat by trying to stay cool, the happy summer noises of children out of school.

The subtly changing cloud patterns near summer's end foretell the coming cool weather. The bright green glistening of the tree leaves starts to dull ever so slightly. In a cornfield, brown leaves around the bottom of the stalks are quiet, gentle harbingers that almost escape our notice.

Everywhere and everything, as Shelley has said, becomes "in harmony" by the hazy golden glow that softens the edges of our afternoons.

It is to the beauty of a fall afternoon that my senses are the most cajoled and courted. Fall afternoons need to be spent visiting a roadside market, enjoying the back porch company of an old friend, taking a walk, reading a book at the picnic table, and daydreaming.

My most favorite spiritual pastime for golden, hazy afternoons is to plant tulip and crocus bulbs. Could this be a commercial for the Burpee Seed Company? No. It is a spiritual communion with the earth and all who ever walked it and loved it and returned to it.

My yard is a landscaper's nightmare. It could be the setting for a horror film called "The Crabgrass That Ate Cleveland."

Thirty drums of Agent Orange would start to improve my yard immensely. In spite of its body-snatching Virginia Creeper and its majestic stands of maple trees carpeted by poison ivy and nettles, I always manage to find a couple square feet of unclaimed earth in which to plant a few new bulbs each season.

To dig in the earth in spring gives forth a wonderful earthy fragrance of moist soil sweetened by new green grasses. Digging in the fall soil gives off an aroma that is an autumn potpourri of dried grasses, leaves, marigold stems and seedpods. The soil is warm and breaks up to your touch in such a giving way.

A bulb, if we listen to it, can preach to us a beautiful, silent sermon of the miracle of life after death and the renewal of all that is in nature. It is all there for us to observe, to muse over, and to have, which is given to us in this most simple, unassuming way.

That this brown, crinkly-skinned object will yield up to us a slender tulip, or delicate, small crocus, is to sense, to know and to feel a plan for us all.

When I plant bulbs, each one has to be personally placed in its own spot and cajoled and talked to. If you have to rush, better wait till another day or else go scatter grass seed with your spreader. Of course, sowing grass seed by hand in dramatic sweeping gestures is marvelous fun also!

After I've dug up an area, I love to sit or lay along its edges and break up the soil with my fingers. People think you are working when, in fact, you are really sort of playing. I guess I equate the whole thing to putting a child to bed and the care and tenderness that should go with it. In whispered conversation between the bulb, the earth and me, we arrive at a decision as to why and where the next one will go.

With my fingers I loosen an area and fluff it up with some bone meal, and it is into this "comforter" of warm soil that I tuck the bulb.

I am positive that after conversing with the bulb, and our time together, that, come the spring, I shall remember each and every one, but I don't. As I cover them over and smooth the surface, I give them a final "pat on the bottom" then move on to the next.

Perhaps I do not give my yard its just due. Maybe it functions best as a sort of large dried flower arrangement and not as a summer garden from the July issue of *Better Homes and Gardens*.

This time becomes a wonderful reflective time as the peace and quiet and beauty of this kind of fall afternoon lulls me into mind musings and ramblings. I think of the first lessons my mother taught me about planting and I hope she is watching over my progress now.

I like to look at all the insects I come across and I wonder if they'll make it through the long winter ahead. A squirrel stops to eat an English walnut atop the picnic table and I worry about the field mouse who will try to winter over in my cereal drawer. My yard becomes my own version of "Wind in the Willows."

This sense of a closeness to nature causes me to think on the spiritual relationship that the Indians of another day and age felt for the land. How deeply their lives were linked to it and regulated by it. How they loved to have their bodies in contact with it and they spoke of feeling its spirit and powers as they sat upon it or walked barefoot across it.

We call this beautiful time of year Indian Summer – a set of words that brings to us a longing echo from the past of a special people's holy reverence and gratitude for all that existed in nature.

As the afternoon wanes, the yard becomes soft and diffused in a moody twilight world where shadows of blue and violet fall over brown and red and yellow leaves.

The sky is streaked low on the horizon with fiery reds and yellows, with dusky gray and violet clouds above. All this color brilliantly contrasts with the silhouetted lacy shapes of forsythia and thinning trees.

High, high above the gorgeous sunset, where the sky goes from gold to yellow-green to deep rich blue shines the evening star, the wishing star. On this first star of the coming night I can make a wish, a very big wish . . .

Today's Sunbeam, Salem, N.J., Sunday, October 8, 1989

A Sense of Community Makes Our Area Special

While visiting the other night with a group of people in Wilmington, Del., a fellow overheard me mention several of the things I enjoy about living in a small town. He then went on to say how he envied me because I live in an area that has a sense of community about it.

I found out that within the past year he had moved to Hockessin, Del.

I shared with him a reflection that I had as a kid of Hockessin being just a patch in the road with one gas station and a few homes. He laughed and said it still has only one gas station, but now it is loaded with homes.

While happy with his new home and locale, he felt it lacked a spirit of community. He said that in the developments, people tend to live very independently of each other. There is no central focus to life there, no town to build around, no sense of history or tradition, no feeling or sense of belonging to anything.

We read so much about the reports, findings, and surveys that are being compiled on the collective health of society today. The results tell us that a lot of today's problems stem from a variety of breakdowns in society. Society as our parents knew it is very rapidly being eroded.

Divorces, transient employment patterns, people too busy or afraid to meet their neighbors, and the list goes on. All of these are indicative of our inability to have any sort of permanency in our lives and our relationships. There are a lot of insecure folks out there apparently.

In an effort to seek a sense of belonging and a sense of identity, people are trying to return to a "small town" lifestyle and the values that have been pushed aside over the last 20 to 30 years.

Salem County has certainly not escaped these social problems. We are not always a happy-go-lucky bucolic bunch of country bumpkins, now are we? But we sure have a marvelous head start over a lot of other places whose pastures appear to be a lot greener than ours.

Our area still maintains a lifestyle that allows for so much interaction between people. The potential to build relationships among a wide variety of people and along many lines is still such a vital and beautiful reality here in Salem County.

How linked and interconnected we are to each other, in so many ways, regardless of our age, our race, our gender.

"Hey! How's your brother? We were in school together."

"We lived next door to you when we were first married."

"Your mother was my third grade teacher. Boy, did I love her!"

"I watched you grow up . . ."

Our interests and philosophies are another bonding device that gets us together to meet one another. The rich historic heritage of this area has created many organizations whose membership is culled from a real cross section of the area.

To our credit, many volunteer agencies and organizations flourish and you may find yourself working next to your plumber or bank manager. You may go to the same church as your insurance agent or former teacher.

All our towns seem to be separated one from the other by a periphery of rural areas which help us to sense the boundaries and limits of our various communities.

We are allowed a feeling of this being our town, our little piece of the world. We are imbued with a sense of belonging to another unit outside of our home and our family.

And to this "something" we can bring a sense of allegiance and caring if we can find it within us to do so.

As a freelance artist and a "stringer" for the newspaper, I work alone in my studio at home. I value my "aloneness" and solitude, but with equal fervor I relish my trips to the post office, the Acme, the bank and anywhere else I may have to venture just for the social aspects of being with people.

These errands can afford me wondrously joyous times when I can laugh and joke or get into a heady discussion with those I run into! My criteria for a place to have lunch is based mostly on where I'll see the most people!

All of these places and more, as well as just walking on a city sidewalk, afford us such wonderful opportunities of sensing that we belong and are a part of it all.

Small towns have very few secrets and this really bothers some people. Yet I have seen great outpourings of love and care and concern when word got out concerning another's misfortune.

We live in a world that could be so much happier if people would only take the time to try to get to know one another and show some genuine concern for each other's well being. I am totally convinced that Salem County has a real corner on the market of good, caring and feeling people.

Have you ever been in the hospital? Same day out-patient surgery gets you on at least three church prayer lists, let alone all the ones you're on for an extended stay! People do take the time to care in Salem County!

A special friend of mine goes jogging at some incredible early morning hour and just loves to spread "Hi's" and "Hellos" to everyone she meets. She's doing a better job starting people's mornings than breakfast at McDonalds!

Her only motive is to just let the other person know that she respects his place on this earth and since they have to share it together, they might as well smile and be pleasant to one another.

Donna is sort of a den mother to the world! She goes through life with the attitude that you treat others the way you wish to be treated. She is very successful in the giving and is a real "find" to have as a friend.

There are other "finds" in the area. Folks who are just really good for my soul and sense of well being. I don't have a franchise on their friendship. They are out there for all of us to share and enjoy and feel good over.

They attend this church or that. They work here or there. They shop over there or down the street. They are in an evening art class. They collect in post office lobbies or at drug store counters. They visit the same doctor. They are all over this county and they are all treasures waiting to be discovered.

If we grunt and growl and groan our way around this marvelous place, we'll never find them. We might just as well go live in the cities and lose ourselves in the bustle and rush.

Today's column is for all you caring, super neat folks out there who make life so loving and fun for the rest of us.

Thanks for making us laugh over postal increases. Thanks for the sweet smiles in the market checkout line, for the hearty hello and handshake at last night's meeting and for coming over to our table at the diner.

You are, with love and laughter and light as your loom, the brightest of threads on the tapestry of life in Salem County.

Today's Sunbeam, Salem, N.J., Sunday, October 22, 1989

Halloween Parade Puts Fun Back in the Holiday

The mood is created by the setting sun and twilight sky at my back, and a full moon on the rise in the deepening night sky ahead. I find myself alone, driving among the woods and fields of Quinton and Alloway townships.

Lengthening shadows are making patterns across the golden brown landscape. Suddenly off to my left I see a lone figure striding through the stubbled rows of a cornfield. As if in a vision out of the Dark Ages I imagine I am seeing the hooded, robed figure of a Druid priest, all backlit by the setting sun, leaning on a stout staff upon whose top is placed a candlelit carved gourd to light his path.

A small owl festoons his left shoulder, a black cat lies in the crook of his arm and a she-wolf stands cautious guard by his side. They turn and walk on and are slowly absorbed by the mist ebbing and swirling about them in the now darkened fields. My spine tingles over the thought of the Halloween rite or perhaps the Feast of All Hallows Eve toward which they are plodding their lonely way.

And now passing through the encompassing and possessing darkness of Muttontown Woods, the wind swirls a banshee's cry through and around my car causing it and my heartbeat to rapidly accelerate!

Thank goodness! Just ahead over a few rolling hills I see the beckoning glow of lights! Saved! Alloway!

Alloway. A quiet little crossroads slice of the American Pie. Tonight this town becomes the greatest place to celebrate Halloween this side of Transylvania and Castle Frankenstein. I now find the specter of a headless horseman filling up my rear vision mirror! In his hands he carries a pumpkin carved to resemble a local politician. If I can just make it to the Alloway Creek Bridge first! Before my religion and rationale leave me completely, I pray that I can made it to the township office and then I know I'll be OK!

It is to my sheer enchantment and bewitchment and delight that I am one of several judges for the annual Alloway Halloween Parade.

I have to arrive very early this special night and so it offers me the chance to drive in the twilight through all those beautiful, empty and ethereal back roads with only my imagination to keep me company.

The rest of you will come in the dark amid the traffic created by the folks who feel that Alloway is the only place to be on this night. By this time all of those lost souls of the spirit world will be deep within the woods and meadows and long into their revery and pagan rites of this magical evening. An evening in which the gate connecting this world and the *other* is open for the span of a few brief, chilling, and mysterious hours. Be sure to count heads when you arrive and then again halfway home!

Over the last several years Halloween has lost so much of its spirit and fun. Because of many greedy and grabby people and a need for curfews in many towns, its sense of fun and merriment has vanished like a vampire at sunrise and everyone misses out on a centuries-old holiday.

With what should be heartfelt gratitude from every person in this county, the quiet, unassuming crossroads of Alloway gives to all of us the gift of a magical night once again.

What a fun-filled festival and carnival-like atmosphere abounds on these normally placid streets. Strings of light bulbs creating thousands of little halos in the evening air. Bright confetti colors of a vendor's balloons twist and dance against the night sky. Scattered here and there, food stands create islands of the wonderful warm smells of hot chocolate and popcorn.

A child's mask is lifted to allow a space in which to devour wispy wads of cotton candy or caramel corn. Adults in costumes have personality make overs and are transformed merely by being able to hide behind a mask and for a little while can be a clown or a goblin or a ghoul.

What a wonderful night. The whole atmosphere is filled with awe and everything that says Halloween! Floats filled with spooky scenes of ghosts and haunted houses, skeletons and tombstones.

Bands in costumes, feathers and sequins, a whole bunch of horn-tooting, drum-thumping hobos from Pitman! The streets are loaded with pumpkins, black cats, scarecrows! The air is thick with a thousand spells cast by all the witches and warlocks that this parade attracts.

The judges are all treated to a seat on a decorated flatbed trailer. While I miss the fraternization with all the folks on the street, we do get a great sort of aerial view of everything. What a great panorama you all become!

Streets are lined with a myriad of people, laughing and having a great time, down through which passes string bands, groups of clowns, beauty queens in shiny cars, and floats of wonderfully inspired bits of Halloween foolery. All are a marvelous visual delight!

Walking and working the curbside will be a witch or a Frankenstein or a hobgoblin. They will be drawing out laughter and shrieks depending on his or her ability to scare and frighten with an element of surprise. Halloween is to home decorating in Alloway what Christmas is to home decorating in other towns. You will see funny stuffed creatures guarding a front porch, spooky spider webs made of string or clothesline all anchored by pumpkins and corn shocks, appliance box coffins, while newspaper-stuffed bed sheet ghosts haunt their spooky way from tree branches. Even an undecorated house has at least one carved pumpkin to ward off any spirits or evil doings of the night.

Besides being festively decorated, Alloway homes are renowned as well for being great havens of hospitality on this night. If you follow this column with any regularity, you know by now I always associate food with just about any social event you can name in the county. Well, this night has been made for plates of glazed donuts and apple cider, and while you're up, I'll take a side order of ginger snaps, if you please! Ah! Yes! Be a nice ghoul and hand me a candy apple!

Well, it's an hour or so till midnight, the parade is all over and I still have all those back roads to travel to get home. How vivid are my memories as a kid of coming home dragging my trick-or-treat bag. How I would gaze at the moon and try to imagine a real witch on a broomstick gliding by. I could and would get myself so caught up that I'd end up running home thinking every goblin and ghoul in the world was right behind me! I even had a cemetery across the street to add to the atmosphere!

And so now as I drive home alone amid corn stalks silhouetted against a bright orange witch's moon, and I see dark shapes amid the trees and across the frosty starlit fields, I get to be nine years old for a little while again. The magic and the spell returns.

I forget that I am driving a car and not walking. The policeman (Halloween's answer to Ebenezer Scrooge) who clocked me doing 95 mph in a 35 mph zone assured me that the only thing that went "bump in the night" were the three mailboxes I took out on the curve in Penton! May the Great Pumpkin turn his patrol car into an aardvark.

The Alloway Parade Committee works very hard all year long to raise the $15,000 needed to have this wonderful parade. The money is needed for prizes, trophies, school bands, string bands, float prizes, celebrities, etc. The committee really struggles to raise this sum. If you liked this column and attend that great parade, I'd really appreciate it if you'd consider sending a couple dollars to the committee at the following address: Alloway Halloween Parade, Box 575, Alloway 08001.

Thanks! I truly hope the Great Pumpkin visits your patch this year!

Today's Sunbeam, Salem, N.J., Sunday, November 5, 1989

A Loving Farewell to One of Salem City's Great Men

Dear Mr. Pedersen:

Please forgive me if I embarrass you by writing today's column as a farewell letter to your memory. All that I am hoping to accomplish with this column would be for naught if I failed to record and take note of your life and your passing.

We thank you with all our hearts for the pride and honor you brought to this community and this county, and to all of us at a time when we really needed a shot in the arm. You really did it!

I shall always remember that day while on a typical errand about town, I passed by the courthouse and Market Street was filled with news teams and television and radio vans.

What a wonderful profusion of hoopla and excitement! A Nobel Prize had come to Salem. Salem, the last place anyone would have ever thought would raise up a winner on that grand a scale or magnitude.

And finally Salem got to meet its prominent, newsworthy citizen and your first appearance really won over our hearts!

Television has conditioned us to expect celebrities to be demigods that smile great flashy smiles, possess gorgeous builds, wear trendy clothes and usually have some sordid history.

Salem was presented with a gentle, delicate, sensitive, poetic man who charmed and enthralled and won our respect by his quiet unassuming ways. A man whose standards and ethics were beyond reproach.

What a tremendous piece of poetic justice for this city and all who loved it and believed in it! This great gift was given to us at a time when most people were willing to send this city "to hell in a handbasket."

And then you came along, and what do we have? We have a person who has just been given the ultimate reward for a lifetime of devotion to his work, his loves, his dreams . . . a Nobel Prize. An award whose very name stirs the mind to thrilling, glorious thoughts on achievements and accomplishments. Hopes and dreams have been made or shattered by its presentation or denial. And now it has all come home to be forever in Salem, New Jersey.

Thank you for the hope and belief in dreams that your life can and will and should set by its example for all the rest of us who dwell here.

We are so grateful that when fame's light fell on our town, we could hold you up with pride to its glow. You were the epitome of a real and true gentleman. How very fortunate, how so very fitting, how so very privileged we were that you were a part of us all.

You were what is most assuredly a contrast in terms, a scientist with the soul of a poet and a painter. Only in rare instances are those two gifts present or allowed to exist together.

Hermann Hesse (Nobel Prize recipient for literature in 1946) refers to thinkers and artists as creatures of reason and creatures of the soul. One sees the sun, the other the moon and the stars. A wonderful testament to your sense of creativity is that you dwelled in both worlds so very comfortably and were so expressive in each.

Being an artist allows me to be privy to your poetic, sensitive nature and that is what I feel makes you so very special for being our prize winner, our hero, our very own "one of us" here in Salem. Our winner, our Mr. Pedersen, was the best of all worlds and all things, a Renaissance man in the truest sense.

Everyone to whom you ever opened yourself and your life speak of your simplicity, your gentleness and your sensitivity to all those around you. Your actions and poetry reflected the great love you had towards your wife and family.

Everyone of your friends has been totally charmed and delighted and honored to have been a part of your life, or rather that you were a part of theirs.

Perhaps that is the best and ultimate prize, the memories and love that we leave in the hearts of those that are left behind. I think you know that your Nobel Prize did not gain you any deeper love or affection from your friends than that which you already had. What that award elicited from those friends was a wonderful, gleeful, happy, delighted thrill that Charlie really did it!

How happy and content everyone is that you had some time to see and enjoy the impact of your prize on not only the world of science and chemistry, but on your own chosen hometown of Salem.

Thank you for the motivation and inspiration you gave to Johnny Campbell and all the factors that created Stand Up For Salem. In this spirit of rebirth for Salem, I was asked to do this column, and I am very thankful for that also.

In the glow and glory of it all you had the graciousness and concern to say that you hoped the limelight would only help to accentuate the goodness, the beauty, and the worth of Salem.

Mr. Pedersen, it took a long time for a lot of us to discover you in our midst. That, in itself, should teach us the lesson that we need to look around for all those other folk in our towns that perhaps will never be revealed by a Nobel Prize but are there nonetheless, as caring and concerned as you for the world around them.

I was allowed the privilege of meeting you and to later return with my wife and son. I wanted so much for my young son to meet you and always to remember he had met a Nobel laureate and to have held your prize. We all left your home dutifully impressed with your scrapbooks and your reminiscences of your trip to Stockholm and the ceremony.

At home we talked about you from the standpoint of your graciousness and demeanor.

My wife spoke of your sweetness, and your love for your garden, and your concern that the honor and glory fall on Salem and away from you.

My son had a wonderful experience to share with a seventh grade science class of a kind and gentle man who seemed to enjoy our visit very much.

I know of your wish that your gravestone should contain only your wife's name and your name and the loving epitaph, "They found each other." A gentle, caring phrase that speaks volumes of a love now reunited.

This town and its people, for a little while, got to share in your glory and light and we too "found each other." We will never again return to be quite what we were before that wonderful autumn day two years ago and this is good and well and as it should be.

You left us as serenely and peacefully and poetically as you dwelt among us all these years, and we thank God for this blessing for you.

Thank you for having touched our lives, our hearts, and our hopes.

Peace
be unto you,
Ron LeHew, artist

Today's Sunbeam, Salem, N.J., Sunday, November 19, 1989

Get Ready for the Hustle and Bustle of the Holidays

A s you settle back to read today's paper and this column, I do hope all is peaceful and calm at your house. Do savor it if you can because this week is likely to be very close to the last vestiges of peace and quiet that you'll have till sometime around Jan. 2, 1990!

I love this week coming up. Just in case you forgot, 67 people and a big fat turkey (no, I don't mean Uncle Jim) are probably going to show up at your place this Thursday!

Aha! You did forget, didn't you?

Well now that I shot this day's relaxation for you, let's talk a little Thanksgiving merriment.

I take a great deal of teasing from various friends over my enthusiasm for holidays. Hey! Why put them in the year if you're just going to "ho, hum" them by like any other day?

I am so happy letting my imagination carry me away into the spirit of any given holiday. About the only special days I can't get a good enthusiastic fantasy for is Groundhog Day and Be Kind to Cats Week.

My fantasies allow me to completely accept the story of the Pilgrims and the first Thanksgiving as gospel in spite of the way historians really think it happened.

My own Hollywood version affords me great pleasure as I work myself to a frazzle helping with the house cleaning and the shopping.

One of the fun parts of the holidays is the hustle and bustle, provided it is approached with a modicum of sanity and finesse. This takes good advance planning so that almost everything is done prior to the last minute.

I've been known to push an empty cart around the market aisles just to try and absorb everyone else's frantic, last-minute panicked frenzy!

I occasionally will utter phrases like, "Oh! I still have so much to do!" or "Oh! I'll never be ready!" as I pretend to sort of stagger and wipe a supposed sweaty brow.

If all those other frantic, frenzied souls thought for one moment that I was really caught up and finished with my shopping, and that I was just out to soak up a bit of holiday hustle and bustle just for fun, they'd probably beat me to death somewhere between the stuffing mix aisle and canned goods!

For what better reason to be done with the hassle than to have an hour or so to attend the community church service on Thanksgiving Eve. I find that this hour is as special to my Thanksgiving festivities and enjoyment as cranberries, stuffing and the Macy's parade.

To celebrate only the outward show of a holiday and to lose sight of its deeper meaning is to miss out on a wonderful, magical vision that gives the special day its substance and flavor. To delve into its true meaning is to be able to fully live in it and appreciate and be fulfilled by its celebration.

In Salem, as in most communities in the county, the various churches take turns each year hosting Thanksgiving Eve service. Lots of folks from the other denominations gather at the host church for the evening.

How much more into the spirit of Thanksgiving could you ask for than this coming together of people from all across the community?

Among many of the great old hymns of Thanksgiving, we always sing "We Gather Together To Ask The Lord's Blessing." That wonderful homespun hymn conjures up great images of a grateful people thanking God that they came through life for another year.

It matters little whether these musical images are of Pilgrims and Indians or just you and me grateful for our health or the health of a loved one, having a job, or that we spent our year surrounded by the love of family and friends.

You see so many of the folks that make up the various facets of life in your town, but now you get to be with them in a setting of reverence and peace and prayer. You are allowed a whole new viewpoint of that person.

It helps to kindle one of those special glows that a friend of mine calls the "warm fuzzies," a delightful set of words, whatever your heart takes them to mean.

How much fun it is to see how the various churches bring their special traditions to this service. It's so heartening to see and hear the various ministers and to sample all the marvelous choirs that make up the spiritual life of our towns!

To attend these services is to experience a lovely feeling of belonging and being one with each other on this special night. The entire church radiates a glorious feeling of gratefulness and Thanksgiving.

We sense, by our participation and involvement, that spirit of the truth that we are truly all God's children. All titles and labels and distinctions and all other delusions of position are left at home, and we come together and give thanks and praise because it just feels "real good."

There are all the decorative embellishments that enhance the spirit of the evening: program covers with nostalgic hazy photos that become icons of families saying grace or of cornucopias filled with the bounty of the land; beautiful bouquets of fall flowers will decorate altar steps; window sills will hold baskets of vegetables and sheaves of grain.

All these are wonderful, enduring delights for one's heart and mind and spirit. They all fit together to make this last Thursday in November not just another last Thursday in a month, but a special day with a special aura and majesty.

We have not yet begun to talk of turkey and pumpkin pies. Have not yet spoken of the thrill of decades-old rivalries on a football field, nor of the beauty of a candlelit table golden in the glow of a setting sun waiting for family and friends to gather.

So many happy, wonderful qualities connected with its preparation and celebration if we just open up and reach out and be receptive to the spirit of it all!

As an individual I am so thankful for so many things in my life and career.

But writing in the spirit of this column, I am so very thankful for the tremendous beauty of this county, the spirit and goodness of its people and their care, love and concern.

In this same spirit, I am thankful that I write and draw in a free land where I am confined only by the boundaries of my own heart and mind and for the wonderful opportunity to be expressive and to have a voice.

This column is so thankful it has a readership. A few of your names are Mae, Dan, Vic, Jo, Bill, Jinx, Sharon and Rae.

You live in all parts of this county and are such a part of its fullness. Some of you clip this column and save it, or share it with others. You are all so giving and generous in your comments. Be so very assured you are all a part of my Thanksgiving prayers of this week and for always.

Today's Sunbeam, Salem, N.J., Sunday, December 3, 1989

Of Christmases in Our Past, Present and Future

In a very clever book written by Jack Finney and entitled "Time and Again," people who dress in period costumes and surround themselves with the décor of a given time discover that with enough concentration and imagination they are capable of transporting themselves back through time to any period of their choosing.

It's a pretty neat trick if you can do it and I get to come pretty close.

Along with sugarplum fairies dancing in my head, the things I love the very best about the Christmas season in Salem County are the "Woodstown by Candlelight" Tour and last year's recent addition of the yuletide tour of Market Street in Salem. Both tours allow me to act out one of my happiest fantasies.

Several years ago, the Woodstown tour committee was wondering where they could find someone with a big enough mouth and enough nerve to wear a costume and be their town crier for their Christmas tour. A very beloved friend, Marian Biernbaum, without blinking an eye, assured the group that she had just such a person in mind.

Ever since that fateful meeting I have had the role of town crier for an avocation. I daydream my way through eleven months of the year just to get to December and these two Christmas tours.

I have a wonderful costume of pewter buttons, buckles on my shoes, knee breeches, stockings, a wonderful black cape and a tricorn hat. My son, in his costume, comes along with me and is the bell ringer, while I "cry out" a Christmas greeting to all the visitors.

This year, good friends on Market Street gave us a gift of an early 1800s lantern which will add to our image just nicely.

These two tours are the all and everything of a festive, decorative, enchanting and charming Christmas season. By this reading, Woodstown's tour will have been over already, but you can still go on the Market Street yuletide tour on Saturday, Dec. 16 from 5 p.m. to 9 p.m.

Each tour seems to have its own special magic, its own distinct flavor and feel.

It is nothing short of awe-inspiring to walk down Main Street in Woodstown and see literally every window aglow with candlelight. As you visually thrill to this sight, your ears start to catch the faint notes of a Christmas carol played by a brass ensemble echoing from someone's porch.

While lost in a mist of total enchantment, someone hands you hot wassail and sugar cookies . . . Does it get any better than this?

The message of Christmas is abounding everywhere this night. All the beauty and the merriment and the joy of the season are the hallmarks of this tour.

And Christmas comes to historic Market Street in Salem. This is only the second year for this tour and its promise is magnificent and enthralling.

To walk Market Street in this season, this night, is to live out the poetry of a Christmas that speaks of charm and elegance and peace. It is a beautifully carved music box just waiting to be breathlessly opened and lovingly experienced.

Last year as we walked amid those beautiful homes and peeked through original glass windows at the Christmas scenes within, it was impossible not to imagine that one was lost in time. Its peace and serenity seemed a living illustration of the beautiful words of the Christmas hymn: " . . . how silently, how silently, the wondrous gift is given."

When speaking to one another, visitors spoke with much excitement and used phrases tinged with sheer delight to describe the various homes they had visited.

They seemed so moved by the antiquity that is found in these homes. Combine this with a garland-bedecked fireplace, a beautiful Christmas tree and some holly and these folks felt they had a spiritual experience of the first magnitude!

A handbell choir and dozens of candles in wrought iron holders brings a loveliness to St. John's Church that is beyond compare.

The magic of these tours, the history that is so pervasive, becomes very intensified for me and I hope for my son. As we rest against a stone marker in St. John's churchyard, we note that it has been there since 1772.

At the home of a friend, I sit for a while at a desk made right here in Salem County in the 1700s. I am enveloped in an interior that is a perfect setting for a cape and a tricorn hat. As my knee blocks out part of the view, I see burgundy breeches and white stockings against a beautifully carved fireplace whose light reflects in my shoe buckles.

In the next room is a marvelous lady from Pennsville who sits spinning wool in lovely solitude, illumined only by the glow of the fireplace. She looks transformed by her colonial dress and cap. She appears to have that same wonderful feeling that for a fleeting, brief moment could return her to a Christmastide 200 years ago.

The room is empty of visitors, no cars go by to disrupt the quiet and a grandfather clock chimes the hours . . . you are hearing the very same sound that someone else heard two centuries before and it is so hard not to sense your place in the long line of humanity that has come down through the ages.

Your mind and heart yearn to hear the tales that a walk-in fireplace could tell of this home, all the human dramas it bore witness to. It heard the laughter and happiness of young children, the fears and sorrow over ill and dying family members. Did it warm the breakfast of a young girl on her wedding day perhaps?

After the Woodstown tour, there is always a wonderful party for all the people who worked as part of the evening. Lots of good food and refreshments and a host of laughing, happy folks make a wonderful warm ending to a lovely night.

As I leave, I find that I am alone in the midnight quiet of North Main Street. As a fond farewell gesture to Woodstown, I do wish I could ring my bell and cry out my Christmas message one last time till next year, but all the town is asleep by now and so I stay this desire.

As I pause for one last look around at Woodstown by candlelight, I amuse and warm myself with a thought that someday perhaps, a hundred years from now, that late at night on the first Friday in December, people will say that if you listen ever so carefully you will hear the faint sound of a ringing bell and a far away voice echoing out the invitation ". . *to come and find the warmth and charm of the yuletide season that is Woodstown by Candlelight.*"

Surely one day this column is bound to create some sort of an award. This way I could give recognition to those who I think make life in this county so much the sweeter by their contributions.

Maybe a "LeHew Loves Ya" button or pin, etc. Till then, and for right now, I wish to give about 86,000 pounds of love, praise, and adulation to Hazel Davis and the Salem City Singers for their wonderful holiday performance at the Old Courthouse last Sunday afternoon.

You folks, along with the Johannes Brass, gave a Christmas gift beyond value and measure to all of us who were there. What a treasure are your voices and talents and how very grateful we are that you belong to us.

Today's Sunbeam, Salem, N.J., Sunday, December 17, 1989

Eight Days Before Christmas and Not an Idea in Sight

'Twas eight days before Christmas
And all through the town,
I was shuffling and mumbling
And feeling quite down.
It was soon to be press time
My deadline drew near,
I had no idea
For a column, I fear!
I screamed at my paper
And kicked the typewriter,
Never let it be said
That I wasn't a fighter.
Well I stamped and I stomped
And I bit through a rock,
I guess it is settled,
I had "writer's block."
I moaned and I prayed
Then I sunk into gloom,
When all of a sudden
There was a glow in the room!
I staggered and stumbled
And clutched at my breast,
Hang on just a minute
I'll tell you the rest . . .
Because of the season
I had reason to pause,
And expected to see none other
Than old Santa Claus!
Well, I quickly recovered
And opened my eyes.
I truly was in
For one big surprise!
She was gorgeous and blond

And right sure of herself,
She had it all over
Some fat little elf.
In her one hand a pencil,
In her other a pad,
A paper gown out of newsprint,
Was I going quite mad?
"Where did you come from?
What is your name?
My name is LeHew,
Art and writing's my game!"
"Don't be silly.
You should be more solemn,
I happen to know
You've no idea for your column."
I sunk to my knees
And pounded the floor,
"You're right! There's no column!
Bring it up, please, no more!"
"My name it is Mona,
To your luck and delight,
I am the Fairy Godmother
Of all those who write!
Now pick up your pencil
And write what I say.
We'll have you a column
By the end of this day!"
"Oh, thank you. Oh, thank you.
Oh, thank you, indeed!
"Dear Reader," she started,
Now here is the score
Concerning the latest
On the Middle East war!
And taxes, aagghh, taxes,
What can I say?
They continue to rise
We continue to pay!
The stock market faltered,
They say it might crash.
Some greedy stock broker
Just ran off with the cash.

If this ain't enough
About our problems today,
Here are a few others
I think you should say . . .
Some charming young preacher
Who preached of salvation
Tried to lease me a place
To take a vacation!
He took all the money
I had in this life,
Bought make-up and mink coats
For Tammy, his wife!
Of crime waves and drug busts
There's never enough,
Readers really seem
To groove on this stuff!
Aren't my ideas super?
Don't you think they are great?
So start on your column,
Bet you cannot wait!"
The sweat beads they trickled
From my head to my collar,
Getting up my nerve
I leaped up and hollered,
"Now hang on a minute!"
I started to say.
"I really do think
There's some better way
To write up a column
For people to read
Without having to write
About crime, war and greed!"
With her hand to her forehead,
Her brows were all knit,
She screamed, "Don't be a dimwit!"
Don't be a twit!"
"I hate to upset you,
You'll just have to see,
I don't think your ideas
Are quite right for me!
I write of happenings and events

And things that are neat,
And all the good folks
You meet on the street,
Of fairgrounds and parade routes,
And all of that stuff,
Local traditions and color,
And if that's not enough . . .
I write of a landscape that is lovely indeed,
We are friends,
We are neighbors,
What else do we need?"
With a look of disgust
She stood up on her toes,
And placing her thumb
On the tip of her nose,
She wiggled her fingers
And through my skylight she rose.
And she exclaimed
As she flew out of sight,
"You're just too provincial,
And your ideas a fright!"
Well, my dear readers,
What can I say?
Still I haven't an idea
For a column today!
I am filled with despair.
I am loaded with dread.
I only can write –
MERRY CHRISTMAS! instead.

Today's Sunbeam, Salem, N.J., Sunday, December 31, 1989

A Year of Unforgettable Images from Salem County

Inspired by two friends of mine, I have been diligently keeping a daily journal ever since last spring.

While going back through several pages, I became really excited and caught up in a lot of things that are now a part of a year gone by, never to return.

I was thinking about writing my column on this sort of "rerun" of my days in Salem County.

In the height of my trying to arrive at a decision, I discovered that the appointed Psalm reading for the day was Psalm 45 and that its very opening line is, "My heart is stirred with a noble theme."

Upon that discovery, I decided that this was too good a sign to ignore and, so, here goes.

What a wonderful year this has been here in the county–a great year, a fun year, one of beautiful, loving, spiritual experiences.

Some of these are the following:

Great moments brought about by nature's return each day with something new to experience, the meeting and making of new friends, and rediscovering the love of old ones.

I've been to Disney World. I shook the hand of President Carter and had Beverly Sills cast her smile on me. Once I had all the shrimp I could eat in Carlisle, Pa. One time I even got money back from the IRS!

Nothing can compare to just about any given day here in Salem County.

I share with you one of the sweeter visual "highs" of the past years. My entry for July 29 reminds me that I had lunch at Hudock's. (Yes, the place with the great chicken).

It goes on to say, "Against a backdrop of tall, green stalks of corn, I watched as a young mother lifted a beautiful young child in the air, her white-blond hair swirling about in the wind, her hair glowing against the dark background.

"Both of them were lost in each other, giggling and hugging, and laughing and loving. Suddenly, a wonderful orange and yellow and black butterfly came to rest on the baby's blond hair for just the instant and then if flew away as merrily as it appeared."

I think God must have had lunch at Hudock's that day.

Because I was giving early morning drawing classes to a wonderful group of Woodstown ladies last April, I had to drive through Mannington Meadows on Old Kings Highway about 7:30 each morning of class.

The souls and pens of a hundred writers could never fully describe the beauty of Mannington on an early spring morning. My heart and spirit long to see it again. Its memory brings a joy and an ache to my heart.

A low, clear and brilliant sunlight sweeps dramatically and forcefully across the fields. It shimmers off a soft, pale gray-violet mist that diffuses the first several inches of everything that grows or is built upon the land.

To sense this contrast of cool blues and greens of shadows against the intense, sunlit surfaces of trees and flowers and barns, is to thank God for the gift of sight, and mind, to perceive it all. There is a joy and beauty to this panorama that brings tears to your eyes.

My journal recalls for me that on March 15 in Elsinboro, I heard the first of the spring "peepers" making their wonderful chorus that is synonymous with the coming of warm, wet earth and tulips.

There are the notes on seeing the red haze of the buds on the apple and peach trees over around Shiloh and up in Mullica Hill. These same orchards which so soon will burst into full bloom cause us to love and long for the paintings of Van Gogh more than ever.

There was the evening when the only soul on all of Main Street in Woodstown was a suspendered shopkeeper sweeping his walk with a push broom at the quiet close of a hot July day.

I waited expectantly for a Mickey Rooney newspaper boy or a Jimmy Stewart businessman to come along . . . but there was just my son and me to offer up a smile and a hello.

During the vesper hours on a drive between Alloway and Elmer, I enjoyed the dark green fields of corn waving against a sky of pinks and lavenders.

There was the summer night driving through Pennsville when the sun appeared as a perfectly rounded, red-orange, surrealistic disc, glowing out of an evening of South Jersey humidity.

Happiness is the beauty and fun of a spring Saturday morning at Butler Gardens or to note the gorgeous, picture-perfect autumn scene created by "Dad's Produce" on Pennsville Road.

I fell in love a lot this year. Sometimes it was brand new and sweet, and sometime just rediscovered and warmly treasured.

For some of these people, I haven't even a name. For others, there are far too many to name.

There is the checker at the Acme who looks like Michael Jackson, only much prettier and so very nice . . . just *everybody* at the county nursing home . . . the Revs. Rolle and Root . . . nurses at the hospital . . . waitresses at the Salem Oak Diner . . . Harry Suter . . . "Fattie" and Marge . . . so many more.

I was especially drawn to a 15 year-old sweetheart named Tina Johnson from Woodstown who went through, wrote and published a book about her back surgery, and helped us get through the same ordeal for my son, Christian.

Speaking of "super citizens," every optimistic bone in this artsy old body tingled to read about the Penns Grove folks who took it upon themselves to put up the town's Christmas lights!

There is great news from Carneys Point with its Dunn's Park renewal and all the pride and positive feelings being generated by that project. Salem will soon be starting the construction phase of "Stand Up For Salem."

I had wonderful gifts given to me throughout the year.

The night of the Halloween Parade, Bill Haskett gave me an "I Love Alloway" button and sent it via Charlie Ahl.

What guaranteed "Men for All Seasons" are they!

Norman Fisher gave me a wonderful tile with my portrait on it copied from the newspaper by his mother, the late Esther Fisher, a dear friend and a very talented china painter.

My Christmas was made all the sweeter by a lovely cut-paper Christmas picture from, and by, Doris Dague because she is just the dear person she happens to be.

We experienced a tremendous outpouring of care and love from St. John's Church for my son's surgery and my Dad's passing.

My Dad never got to read any of my columns. He would have cut each one out and then hung out at the Acme or post office for days and showed them to everyone! I guess it is from him that I developed my love of "cruising" the aisles of the Acme!

I said good-bye to my neighbor, Tom, who wrote the book on what being a neighbor is all about. As long as I write of caring and helpful people, his spirit shall always be part of my life and of this column.

I am an artist by trade. I make pictures to sell my product, to tell the story, to convey the message.

This column on this New Year's Eve 1989 is meant not so much to talk about my year, but to make a picture for you that is heartfelt and love inspired.

I have New Year hopes and wishes and love abounding for all of you. I hope today's "picture" will inspire you to a great year of your own in Salem County where you will open up the doors and windows of your soul and your senses, and let all of the beauty of this area enter in.

I hope you find not only the beauty of nature that is God's gift to us, but the beauty of the people who live here. We all have a touch of the Divine within us and nowhere does it flourish any brighter or sweeter or more evident than here at home.

Though I don't know who penned these, I leave you with a wonderful set of picture-making words for 1990 . . . "I wish you butterfly mornings and wild flower afternoons."

Today's column is the 18th one I've done. Without the support of Mae Allen, my former English teacher, I'm afraid I would barely appear literate! Thanks, love and gratitude to you for keeping me on track.

Today's
Sunbeam
Columns

1990

Today's Sunbeam, Salem, N.J., January 14, 1990

'Home' Not Always Where Ancestors Put Down Roots

One of the more depressing cliches we have as part of our language relates that, "You can pick your friends but not your relatives."

I guess I just feel that to arrive at such a determination is to be in a very sorry state of affairs. Should not the love and caring of the family, one member for another, be sort of a buffer against some of life's whims and vicissitudes?

Well, just let me say I've had quite a time of it with my family! I recently went very far out of my way for them! And I've had them up to here (columnist indicates with hand gestures that he was surrounded by various heights of people up to his waist, shoulders, above him, etc.)!!!

And I loved and reveled and gloried in every minute of it!

"Going out of my way" is in reference to a 477-mile trip I made to Lancaster, Ohio, to attend a family reunion.

My family, on my mother's side, has a mutant gene which dictates, "Why plan for months what you can throw together in about three days?" It is a very spontaneous family grouping I hail from.

Late one evening, the phone rang and much to my delight I discovered that the caller was one of my very favorite cousins. Well, being doubly delighted to discover that another cousin was with her, I proceeded to try to find out who died, got married, hit the Ohio Lottery (do they have one?) or just what was so catastrophic a calamity that it took two cousins to break the news.

They proceeded to say that very soon a literal cast of thousands were to assemble in central Ohio for a family reunion.

My first thought was that in all the intense planning I had been overlooked and they forgot to mail my invitation. Being of a very forgiving nature, I was willing to forgive the oversight, and I asked how many weeks away this epic event was to take place.

The answer: Not weeks, it's this Sunday! Well, after righting my chair and getting up off the kitchen floor, I asked how many months ago had they decided to have it, trying to determine just how long I had been slighted. The answer: Not months, just three days before!

Let me tell you, these gals had a phone campaign going that made "Dialing for Dollars" look like child's play!

With love-laden voices, I was begged to come "home." They said I just had to make the pilgrimage "home."

"Home" now in my mind's eye was being manifested as something akin to the New Jerusalem!

With trembling lips and tear-stained cheeks and soggy beard, I joyfully acclaimed my acceptance that, "Yes! Yes! Oh, Yes! I'll be there. I'll come 'home!'"

Well, it wasn't till after I hung up that it hit me. I was "home!"

Salem, New Jersey, is my home. The same as Lancaster, Ohio, is theirs!

I had been duped by my own family! A great sense of the dramatic runs strong in this family.

What wonderfully warm and loving people these "Buckeyes" from Ohio all are. They are the type of people I would choose for friends. When I need to laugh and have my heart set aglow for a few moments, it is to memories of them I often turn.

Out of a family of nine brothers and sisters, there is still one aunt and one uncle going great guns. It is the next generation that now makes up most of the family.

Our parents were all such marvelous characters and personalities that we all wish to keep their memories and spirits alive by trying to get together. This generation seems to show a wonderful talent and potential for being just as "whacko" as the last one!

For those of you who knew my mother, just multiply by nine and you'll get some idea of what kind of lineage my cousins and I are descended from.

As a young kid, I was always so envious of my friends who had, seemingly, multitudes of aunts and uncles and grandparents nearby. At holiday time, they spoke of going to grandma's house for special family dinners or great gatherings around a summertime cookout.

My only living grandma was a lot further away than just "over the river and through the woods." There is nothing very romantic or homey and warm about a 12-hour trip hauling down the Pennsylvania Turnpike, is there?

When we made the trip, Dad always specified that you had better be coordinated with the car's fuel consumption. When the gas gauge said "E," your bladder better be reading "F" or you would be out of luck later on.

My folks were both born and raised in Lancaster, Ohio, and moved to Salem because Dad worked for Anchor Hocking. They came here in 1941 and I was born a few years later. Due to this turn of events, I am able to stake my claim as a birthright Salem Countian.

Every immigrant family of the latter 1800s came through Ellis Island, waved teary-eyed at the Statue of Liberty and docked in New York City, the gateway to American!

My great-grandparents missed all this and landed in Baltimore! Maybe they got blown off course or something, but Baltimore?!? Harbor Place and the Aquarium weren't even opened yet!

Can you picture a bunch of Austrians trying to figure out what to do with a Chesapeake Bay crab? I am still devouring crabs in silent tribute to their first adventure in the New World.

While I am not a part of a family name that locally goes back many, many years, I nonetheless love the lore and legends and mystique that the old family names conjure up.

Names like Cuff, Hassler, Waddington, Layton, Sparks, Acton, Gross and so many more. There are so many marvelous local stories associated with these names that add color and life to our local histories.

Salem Countians have that knack of being related to just about everyone else in the town or county. I have one set of friends who share the same grandparents about five generations back. There are friends who, before, as well as after the wedding, shared the same last name.

I truly admire the folks who will hear a name and then proceed to say something like: "Oh, yes! She was a Dixon and married a Smith and his mother was one of John Jones' daughters and you remember how her brother married one of the Green sisters whose grandpa was married to . . . "

This is similar to the oral histories that primitive tribes use to keep their histories recorded for succeeding generations.

With society today being so transient and mobile, as well as with the increasingly high rate of divorce and single parenting, perhaps this wonderful gathering of names and lore will suffer in the same way that other traditions have suffered as society's structure changes.

A wonderful local mannerism is the way in which some of the older folks will refer to others as "Cousin Howard" or "Brother George" or "Sister Sarah."

This gives a wonderfully warm and cozy feeling to people's relationships and a sense of pride in their belonging to a family that they love enough to publicly claim.

To recall some of the old family names adds a sense of stability and familiarity to our communities. While a lot of us are not members of a stated "old family," we all seem to be able to recall the role that a family played in the history and growth of our towns as shopkeepers, doctors, lawyers, factory workers, farmers or politicians.

A few years ago I took my dad back to Lancaster for his 65th class reunion. One of dad's classmates came up to me and said since I was not a native, he thought I should know of the good name my parent's families held in the town's history.

He had known all my grandparents and great-grandparents. He spoke of family members that I knew only through antique photographs. To me they were people of another time and era and he made them so wonderfully real for me!

He described their personalities, physical builds, quirks and traits; all things that allowed me to see them as real people who walked these streets and dwelled within these houses.

He so charmingly recalled that my Aunt Peggy broke his heart in the first grade in 1911!

He ate in restaurants owned by my grandfather. As a boy he admired the horses and carriages in the livery stable once owned by another grandfather, who was put out of business by the automobile.

To share in a family life is a wonderful thing. Many of our friends have "adopted" us and we now have wonderful extended families. We have Thanksgiving dinner with 20 other folks. We are part of birthday parties and anniversaries, and we love it!

Christmas festivities are shared with another family group that we help to swell the ranks of at holiday time.

When they landed in Baltimore, my great-grandparents used all of their money to buy train tickets for as far west as they could go. They were able to go as far as Lancaster, Ohio.

Just think, if only they had just gone 65 miles up to Wilmington, Del., and turned right into New Jersey, they still would have been in the Land of Opportunity, had a few bucks left over, and best of all, 100 years later I wouldn't have had to drive all day on the Pennsylvania Turnike just to get to a reunion!

Today's Sunbeam, Salem, N.J., Sunday, January 28, 1990

Salem County Sired Its Share of Wonderful Artists

It is during my ramblings and wanderings through the quiet beauty of the Salem County countryside that I come to feel as a kindred spirit to all the artists that this county has produced.

Artists feed off their environment and the various influences that their surroundings provide. Each sees it and expresses it in his or her own way. The sheer joy and thrill of being an artist is to know that the act of living and breathing and seeing and feeling is a creative action. It is so important for artists to be able to sense and know their relationship to the world around them.

In the first half of this century so many artists left America to reside in the great art centers of Europe. It was in Paris and Munich where all the great art movements were being explored and digested and discovered.

So many Americans returned home discouraged. This was especially true of those young painters from the Midwest. These were artists who grew up amid the wheat fields of Kansas and tent revivals on summer nights, barn raisings and square dances. They could not get the knack of wrapping their hearts and souls around Parisian cabaret scenes and the harshness of German Expressionism, or the simplicity of Bauhaus design.

They came to realize that "home," for better or for worse, was what they knew, loved and understood, be it Iowa farmers or New York City street scenes. They learned techniques and mannerisms from their European counterparts but they applied them to familiar themes from home.

I have many times argued against the belief that someone is born an artist. Those of artistic temperament are perhaps given the sensitivities that are needed to be creative. Some take their sensitive natures and express them as writers, actors, dancers and some become artists.

My mother constantly fed my senses because she herself was of a similar nature. In the summers during art school I worked a 12-hour night shift at the Heinz plant. Even though I was reeking of dirt and tomatos, she would pick me up at the end of my shift and we would take a drive through the countryside. It was her belief that I needed to see the beauty of the early morning after enduring a 12-hour shift at the plant. I may have learned to cruise an Acme aisle from Dad, but I developed a sense of beauty and romance from my mother.

I never tire of talking and thinking about the influence Salem County has had on my life and my career. I oft times think and wonder about the other artists that were born and raised here. This county can be so proud of the artists it has fostered and nurtured over the past two hundred years.

Everett Shinn was written up so wonderfully in the late Edith DeShazo's book of the same name. Everett was born and raised in Woodstown and became part of the only true American art movement in our history. While having the dubious name of "Ashcan School," this movement nonetheless made its own great contribution to American painting.

Tom Sinnickson sidestepped a business career to pursue one of being a commercial artist. During World War II Tom was in Greenland and it was there that a German submarine sunk the troop ship Dorchester. It was upon the sinking ship's deck that four military chaplains gave up their life jackets so that others might survive. Tom painted some of the first canvases of this heroic and inspiring moment in American history.

While speaking of selfless and unselfish acts, we need to mention Woodstown's Lydia Austin Parrish. Lydia, while an art student in Philadelphia, met, fell in love with, and married fellow artist Maxfield Parrish. Parrish became one of the glowing lights in America's Golden Age of Illustration. She gave up her own promising career in order to allow him to follow his while she kept him, in her words, "sheltered from the world."

Alice Barber Stevens of Mannington began her career in Philadelphia in the 1870s and became an illustrator for the famous Harper's Weekly and did many illustrations for the works of Bret Hart and Nathaniel Hawthorne.

The mid-to late-1800s spanned the career of Salem's George Petit. Petit became a popular historical and portrait painter in the American art scene of this period. He returned to Salem each summer and stayed at Ford's Hotel. He loved to write and composed a poem entitled "Old Salem Town."

George Washington Canarroe became a very successful portrait painter. Many of his portraits of early Salem citizens can still be found in county homes and in the Salem County Historical Society. He died Easter morning 1882 and the Pennsylvania Academy of Fine Arts passed a resolution acknowledging his passing and his contributions to American painting.

Lucy Holmes grew up in Elsinboro in the mid 1850s and studied with the great Thomas Eakins in Philadelphia. She was considered "odd" because she would traipse through the fields of Elsinboro and set up her easel to paint outdoors. In the Pennsylvania Academy exhibit of 1883, she exhibited "Elsinboro Meadows."

Lucy received an honorable mention at the Chicago World's Fair of 1893. She returned to Salem in her last years, passing away in 1928.

Morris Hall Pancoast left to study in France in the 1890s and spend most of his life in New England. Two of his local works are of "Major's Wharf" and "Elsinboro Point."

As a young girl, Libby Fogg, who is now the head of the Salem Free Public Library, took drawing lessons from Mary Figlestahler. Mary was not originally from Salem but spent about 20 years here. She formerly owned my present home and had a studio in the same room as I do. When I first returned to Salem, I met a wonderful old woman who, in a lovely, wistful way, mentioned that every day as she walked past my house she would look up at the bay windows and my studio and smile, knowing that this house and Salem once again had an artist living in it.

I am so very lucky that I can live in Salem and yet pursue my career. In my time frame I have telephones, fax machines, and overnight mail delivery systems that allow me to deal with clients all over the country.

All the wonderful influences of my early years are still around me. They are here to renew me and inspire me all over again any time I need them.

There are all my beloved landscapes, the great skies that the flat land affords us, the humidity (while not always so pleasant) that softens and modulates nature's colors, the wonderful sculptural forms of this county's architecture and the people . . . always the people.

I spoke of and gloried in Salem County's artistic heritage of another time. It is now my time and my moment to try to strike a blow for my life and my career and to try to let it reflect on Salem.

While working and praying and hoping so much for my own career, my heart turns to another group of artists who reside and work in the county. They are artists who grew up here, were influenced and nurtured by all the same thing that I cherish artistically. They have come home to be teachers of the craft and not always to practice. Where would I, or any other artist, be without the nurturing and nudging and caring influence of these artists? They exist in such unassuming ways in the public schools all over this county. At the Teen Arts Festival in April, we can see the results of their love and dedication and determination reflected in the works of their students.

A few nights ago, on a drive down from Carneys Point, I stood by the roadside in Mannington and watched the full moon play hide and seek aided by wonderful small puffy snow clouds. The beautiful silver light ebbed and flowed and raced in great arabesques across the waters. One time the glow was here! Another time it was there! When it illumined the fields, wonderful lacy patterns of leafless tree limbs danced in the wind and etched themselves against the cloud forms . . . what a sight. What a thrilling piece of God's creation to behold.

In the splendor and the glory and the romance of this wonderful few moments in time, I again felt the kinship of all those artists whose souls and spirits ever paused to fall in love with this land that is home.

They may have left to pursue careers in more metropolitan areas, but it was here among this landscape and people much like you, and you, and you, that the seed was sown, the spark was blown aflame and the journey started. How so very blessed and fortunate were they that this was their beginning.

Today's Sunbeam, Salem, N.J., Sunday, February 11, 1990

Behind the Zaniness, Hearts Full of Love and Concern

What a wonderful piece of planning it is that, amid the dreariness and weariness of a February day, we should have the opportunity to celebrate the warmth and light and magic of love.

Ah! Love . . . that wonderful, joyous affliction of the heart that drives us all headlong into deliriums of ecstasy and delicious pain.

However and wherever we may find it, and however we do fare by it, thank God we have it.

I send one big Valentine and 87,000 pounds of chocolates with raspberry centers to all of you. Salem County runs wonderfully rampant with signs and examples of love. Acts of love, like lovers, come in all manner of forms and shapes and degrees of depth and color. I will not "kiss and tell," for rather, I would that you search out and discover them on your own. Their discovery then becomes a wonderful warm little secret for you to muse over and tuck away in your heart, to save for a rainy day, a gloomy day in February all your own.

As a Valentine from me to you, and to help start you on your way, I wish to share but one of the many inspired acts of love that our area generates. It concerns a group of my friends. These guys are just a big bunch of clowns. I mean it, really. These guys are always acting silly and goofy and just downright ridiculous. So what's the big deal about a bunch of guys cutting up, you may be thinking?

Ah! Dear and gentle reader . . . it is out of this "clowning around" that comes a wonderful example of warm, selfless giving and giving and more giving of love. I so proudly point out that my friends in question are the Pennsville Tall Cedar Clowns.

Locally, the clowns get their biggest exposure by their participation in all the local parades here in the county. On Thanksgiving Day, they can also be seen escorting a huge helium-filled balloon down the Parkway in Philadelphia's big televised parade.

In all of their parading, they add a wonderful sense of dazzling color and fun and zaniness to the day. But it is their work between the parades that is a story of love and care and concern for others in the world around them.

Most of you will never see the real work that these guys do for others, but you can be so very thankful for their work.

They bring laughter and love and joy in huge, wonderful overflowing armfuls to wheelchair-bound children at a summer camp for kids with muscular dystrophy. They are a regular fixture at the Alfred I. DuPont Institute, which is a children's hospital in Wilmington, Del. Would Christmas truly be here without a visit from the Tall Cedar Clowns at the Salem County ARC Center? The clients there don't think so! A group of kids with spina bifida are swept into happy, bright worlds of magic tricks and where clowns turn 5-foot-long balloons into poodle dogs and parrots. I can imagine the merriment and excitement they must bring to the residents of the Friends Home or the Salem County Nursing Home!

The group started in 1986 with nine men and has now grown to 22. The "tie that binds" is the all-consuming dedication that each man has to raise money for the fight against muscular dystrophy.

Three years in a row they have raised over $7,000 a year for "Jerry's kids." To help raise money, they hire themselves out for parties and picnics and other social affairs. On Labor Day weekend, they haunt the boardwalk in Wildwood handing out silk roses to seek donations for MD.

Roses and balloons go hand in hand at the Salem County Fair as the Tall Cedars set up their "rose" booth, always with a few clowns each night to help attract a crowd.

The visits to the hospitals and children's camps are their gifts and acts of love for which there is never a charge. They have a real propensity for bringing happiness to others. Smiles and laughter are the only payment they seek.

How really good are these clowns as clowns? For three years in a row they have won first place in clown competitions with other Tall Cedar clown units from all over the East Coast. Tall Cedars is a branch of the Masonic fraternal organization. All Tall Cedars support work on MD financially, but the clowns have really devoted themselves wholeheartedly.

They are very proud of their clown work and the part they play in the time honored tradition of clowning and making people laugh. It is very important to them that I mention the support they receive from their wives. When they march in the parades, their forces are joined and supported by many of their wives who are in costume with them, not to mention their help in designing and making of costumes.

All but two of the men are from the Pennsville-Penns Grove side of the county and most of them work at DuPont. Their oldest member "Pappy" Endres is 75 years young and can run circles around the rest of them!

Each one can share in wonderful memories and reasons they have for going back for more work with the kids. They thrive on seeing the happiness they bring to children in heartrending physicial condition.

The group, to a man (or should I say to a clown?), knows that this is the best thing they have ever done. The smiles and laughter and happiness they bring are, for each one, their "finest hour" of being a man, a Mason and clown.

"Socks," the clown, tells the one story that best sums it all up for the group. Ending one of their many visits at the DuPont Institute, he realized he had left his "box of tricks" in one of the kids' rooms. As he quietly stole back in to get it he heard one little girl say to another little boy, "Wasn't that the most fun you ever had?!"

Someone once defined religion as "the love of God in the life of man." Here you see God's love born out and aided by greasepaint, fright wigs and red foam-rubber noses. How so very, very content God must be with these clowns.

Today's Sunbeam, Salem, N.J., Sunday, February 25, 1990

Each Visit to the Salem Library Is Filled with Magic

While in special moods on special days, when conditions are right and time allows, I have any number of favorite places around our area that I love to visit.

Some days the feeling is manifested by an impromptu drive down a favorite country road. Other moments might inspire a visit to the Oak Diner and Butler Gardens.

I love any opportunity to go to McCoubrie's Pharmacy and joke with all the fun people who work there. A visit to the tax office, while excruciatingly painful, can be softened and soothed by a few minutes of passing banter with all the office staff.

I deposit money a few dollars at a time just to have an excuse to visit and flirt with all the marvelous tellers at my bank.

All these places and so many more just like them can be wonderful, bright, happy spots that color our days and memories of life here in the county. They can bring to us a sense of warmth and contentment and joy.

One of my favorite spots that can really set a tone to any day is to head over to the Salem Free Library. That wonderful old building is the epitome of the "home away from home." It is like the willing and waiting friend who you know is always there. As I step within, I find I always breathe a sigh of happy arrival.

Our library reminds me of the wonderful old traditional bookstores that you used to see in Philadelphia. Places like Leary's and Sessler's which have given way to modern, brightly lit bookstores such as we find in the malls. A visit to our library and the old book shops was like stepping into an engraving from Charles Dickens' England. These places seem to have a marvelous fragrance about them that stems from a combination of leather, paper and printing ink, and perhaps a modicum of dust!

Modern libraries with their flourescent lighting, dropped ceilings and indoor-outdoor carpet have a completely different ambiance about them for me. I certainly do appreciate the efficiency and convenience and modern facilities of the newer libraries and bookstores. It's just that they tend to lack that special patina, that lustre and charm, of the older ones.

Our library lends itself in such a warm way to wandering and rambling amid tall shelves of books. I guess "browse" is the truly suitable word and verb for this marvelous pastime. I always just wish that I could lay on the floor between the shelves and read a bit from this book or that, whatever happens to be within my reach.

Reading, to my way of thinking, is something that is always done in a prone position. Only newspapers are read in an upright pose unless, of course, it is Sunday's edition.

As a young kid, I remember cutting my artistic teeth on a beautiful spot within the library reading room. This scene focused around a certain tall, deep window which is unfortunately now blocked by a desk and some file cabinets.

On Saturdays about mid-afternoon, wonderful slanting bands of sunlight streamed through this lovely tall window and cast a beautiful fairy light over all the immediate area.

Peering between the sunbeams and panes of glass, you saw the Old Oak and the Friends burial ground in a very special kind of beauty. It was a very special way to see such a familiar scene.

Several years were to pass before I discovered that Vermeer, the great Dutch painter, saw the whole world bathed in just such a glow of sunlight. This window, among many things, was a wonderful, marvelous benefit to owning a library card.

My awareness and ongoing love affairs with the staff began in the early 1950s. To me as a young kid, the late Miss Frances Norton, who was head librarian, was a bit intimidating. As the years grew on, I came to care for her and enjoy her so very much for the wonderful person she was.

And the complete antithesis was Eleanor Rumsey, who worked with Miss Norton. Miss Rumsey was all charm, sweetness and light. To this day, when I think of grace and charm in women, Miss Rumsey is still the measure I go by.

It is all those varied and interesting personalities that the job seems to attract that really make the place hum. The current staff, with Miss Libby Fogg as head librarian, is just sheer delight! They have as much charm and character as the building does!

I say that with tons of love, respect and admiration for all those ladies who work there. It is just a marvelous potpourri of personalities and I am hopelessly infatuated with all of them.

Nothing ever is too much trouble, regardless of what you need or ask for. They all continue to help keep my career afloat with untold amounts of work on their part in providing research for my various job assignments.

Their great ability to provide information to the public just earned them the highest grade in their classification. This recognition for outstanding performance was just announced by the South Jersey Regional Library Cooperative.

To add to the library's continuing glory and honor, it has just been announced that Miss Libby Fogg, head librarian, has become one of eight recipients of the 1990 Women of Achievement Awards sponsored by the Salem County Commission on Women.

See how well documented my admiration of the library staff is. No hollow accolades in this column!

One never knows who you will run into during a visit, and I find that in itself is a great inducement to visit there. Everyone tends to join in the conversation and laughter that flows so nicely in that setting.

The staff, bless them, are always ready to laugh at some inane piece of teasing that I readily force on them. They do have to tolerate me though because my huge overdue book fines help make the payroll on any given week, or so it seems!

Books are so important to my life. I really know of nothing that has had the impact on my being that the love of books and reading has had.

Our library has a wonderful collection. If they do not have a particular volume, they are part of a great system that within days can supply you with the desired book.

As a current touch, you can even borrow video tapes from a list that changes monthly. They provide so many marvelous services to the area. They do a super job of keeping abreast of all the current books that everyone is reading. They readily accept recommendations from the reading public.

It is a truly marvelous place. It can become a wonderful refuge to flee to amid a noisy, frantic and busy world. Again, the gals there make it so comfortable and warm, and they all add such a special flavor to one's enjoyment and delight in the old place. What a sweet jewel in our crown.

As much as I love books, reading and the library, I'm afraid I am entirely upstaged and outdone by George Abbott.

George developed an endearing and lifelong passion for books at an early age. It was a lifelong wish of Mr. Abbott's to be buried as close as he could be to the library building that he loved so much.

George got his wish when he passed away in June of 1955. His grave is only a few feet away from the west wall of the library.

To this day, members of the staff are positive that, in the quiet hours before the building is opened, you will hear his spirit walking amidst his beloved books and library.

With my abiding love of the place, I thought his wish was really fantastic and not the least bit unreasonable. I myself plan on being cremated and, now that I think about it, the library does have that wonderful mantlepiece . . . maybe a small piece of empty shelf over in the art section?

Today's Sunbeam, Salem, N. J., Sunday, March 11, 1990

Embracing the Churches that Embrace Our Town

The other day, taking advantage of the fact that March came in like a lamb, I walked over to one of my favorite lunchtime haunts.

The air was bright and crisp and snappy, a few horn-honks here and there, a wave or two from some friends, all was lovely in God's world under a bright sun in a Kodachrome blue sky.

Kodachrome blue is the way artists describe those intense blues that Kodachrome film produces in your photos. When painting this type of sky, it can tend to dominate your canvas and thus it becomes a tricky type of sky to paint.

Against this intense blue sky, I viewed a scene that I've seen hundreds of times before and yet I thrill to it anew with each and every experience. What is lovelier and any more striking than seeing the tower of the "Town Clock Church," otherwise known as the First Baptist Church, against almost any kind of sky condition: late fall afternoon, a summer storm sky, any noontime such as today. It is always so stately, so powerful, so dynamic.

In Salem, your age and memory are challenged and determined by your ability to remember where you were and what you were doing the morning of Jan. 22, 1947 when the tower caught fire! Dan Harris tells one of the best stories I've heard of this historic event. Ask him about it sometime.

In my own little " Mary Poppins" world, I tend to bounce off the buildings and curbstones of Broadway relishing in the delightful mood this beautiful building has put me in!

Do you know how many churches you can see from Salem's main intersection at Broadway and Market? Six churches! All are beautiful examples of period architecture and construction. You can see Broadway Methodist, First Baptist, St. John's Espiscopal, the First Presbyterian, Friends Meeting and Memorial Baptist! All this from one viewpoint! How bad off can a town be that has this much spiritual presence in evidence?

It is so wonderfully inspiring to look around and see all of these magnificent buildings and to realize historically and spiritually just how important they are to our town's heritage. And these were just the ones in mid-town that I could collectively see. Salem has so many wonderful houses of worship all around us.

Very recently my son, for a school religion class, had to pinpoint the churches in his community on a map. We drove around one afternoon and found at least 20 churches and I'm sure we missed at least a couple more.

Wonderful, happy, endearing memories have always been associated with the various churches about town. The Quakers who feed the multitudes with chicken pot pie each Spring. All the wonderful ministers from Broadway Methodist who lived next door to us on Chestnut Street. The beauty and excitement of the "Walk A Christmas Mile" and viewing the churches on the walk in all their Christmas glory. Easter sunrise services under The Oak Tree! Wonderful! How ecumenical Salem folks seem to be.

I have always gone to St. John's and so much of my life and my family milestones are anchored to it. Christmas and Easter for me can only be celebrated there. It is most assuredly a wonderful, beckoning, loving home away from home for me.

How many hours I wiled away during the fourth grade at the Grant Street Grammar School as I longingly gazed out of the window and daydreamed on the beauty of the Presbyterian Church steeple. Stately tall trees that grew in the schoolyard made a beautiful base of fall color or spring blossoms out of which rose and rose this marvelous ornate steeple. Truly a silent finger pointing to God.

During art school, I commuted to Philadelphia via the 7 o'clock bus out of Salem. The bus was always parked and waiting over on Belden Street across from the Walnut Street Methodist Church.

Every morning I would climb aboard and somewhat wearily drape my body over a rear seat and study the quiet serene beauty of the church as it waited to receive the rays of the new day's sun. The homes were lost in a blue-gray light.

As the sun climbed a bit higher and cleared the homes, the steeple glowed brilliantly and the golden light set the windows to a sparkling shimmer.

Inspired by this scene, how many prayers on how many mornings did I offer up for the hopes and aspirations of the school day ahead? Lucky and truly blessed was this art student who could begin his day learning to draw and paint with such a wonderful example of nature in such striking splendor.

I grew up a block or two from the Ohab Shalom Synagogue. As a kid I was mystified to see everyone going to the "Jewish Church" on a Friday evening. Even though I had several Jewish friends at school and in the neighborhood, I had no idea what their service was all about. How could you spend your allowance downtown on Friday night if you had to go to "church?"

It was to be many years before I had the opportunity to attend a service there. Sadly enough, my first experience was to be for the funeral service for Sam Grechesky, a very beloved family friend who died a few years ago.

The front steps of St. Mary's Catholic Church will always hold tender heartfelt memories for me of my days as a lovestruck 11-year-old boy. How well I remember when a skinny, tomboy playmate became a veritable angel with red hair. I was allowed to breathe in the essence of love's rapture by walking her to Confession on Saturday afternoons.

I perspired in 90-degree heat for love, I caught pneumonia-like colds for love, I shivered alone in the darkness for love, and all on the front steps of St. Mary's Church. She threw me over finally for another guy. He was a Catholic boy and they probably met inside while I waited outside!

The '90s are projected to be a decade where the values of an earlier day are to return. Hopefully we will be putting aside our greedy rushes for things material and instead turn our thoughts and hearts to things that require a more spiritual approach. Perhaps then all these wonderful buildings will be filled to the rafters!

All these heavy and heady thoughts were contemplated while stuffing myself with pizza and root beer at Pat's. I sat where I could see across the street to the empty area where soon the Fenwick Plaza shopping area will be built. As I toasted it with my root beer, I was filled with many silent hopes and prayers for its success.

Stand Up For Salem and so many other local groups spawned by SUFS are working so hard to make this dream of a better day for Salem a reality. And I think we should all be saying a prayer every day for their success.

In my mental musings and meanderings, I could not help but note that all the midtown churches seemed to completely encircle the business district and the soon-to-be Fenwick Plaza. They appeared to take on a feeling of being like protective big brothers and loving sisters as they lent their strength and beauty to the business district around them.

They symbolize so much grace, majesty and endurance. They seem to fill our hearts and souls with a wonderful spiritual strength and belief of things that withstand the passage of time and create flow of continuity in spite of various setbacks that happen every couple decades. They have the potential to preach wonderful silent sermons to us if we would only listen.

While I would never care to replace a pew at St. John's with a table at Pat's Pizzeria, on that beautiful, early March day, God's presence was wonderfully real amid the streets of our town, and I was so grateful for the moments we shared.

Today's Sunbeam, Salem, N. J. , Sunday, March 25, 1990

With Spring, the Sweet World Around Us Awakens

As the tractor makes its furrows, turning up the damp dark earth that lies in rich contrast to neighboring green pastures, it appears as if the sea gulls streaming behind have been released from the earth. Is this where gulls go to spend the winter?

The Bradford pear trees with their lovely white blossoms give a beautiful, delicate softness to the downtown area. Daffodils, azalea blooms, dogwood blossoms and tulips are longed for and expected in the days ahead, the weeks to come.

Combine all the above with glowing warm sun, a gentle balmy breeze, temperatures in the 70s and our hearts leap within. Spring and all its symbolisms are not lost on us: rebirth, renewal, death awakening to new life, darkness has become light! Our weary, winter bones and mental processes rejoice and are invigorated and rejuvenated! Our souls are in love with life and become gentle and poetic. We have arrived at another spring in our lives.

Hallelujah!

When I dream of autumn, my feelings and longings recall the golden glow of late afternoon. It is the time where the world eases graciously and whisper-like into slumber for a while, truly the season of the romantics.

Spring is the morning of life, it is dawn, it is matins, and hours before noontide. One of its first delicious hints is in a gentle breeze. Be still and be aware, this breeze is neither cold nor warm, gentle, not blustery nor windy, it is something akin to a "just rightness!"

On the first night that we keep the windows open I love smelling and feeling the night air as it comes delicately through the curtains. It is so welcomed that I wish to bathe in it, to somehow absorb it within. To drink it in as an elixir.

This welcomed "opening of the windows" appears to be some thrilling little act of spring ritual that has gone unheralded and

uncelebrated. The other day at three different locations I overheard people quietly and secretively whisper to one another
. . . "yesterday, for the first time this season, I opened my windows!"

I wanted to jump right in and add my two cents worth but I was afraid to let them know I had eavesdropped on their whispered words.

How marvelous and wonderful is it to lie in bed and hear the crickets and the peepers making their own special kind of night music. This lulling and peaceful sound allows us to fall asleep in an aura of contentment and bliss, no stress or anxiety, an orchestra of nature whose season has run for millions of years, and tonight brings a symphonic peace and calmness to our day's end, thrilled to as if heard for the very first time.

At dawn a new type of music is heard as we lie abed, our eyes not yet opened, still half lost in sleep, we hear the robins, the cardinals, the finches all performing a sort of concerto with their combined songs. Some bring to us notes very sweet and clear, others sing sharp and quick, others lend to the sound a trilling, all held in harmony by the soft cooing of a dove who perches on the rain spout.

As these sounds gently and sweetly pry their way into your slowly awakening senses, they are wafted to you on that same alluring gentle wind of the night before.

What a gift nature gives to us. The sounds of the spring night and early morning falls over us like a prayer that bids us to sleep, or to awaken to a feeling of grace and thanksgiving. We are so blessed to have the gifts that allow us to hear and to see and to comprehend all of this wonderment.

To lie in bed and gaze out of the window is to read the sky signs and know it is spring. In spite of perhaps a few cold, blustery days still left, spring has made her mark in the heavens.

The wonderful and dramatic cloud laden skies of winter that I love and relish so, have now given way to that same gentle sweetness that caresses the daffodils and rustles through our curtains.

Along the horizon the sky is a creamy white that eases into purer hues the higher we gaze. The sky has soft, wispy swirls of gossamer white that are far too fragile and delicate to be called "clouds." These wisps of white blend and meld and fold their softness into a watercolor sky of cobalt blue that God has painted while we slept. As a final gesture of wanting it to be "just so," He has lightly and deftly caressed it with a stroke or two of rose pastel.

Finally awake, I hang off the window frame and see the crocus blooming in our rock garden. I make a promise that later on, about noon, I will go outside and study and love them a little. I love to sit or lie in the grass and enjoy the purity of their color and shape. Some have such fine stripes of color on them. Others are a pale lavender, most are rich purples and oranges. Noontide seems to be the ultimate hour for the crocus. It is so marvelous to feel the warm rays of the sun on one side, as your other side rests against the damp earth and cool grasses.

Spring flowers have a delicate translucency to their petals that allow the sunlight to pass through which makes them glow with a shimmer and intensity and beauty that one seems to see only in the hues of a piece of stained glass. To lie in the new grass amid the wild garlic and crocus, the weeds and the daffodils and to view the world from this eye level is to see a richer, fuller and more dramatic viewpoint of a simple backyard.

When we stand, we see a clump of grass here, some crocus there, a rock, some weeds, as we look down we see small sections. When you lie down and view it all through the blades of grass the world falls into wonderful layers and patterns like the backdrops and stage sets of a theater.

Patterns of light against dark, and dark shapes against the light; purples and oranges against tan-gray rocks against 10 shades of the green of new grass and foliage; the brilliance of red tulips set against a brilliant blue sky and the golden glow of sunlit daffodils against the pale pink buds of an azalea bush and the stage set goes on and on and on.

Sitting here amidst all of this happiness and world of light and color, bittersweet memories return of a long stay in the limited world of a hospital bed as the rest of the earth celebrated spring.

My doctors figured I was six shades of crazy when I told them I needed to get home very soon so that I could lay in the new grass, amid the wild garlic and watch the crocus shimmer in the breeze.

Doctors who spend eighteen hour days in the twilight land of big city hospitals are not really into crocuses, soft winds and sunlight. It's way down on their list of priorities. As I sit here today, in my own weed rampant patch of earth, I revel and rejoice and feel wonderfully inspired by all of this beauty that surrounds me . . . I thank God for all of those wonderful truths that the love and joy and appreciation of a day in spring can teach us.

On this most beautiful day in a very lovely world, I think of all the hospitals that are filled with patients, and with doctors, some of whom I owe my life to. And in spirit I will love and appreciate all of this a little deeper, and a little sweeter, and a little more prayerfully, just for them.

Today's Sunbeam, Salem, N. J. Sunday, April 8, 1990

Dedicated Group Brings the Thrill of Broadway Home

How much fun it can be to return to old familiar grounds. One can return to a favorite poem, an old worn piece of clothing, a long-forgotten recipe, a childhood memory, a visit with an old friend. What warm and comfortable feelings. What peace they can bring when all else is a jangle and jumble of chaos in our lives.

The subject of today's column allows me to return to a familiar piece of ground, to return to an early theme in my writing, to return and revive a "first love" that is never very far away and is still very special.

Long before someone got the dubious "bright idea" of having me write a column, I loved to write letters to the editor about all the wonderful plays and musicals presented by Oakwood Summer Theatre. And now from my very own soapbox I get to trumpet and extol all my feelings about this great group which treads the boards at OST.

In celebration of their 10th anniversary last weekend, Oakwood presented a wonderful evening of entertainment to a sellout audience. It was held in a cabaret-type setting in the cafeteria of Salem High School.

For an hour before show time, folks were able to mingle and enjoy a buffet of hot and cold hors d'oeuvres all amid a lovely setting of candlelight and flowers.

The entertainment for the evening was selections of songs from all the musicals OST has performed over the last 10 years. It was a truly wonderful journey back through the many memorable evenings that we've spent enjoying the talents of this local theater group.

1980 was the founding year for the Oakwood Theatre under the direction of Bill Donald.

Bill taught theater arts and English at Salem High School and wanted a vehicle for his graduating students so they could continue on with their theatrical interests beyond high school. He was in the audience last evening and, during intermission, he was presented with an award for his contributions to the successful 10 years OST enjoyed.

Bill is now in northern New Jersey, having moved after the 1985 season. Before his departure, Bill had set in place a viable and dedicated board of directors which continued to nurture and guide the group in the wake of his leaving.

The anniversary program was done on a small stage in the cafeteria. Through the clever use of very simple, yet effective devices, a very total and complete stage setting was accomplished. The stage was "framed' by an exciting visual display of play titles set on a variety of colored background shapes.

Play names were lettered in the original logo-type designed for that particular title. As a foil to this look, the stage held three large white panels and a set of white steps. These panels were used to great effect by coloring them with various hues of spot lights.

The colors complemented the feel of the music and helped to create a mood for each performance. All of this worked whether using one or two performers or a crowd scene. Really nice job!

Out of the musical "Cole," which is based on the career of song writer Cole Porter, there is a line that exclaims, "I get a kick out of seeing you stand there before me!"

It is one of those bouncy, wonderful songs and that line speaks to me in a thousand ways about my thoughts on Oakwood. I always get a tremedous "kick" out of seeing them on stage.

What great strides the Oakwood Summer Theatre has made throughout the last 10 years! The artist in me relates and responds to your sense of drama and impact and effect that seems to me to be a hallmark of OST.

I always choke up in all the wrong places, and even in the right ones, just because of the thrill you give as I watch you go through your paces. All of your combined efforts give way to wonderful moments of expression that are so thrilling to see created on stage before the audience.

After 10 years I know a lot of you personally, which only intensifies the delight and enchances the emotions. What a neat feeling to react to all this talent and beauty and then realize that the voice of a school teacher just gave me goose bumps!

With a saucy swing of a feather boa and the flutter of eye lashes, the young college student/cashier at the Acme has just charmed and electrified an entire audience. We are privileged to experience the beautiful voice of the young office worker whose song has brought unabashed tears streaming down our cheeks.

Each and every one of you in OST, whether you work in front of the audience or behind the scenes, makes a contribution not only to this theater group but also to life in this county that is beyond measure.

Some of you I see only on stage, others I see more often about the county, but I know you are all out there somewhere at any given moment. You are out there making life in this county all the richer and happier by your existence and enthusiasm to just being alive and making things happen, be they in life or on stage.

To miss an Oakwood Summer Theatre season is to miss something wondrous and delicious. It is to miss something that can be thrilling and expansive to your existence.

I can reach back into my memory and be thrilled and excited and go crazy once more over remembering how a real brass band marched all through the audience at the finale of "Music Man!" I can cry once again over a red-headed Orphan

Annie singing in vain about how someday her real parents will come to find her.

In "Godspell," the portrayal of Jesus gave a new meaning and sensitivity to my Christianity. To recall hearing the chorus sing the theme to "Brigadoon" is to hear it echo and re-echo every time a summer sunset casts its enchanting glow over a patch of woodland.

Thanks to this group for giving me the opportunity of returning to familiar ground for a while once again. My love affair with and for talented and dedicated Salem Countians will always assure that Oakwood's name will return time and again to this column.

It is so hard to write about all of you in this group without naming people for fear of leaving someone out. Forgive me this worry. Each and every one of you give 800 percent effort and this day I hope you each feel that any love and admiration you find in these lines is just for you . . . be it that you build sets, sell tickets, sling a paint brush or break my heart with a song.

•

A cryptic note to two friends: For any good or glory this column may bring to Oakwood, these words are lovingly dedicated to my "hero" and the "Jersey Lily!"

Today's Sunbeam, Salem, N. J., Sunday, April 22, 1990

Handwritten Notes a Rare, Treasured Possession

Junk mail . . . bills . . . catalogues . . . soap samples . . . but wait! I hear angelic humming! Do I see a glow coming from between a computerized bank statement and a water and sewer bill? Could it be? Yes! Oh, yes! A plain envelope. No little address window. No postage meter markings. It has a real licky-type stamp and an honest-to goodness handwritten address . . . a real piece of personal communication. Be still my heart!

While I shall never grow rich being a columnist, the payment that has been the sweetest and the best and most unmeasurable has been the wonders it has done for my daily mail.

Over the past year, I have received many wonderful and exciting notes from several of my readers. I always answer my mail because I appreciate that people are still willing to share and give of their time and thoughts by simply expressing themselves in a note or a letter.

My career began as a designer for Hallmark Cards. As part of the orientation we learned that Hallmark's success was established via one premise: Mr. Joyce Hall, Hallmark's founder, convinced people that he could do a better job of expressing their feelings than they could.

So for the price of a card, you can be the proud owner of a few expressive lines for your sweetheart, a friend, your mother, a graduate, etc. All you have to do is sign your name and the recipient is delirious that "you cared enough to send the very best."

I owe much of my career to my beginnings at Hallmark, so I don't wish to imply that we should stop buying greeting cards. I just wonder if we have grown complacent about expressing our feelings to each other in our own words.

Is it easier to let Hallmark do our talking for us? Apologies to all my artist and writer friends who are still part of the profit sharing plan at Hallmark!

When was the last time we may have received a real handwritten note from someone? Perhaps we also have to ask ourselves: When was the last time we sent a handwritten note to someone?

The sending and the receiving of handwritten and heart rendered notes can add so much beauty and joy to our lives and to the lives of others. Our existence can be so enriched by these wonderful few lines that show someone else is thinking about us in a myriad of ways. I like to think of notes as a loving little whisper in one's ear.

Their size alone makes for a gentle and intimate experience. They are a bit of love or humor or tenderness when it is the least expected and they leave a joy in our hearts that can only enhance our life in untold ways.

I love using a telephone. It is instant gratification when I wish to vent my emotions to someone special in my life. I can laugh, or cry, or receive and give love and affection. But, to me, it is a fleeting experience.

Unlike the written word, it is so easy as time goes on to lose the drift of the conversation. What did I say? What did they say? Did I mention this or that?

Is it possible that telephones have replaced the art of the written word?

While being a true marvel and offering expediency and instant verbal contact, has it robbed us of something more endearing and personal?

In our shoe box or bureau drawer treasure troves, we can lovingly keep our collection of notes and letters. They are there always, awaiting our return and perusal; to be read over again, held close and even embraced for the messages they contain.

I love the feeling and the dreaming that it was once touched by the friend or loved one who sent it; it was once in their grasp, their presence, their life and world, and now it remains here to stay as a part of ours.

I have friends and loved ones who have passed on and, while I am not always able to remember our last words together, I do have the last note or letter that they sent me.

What wonderful, precious mementos of their lives and love do these few lines across a page become. We are allowed to be together, to laugh and smile, and be happy and content for a little while once more.

Because I am so aware of the happiness that someone's note brings to my life, I love knowing I have the power to give that same sense of delight and surprise to someone else. A power and a love force that is ours in exchange for a few moments of time and effort.

I delight in knowing that I am going to surprise someone by dropping in uninvited by way of their mail box 1,500 miles away! I want someone else to know that her cooking makes her the "Crab Imperial" queen of the universe. I want to share with those in sorrow the feelings and the memories I have of their loved one.

I just can't see myself signing my name to someone else's poetry that 6,000 other people are going to use to say "Happy Birthday, Mom!"

If we "care enough to send the very best," we should send ourselves, our love, our congratulations, our heartache, our silliness, our "whatever" that makes that relationship exist as the special thing it has become.

It is not necessary to be a gifted writer or poet. Words and thoughts that are heartfelt in origin always have their own grace and beauty and style. Think for a moment on the love that exudes from a Valentine made by a 5-year-old child to his mother.

The pens of a thousand poets could never replace those scribbled words. It's all in the thought. It's all in the effort.

Samuel Johnson wrote, "An odd thought strikes me: we shall receive no letters in the grave."

I like this phrase. While a bit obvious, it serves as a reminder not to tarry or put off any show of affection or appreciation we feel for another. Do it now, this moment, at this time. Never be reluctant or feel strange for doing it.

I think of notes as mini-love letters and I take that thought into play whether I am writing to a friend, a client, someone I only met once or perhaps who I never met at all except through their note to me.

Across the ages, John Donne's words come down to us, that more often than kisses, letters mingle souls.

By having read this far, you have allowed our souls, yours and mine, to mingle once again, and for this I am very appreciative.

Today's Sunbeam, Salem, N. J., Sunday, May 6, 1990

Sharing the Joy, Beauty of an Artist's Special World

It is an early hour as I round the long gentle curve that leads into Quinton. My eyes are caught by the silvery twinkling of Alloway's Creek reflecting the early-morning light.

On its far banks beyond the bridge, bathed in soft blue tones, are the few homes and buildings that comprise the main intersection of this quaint country town. Golden tan foxtails waving in a soft gentle wind create a rich note of color and movement in this tranquil scene.

I am reminded of my long-time enticement of small country towns. On vacation trips, even as a child, I'd find myself wondering about the people who lived in whatever town we were traveling through. What were they like? What did they do all day? The mystique would be heightened if I actually got to see someone walk out of a house, or if I saw people talking to each other on a street corner. Quinton and many of its people are old familiar friends by now, so there is no mystique left. The void is now filled with a deep sense of appreciation for its quaintness and rural setting.

As I turn left at the light, my rear-view mirror reflects the charming character of Smick's office and hardware store. The traffic light silently changing colors, a bridge, soft foxtails through which I can see shimmering colors reflected in the water all support each other to create a picture-perfect scene of Americana at its Norman Rockwell best.

For the next few miles I enjoy seeing the beauty of the sun awakening nature's colors out of early morning shadows. Soon after a small dip in the road, and the ascending of a hill, I am in Alloway. Whatever road I take into this town, whatever the time of day, I always see Alloway as if for the very first time.

There is a sense of "rightness" to this community that I find so very comforting. Alloway is for me a buffer against any chaos and turmoil the rest of the world may hold. Alloway is many loving remembrances of Christmas carol songfests and Halloween parades.

As I pass by the little white frame township office, my mind's eye conjures visions of a parade judging stand, floats and queens, costumes and clowns. Today there is far too much the ambiance of spring for me to remain for long in an autumn realm of goblins and ghosts and candied apples.

As I leave Alloway for more open land, bright green grass creates a striking contrast to the gentle and delicate colors of dogwood and flowering cherry trees, rich vibrant azaleas and the glow of sunlit tulips. Across deep green meadowlands, in rampart swirling and whirling masses grow expanses of wild mustard gleaming in the sunshine. Black and white cattle graze at road's edge, intensifying the delicacy and color of their surroundings by their sheer size.

The road curves and cuts through a small hill leaving a high bank to one side. A large red tractor rumbles and rides this ridge, churning together green grass, wild yellow mustard and brown earth. One senses in the power and strength of this machine and its rider a determination that seems to speak for every man who ever loved the land and tilled the soil. He gives me a wave, a silent "hello," and becomes lost in the fold of another hill.

Every turn of this road offers new vistas of nature in spring–so much evidence of new growth and rebirth–one cannot do otherwise than to thrill to this hymn of life's continuity. My revery of prayerful appreciation and thanksgiving is made totally complete as in the distance I see Daretown's beautiful Presbyterian church. What an impressive sight it is to behold this wonderful building rising and evolving out of the churchyard that surrounds it. No neighboring tree can compete with it for size and majesty and sense of stability. Throw out all those calendar pictures of New England churches in autumn that you've been saving and get thyself to Daretown in the spring! Large old homes and huge stately trees give Daretown a feeling that is all proverbial country village. To gaze on sunlit dappled lawns and a quiet main street and to feel the quietude of it all gives a sense of peace and tranquility to the observer.

I have come to Daretown this day to speak to the children in the local elementary school. In coming to speak to them of my world as an illustrator, I have fallen in love with theirs. The school sits smack-dab in the middle of wide open farmland. As I stood for a moment under the trees in the parking area, I could hear the music of the wind as it blew through the branches. Birds were singing everywhere. Two squirrels stopped their chase to see what I was all about. In an adjoining field was a great old barn that every artist in the world would love to set an easel and canvas to. By my aged standards, this school looked like a real school should look. It harkened back to the old red brick elementary schools I went to as a kid.

Over the course of a few hours, I got to meet and talk to students from four grade levels and I fell in love with all of them! We shared lots of things together . . . they looked at my art, I looked at theirs, we laughed and asked questions of each other. I just hope I was as well behaved as they were that day! Among many good questions asked of me, my favorite of the day was from a first grader who, after hearing how busy I've been lately, asked, "Do you ever get to eat lunch?" I was going to pat my mid-drift bulge, but I thought I'd only confuse him.

After a first time experience of being in a school cafeteria lunch line, I had a marvelous time having lunch with the teachers. I left finally, filled not only to the brim with tacos and potato puffs, but spiritually filled on huge doses of appreciation and caring so generously expressed by the students and teachers.

It had rained late in the morning, and now as I was leaving, the colors of the surrounding fields became more vibrant and intensified by the sheen of rain drops on everything. The humidity softened the distant woodlands and blurred the colors and edges of the meadows. Close up, bushes and trees and wildflowers became sharp and clean and crisp in their contrast to the softened background.

The earlier rain left one part of the sky a soft shimmering blue-gray-violet cast; the rest was all brilliant sunlight and blue sky. This after-the-rain world was so alive. I saw squirrels sitting on split rail fences down in little glades or glens. Shiny black crows and scurrying rabbits always seemed to be popping up somewhere. Soft blues of wildflowers punctuated the deep dark green patches of weeds and other grasses with their color. A leggy black colt was standing along side its mother.

I had a beautiful and wondrous day in the world that morning. As surely as nature gave such joy and beauty to my soul and senses, so also did the children of that country school give a thrill and beauty to my hopes for the future of our world.

Today was truly a "gift." It was too lovely, too wondrous, too exciting to be anything else. I'd like to say to all of the kids who heard me talk of my world of fantasy and silliness and humor, that someday perhaps I can come again and we shall talk and share stories and dream dreams of other special worlds of joy and beauty that artists are so privileged to live in. Today was one of those worlds.

Today's Sunbeam, Salem, N. J., Sunday, May 20, 1990

Bridgeton Symphony Helps the Soul Take Flight

The world around us is filled with many kinds of marvelous and wonderful delights that, when experienced, can give a richness and depth to our lives, can enflame our hearts and give to us beautiful moments of ecstasy.

It is up to all of us to be capable of discerning these meaningful and rewarding experiences as they cross our paths or we cross theirs. Our ability to be open and fluid to these moments have so much to do with our enjoyment and appreciation of the experience.

A gemstone that I would truly love to lay in your pathway has the power to remove you for a little while from this worldly plane to that of another high and loftier one; to lull you, to caress your emotions, to hold you within its embrace, to do wonderful things for your soul and spirit and mind. I am speaking of the magic and beauty that can be yours for any evening spent listening to the Bridgeton Symphony Orchestra.

Bridgeton? Symphonies?

Concerts in a cow pasture? All of this you may incredulously exclaim, but I assure you that the Bridgeton Symphony Orchestra is a very enriching and rewarding experience, in not just my life, but for the 600 or so people who usually attend their concerts.

The very fact that it is based in Bridgeton is one of its great advantages for us. We do not have to fight traffic, pay for parking or bridge tolls, be accosted by panhandlers or any other ills one is likely to experience by going into Philadelphia or New York. To attend the Philadelphia Orchestra concerts one almost needs to remortgage the house to afford the price of a ticket. For the price of one good seat at the Academy of Music in Philly you can attend all four concerts of BSO's concert season and still have a good seat.

Bridgeton Symphony is a fully professional orchestra made up of musicians from all over the Delaware Valley, many of whom play in other orchestras or chamber groups throughout the area.

Many people think of classical music as "high brow" or "long hair" (can't use that term any more, can we?). People say that they don't "understand" classical music so why bother trying to experience it. The easiest and simplest way to begin an appreciation of classical music is to simply listen to it and be appreciative of the musical sound that you are hearing. Let it stimulate your senses, let it speak to you in its various moods of serenity, tumult, happiness, hopelessness, joy, power, and so many other moods that make music so exciting to experience.

To help its audiences deepen their understanding and knowledge, the orchestra provides a special feature called "Preconcert Conversation With The Maestro." In an informal and relaxed atmosphere, an hour prior to the performance, Conductor Russell Meyer and a few musicians discuss with concert goers the background and structure of the evening's music. Also in your program are informative and well written concert notes concerning the individual pieces that afford you great insight into each selection.

After each performance refreshments are served and Russell Meyer and the orchestra members are all present and it affords you a great feeling of intimacy with all these talented people. The familiarity and closeness to the orchestra that is promoted constantly by the symphony is of tremendous educational benefit. I am always surprised that more young people are not in the audience. The opportunity to introduce a youngster to this type of experience is fantastic. Even if a young person only attended a couple of the concerts and talked to a few of the musicians, they are going to go off into the world so much the richer culturally for having had the experience. To expose young people to this experience could be one of the greatest gifts they could ever be given. My teenage son has a room that is papered in rock music posters and other trappings of the average teen, yet he is very aware of the beauty and expressiveness of classical music and loves to attend the symphony.

The Bridgeton Symphony, under Russell Meyer's baton, perfectly illustrates the adage that music is the most passionate of all the arts. This orchestra has a certain identity to their interpretations that is uniquely their own. To my way of thinking, they have a very poetic and romantic sense of flow and timing and I just go ecstatic over the emotional content they seem to produce with their style. Most concerts feature a guest artist or sometimes a large concert chorus all of which only adds "gild to the lily."

Two special and exciting concerts that the orchestra performs are a Fourth of July outdoor concert that features the "1812 Overture" complete with booming cannons and fireworks, and the magical Christmastide ballet performance of "The Nutcracker." The ballet dancers are another local testament to the talent that abounds in this area as they are from the Vineland Regional Dance Company. Both of these performances are so exciting, so alive with beauty and energy, so very typical of all that makes the symphony so special.

I cannot say enough about how wonderful an evening at the symphony can be. To sit in the auditorium as the lights dim, to see the first opening gestures of the conductor as he moves his body and lifts his arms to lead seventy musicians into a glorious sound, be it dynamic and bold or soft and serene. To see his movements that will beg forth the violins, command a brass section, to blend and meld the rhythms and nuances of a composition until it flows and whirls and surges over you and around you and through you, this is truly to know and sense the delicious beauty of music. This is a wondrous experience that opens your emotions and feelings and lets them be alive, allows your inner being to dance and sing and shout for joy in sheer pleasure and ecstacy all because of this wonderful encompassing sound.

The talent and beauty of Bridgeton Symphony Orchestra allows our souls and spirits to truly fathom that music is one of the great glories of mankind. Bravo! Bravo! Bravo!

Today's Sunbeam, Salem, N.J., Sunday, June 3, 1990

Like Our Forefathers, We Return to Till the Spring Soil

Winter's harshness has now given way to soft gentle breezes, and the rains have become lulling and gentle.

The awakening earth fills us with its fragrance, and that of the perfume of lilacs and honeysuckle. We hear the siren song of the great Mother Earth beckoning to us; we are called to her bosom by that same hymn that has lured man to the soil for thousands of years. For a million springs after a million winters, man has gone off to the fields to sow, nurture, and harvest the fruits of the earth.

Today, I too am that "every man" of past millenniums. I go forth with a million spirit farmers of the past surrounding me, their hopes and dreams manifest in me.

I stand in the rays of a slowly ascending Saturday morning sun, prepared to till the soil as my forefathers before me have done. As if some Samurai warrior in an ancient Japanese print, I stand garbed in the array of battle!

My head crowned by an Amish farmer's straw hat and my eyes set in a cold, determined glint as in a John Wayne-like stare. Clutched firmly in my right hand is a spade and a hoe and my left hand holds the serpentine coils of a garden hose. Wedged between arms and torso are a variety of hand tools, bug spray, and a 25-pound bag of 5-10-5 plant food. My feet are planted firmly and staunchly in my L.L. Bean boots.

My heart and soul responding to the lure of the soil, I go forth invoking the spirit of Ceres, the Roman goddess of all growing things. Forward, boldly, I go. Approaching the first plank of my back porch steps, my spade handle hangs up on the door frame, the hoe slides down knocking my glasses askew. I stagger blindly forward, straddling the spade handle while heading toward the next step. I tear out the side of my 25-pound bag of plant food on the hand rake, the hose now sensing I am starting to falter wraps about me its merciless coils, and with a heart-wrenching scream of despair I fall headlong off the steps and into last year's herb patch.

It is quiet now. Only the early morning birds twitter and tweet as background. With my glasses askance, a bug runs across my bifocal and appears ten times normal size. I scream. I lay in a distorted heap. The hose, knowing it is the victor, uncoils itself ever so slowly. With a groan, a moan, and a loud clattering sound, I fling off the spade and extricate the hoe from my back. A constant hissing sound and the smell of chemicals alert me to the can of bug spray implanted in my arm pit. The path of my fall is marked by a trail of 5-10-5 plant food, and the torn remnants of the bag lies by my head, its shifting contents muffle all sounds in my right ear.

I have trod the earth, faced the sun, I have screamed my cry of defiance to nature and for the moment nature has shouted back, "Foiled again, LeHew!"

Two neighborhood kids help me up and dust me off. Lured by greed and not the hymn of nature, they offer to do my digging for ten bucks apiece. Handing over twenty bucks and sensing a collective sigh of disgust from all those long gone agrarian spirits, I leave the two boys in their spiritual care. I go inside to bind up my wounded pride and regroup my energies.

Having solved the turning and tilling of the soil, I decide that my next plan of action involves the purchasing of bedding plants. I love this part of gardening the very best of all! As children, our delight is found in trips to candy counters and toy stores. As adults, at least for me, this giddiness and thrill is transformed to bulb and seed catalogues and Saturday morning trips to any one of several roadside flower and garden markets here in the county.

One of my very favorite places is Butler Gardens in Canton. Part of the fun of Butler's is the drive to get there. From Salem you have your choice of any one of about eight combinations of roads that will take you through a variety of fields, woods, or meadows. Maybe, like ancient Rome, all roads in Salem County do lead to Canton! A drive through this terrain of plowed fields rekindles my spirit to plow and plant and reap.

Butler's sits amid a lovely little rural setting of peace and tranquility. Wind chimes and bird songs offer a lovely pastorale-type music to an array of beautiful plants and nostalgic antique farm equipment. This whole idyllic scene is alive with color: intensified in some areas by brilliant sunlight, in other areas the same colors are subdued by cool, tree-cast shadows.

Many of the bedding plants are set out on table-like structures of planks and cinder blocks which allows you to feel surrounded by them. You get a great feeling of closeness to the beauty and delicateness of the plants which, from a merchandising standpoint, makes me want to buy armloads of them! I tend to "impulse buy" so I always need to be restrained in this delightful setting.

I've noticed that the flower and plant business always seems to attract a special kind of woman as salespeople who are very gentle and sweet-natured, and Butler's is no exception. They have always been so helpful and kind, and especially with me—enduring and patient! There seems to be no question that I can ask that is ever so dumb and inane that they won't answer without a smile or some other evidence of their good natures. This is so important to someone like me who can never remember the difference between an annual and a perennial. The only time I have a green thumb is when I am painting!

To our lovely roadside Salem County, all the other flower markets add wonderful islands of color with their "flats" of purple pansies and red geraniums, the bright yellows and oranges of marigolds, and the rich reds, whites and pinks of impatiens! I enjoy seeing all the contrasting shapes and textures created by rose bushes and fruit trees, azaleas and rhododendrons, all displayed against a fortress-like wall of bagged peat moss and plant food. The wonderful profusion of such places as the Marlboro Farm Market, Dad's Produce, Moore's Market, Hannagan's Country Produce, LaRosa's, Bradway's or any of the others I may have overlooked are as refreshing and appealing to our senses as the garden delights that they sell.

They offer to us wonderful sunny open-air respites from the hustle-bustle hassle of ordinary shopping. Our purchases are living things that we can touch and smell and revel in their aliveness. We smell the damp, rich fragrance of potting soil, the haunting perfume of tea roses or English lavender, the exciting fragrance of the herb plants. We can have happy, cheery, "feel good" conversations with our fellow customers over how to grow the best tomatoes, how much sun will this plant need, do I talk to, beg, or threaten my plants to get them to grow?

In a world where roadsides are being threatened by fast food chains, car dealerships, and convenience stores, I think all of us here in Salem County are so fortunate to have our roadside stands. We have them to help us retain our rural and agrarian roots and our sense of closeness to people and to the land. They can be marvelously therapeutic to browse and muse through. To end on an old cliché, we have places where, in our mad helter-skelter dashes through life, we can truly "stop and smell the roses." Thank goodness. Aren't we lucky!

Today's Sunbeam, Salem, N.J., Sunday, June 17, 1990

Old Church's Serenity Mixes with Nature's Glory

As I walk along by the side of the road, the scene evolving before me is one of peace and solitude. One has a feeling of being wondrously overwhelmed by the sheer beauty and quiet charm that this setting imparts.

Around you and above you are great, green, leafy boughs, blowing and bowing and dipping in the cool June breezes; and there is the serenity of the country churchyard with its orderly rows of ancient gray and tan headstones; amid it all sets a beautiful old colonial church.

Flickering and flowing sunlight cascades over broad, green expanses of lawn, highlighting the curved tops of the taller headstones, the scene is composed of lovely, strong patterns of warm, bright light and cool, deep green shadows. My senses are delighted to smell the sweet fragrance of honeysuckle and to hear the wonderful distant ringing of a bell choir, both carried along on a gentle afternoon breeze.

The church that stands in such quiet dignity is the Old Pittsgrove Presbyterian Church in Daretown. Today, the 57th annual memorial service is being held. This wonderful building was erected in 1767 and is no longer in use save for some special services held in the summer months. Its small size having given way to the "new" church built in 1867 that sets a few hundred yards away.

A few years have passed since I last attended this annual service and having always remembered it as very special, I return this afternoon with the same excitement one reserves for seeing old friends. Speaking of old friends, today's guest speaker is a good and dear friend of mine, so I am doubly excited and blessed. Harold Elliot is a legend, in many circles, as a speaker. Combining a wonderful sense of humor, great gestures, and a heart overflowing with love and faith, I know he will bring a rollicking and inspiring message to the dignity of Old Pittsgrove Church today. Lucky will be those folks who will be his audience this afternoon.

As I cross the broad expanses of rolling lawn and walk through the churchyard, the congregation is singing the great old hymn, "All Hail the Power" in company with the warm, rounded, traditional sound of a pump organ. This country church atmosphere brings to mind phrases such as "Old Time Religion" and "Church Meetin's." Were it not for the cars in evidence, one could be hearing and seeing this scene as it could have been on any Sunday afternoon over the past 200 years!

The quiet and serene beauty of the surroundings outside are met and matched on the inside of this church. I don't know of any other county church building quite like this one. The pews are of a colonial box-like structure each with a little door on the end. The curved ceiling is two stories high and thus allows for a balcony to run on three sides of the church. The pulpit area is at least 12 feet high and places the speaker dramatically above the lower pews and at eye level with the balcony seats. The interior is completely white with only some stained trim on the top edges of the pews. Gorgeous 12 over 12 Colonial windows are deep set in whitewashed plaster walls. The arrangement of windows and woodwork that frame the pulpit give a classic grace and yet stoic dignity to this focal point of the church.

One of the manifold beauties of a summertime service in this church is that the windows are all opened and a wonderful merging of the service inside and the surrounding nature outside takes place. You are constantly serenaded by the sounds of the wind creating a swishing-like murmur throughout the trees; the delightful happy sounds of bird songs fill the quiet moments when no one is speaking or singing. Gazing through these centuries old panes of glass one sees the blue sky and snow white clouds as little sparkling pinpoints of color as the green leaves blow this way and that.

The special joy and beauty of people at prayer and song seems to mingle as one with the beauty of the land that is around us. One senses a "wholeness" to this Sunday afternoon and to this service that cannot be felt nor adequately described. This feeling perhaps comes out of a sensing of the history of this building and the people who worshipped here over all these many long years. Perhaps it is to look around at these walls and wonder what unknown stories of the past they could tell . . . what tragedies and triumphs they bore witness to; so many of those same participating souls are now at rest in the serenity of the churchyard just beyond these walls.

A last hymn is sung, the Rev. William Allen pronounces the benediction, and all of us in a wonderful, buoyant, spirit-ladened tumult of "hellos, goodbyes, how-are-ya's, and nice to see ya's" head our way homeward. In quieter moments, we will realize that the beautiful moments of this afternoon's service that we now leave behind, will become part of a building's collective history that we added to this day. We leave behind a beautiful solo of the Lord's Prayer by William Clark, accompanied by Marjorie Brooks on the reed organ, and the marvelous serenade of a cardinal by God. We leave behind the beautiful sounds of a bell choir and a men's chorus; the inspired and inspiring words of a dynamic speaker. We leave these wonderful sounds to echo and re-echo throughout these walls and across these woods and fields; to mix with all the sounds that are out there, somewhere in the cosmos. But this building shall always remember *these* sounds and *these* moments and be a part of them, and I like that thought.

Knowing that to hurry will all the sooner end the beauty and serenity of this afternoon, I amble along slowly through the churchyard, so hesitant in my efforts to leave. Longingly, I look back several times, just to instill in my mind's eye, the beauty of it all.

I make a promise to myself that I will come back here again, soon, just to be quiet for a while; to bring paper and pens, to either draw or to write; but mostly I will come just to give myself a present of this peace and solitude alongside a country road. I will sit under these wonderful trees; against a headstone in the shade and know, with all of my being, that the happy sweetness of today will only deepen and enhance the hues of the picture that my heart paints of life here in Salem County.

Today's Sunbeam, Salem, N.J., Sunday, July 1, 1990

Delightful Day Heralds Opening of Fenwick Plaza

This rather haunting line of poetry, "Nay, love, 'tis not time that flies but we that go . . ." has always been a favorite of mine. In the "going" I have picked up so very many wonderful memories of friends, places and events; and they color and give a marvelous substance to so many aspects of my being today.

Out of this wellspring of memories, I find that so many of them relate to life within this county and most especially to my hometown of Salem. My mind's eye returns me to parades of a grand scale, the openings of many local institutions, special presentations, favorite speakers at various local affairs and the memories go on and on.

A few days ago I added to my many memories in the most wonderfully festive, positive and hope-filled way. By now, we all know that the Fenwick Plaza in Salem was officially opened and dedicated last Tuesday. It opened amid an air of low-key fanfare but high-key joy, happiness and expectation. It played to an audience of excited, smiling folks who came to see and believe that dreams can and do come true.

On this bright, sun-filled morning I had walked over to the plaza to hopefully catch a glimpse of the events going on and made some written sketches for use in this piece. I was there to just enjoy and absorb some of the atmosphere created by Gov. Jim Florio's visit to Salem and all the excitement that encapsulates events like this. To my complete surprise, I quite unexpectedly ended up being invited inside the courtyard with a front row seat and an exquisite lunch provided by Brigadoon, the new restaurant on Fenwick Plaza. While somewhat mortified about my casual attire, I pressed on undaunted with my quest to totally enjoy this delightful turn of events.

The large gathering of invited guests were composed of many people working as part of the various community and civic groups in the united effort to revitalize Salem. Many city, county, and state government officials were in evidence also. Everyone seemed to enjoy being there and they greeted each other with great enthusiasm. This was an ideal example, I felt, of the relationships that you can build when people pitch in and work for a common and united goal. Being around so many friendly and familiar faces was like the ultimate trip to the Acme Market! I loved it! Nirvana on Broadway!

The excitement was heightened as everyone awaited Gov. James Florio's arrival to the plaza. Regardless of your politics, it's exciting to see the various whirlwinds that accompany one in his position: the press, the security personnel, the aides, the many accoutrements of the office.

Across the street from the plaza were various placard-carrying protesters who created an audible uproar during the formal proceedings and speech making. At their loudest during the governor's speech, he referred to them as an example of "boisterous democracy." I guess I would not make a very good politician because I would have called them rude, ignorant and obnoxious. I believe in the right to protest, but I, and others as well, resented their efforts to blemish something so special and so positive as this ceremony. There is a sidewalk in front of the Statehouse, too!

The atmosphere was wonderfully imbued and alive with the confidence that this project was meant to instill. It was so easy to catch the spirit that things are turning around for this very special and beloved city.

To an already buoyant, spirit-lifting occasion came more good news from Scott Smith, president of Mannington Mills Inc., that the plaza will be 100-percent occupied by summer's end. In Johnny Campbell's message, we were informed that 95 percent of the fund-raising for Salem's soon to be constructed community center has been reached.

All of this heartening news added to everyone's hopes and expectations for the future. For so long, so many things have been talked about and planned for, and today, we got to see a dream come true. We got to be part of the crowd on the dock when the ship came in, so to speak, and it felt wonderful.

This is but one more culmination of the dream inspired by Charles Pedersen, our Nobel laureate, and lovingly nurtured so faithfully by Johnny Campbell. While all of the endeavors of Stand Up For Salem are supported jointly by various local industries and businesses, Fenwick Plaza was constructed solely under the auspices and funding of Mannington Mills Inc.

What an impressive project it all has turned out to be. So many special touches give it a charm that pulls you into its courtyard. Wonderful chords of color are created by the distinctive green awnings to the red and tan brick work. Arched window treatments give a marvelous turn-of-the-century feeling to the Mecum Building. Honey locust trees, with their fern-like foliage, will give a diffused softness to the scene as they mature over the next couple of years. "This lovely area will grow to live up to its function of being a true plaza as it seems so conducive to ambling about its perimeter. Come and see for yourself.

"The optimist proclaims that we live in the best of all possible worlds; and the pessimist fears this is true," wrote James Cabell. I hope all the doomsayers and the grumbling pessimists will come and visit and let this rejuvenating effort speak to them. Let it help you become inspired to accept a bit of hope and light. Never has there been a better time to say that if you're not part of the solution, then you must be part of the problem.

Someone had the soul and the romance enough to suggest that a replica of the star on Star Hall Corner be placed in the Fenwick Plaza. The original bronze star, still located on the corner of Broadway and Market, adjacent to the Security Savings Bank, holds the legend that should you step on the star you will never leave Salem, and if you do, you will always return.

The symbolic replica has been placed directly in front of a display map of Salem County so that when one views the map and reads the list of year-long events, they find they have inadvertently stepped upon the star and, hopefully, will succumb to the spell of the legend.

Last Tuesday, for a lovely, long while, Salem seemed to be the center of the universe for a lot of us; it was a very exciting time to be a part of the life and history of this wonderful place. As a kid growing up here it was the thing to do, on the way home from Saturday afternoon movies, to step on the star. Perchance there is something to that legend, for I left for a few years but I returned. Should I ever decide that I have a few regrets about life, this decision will never be one of them.

To every one of you, wherever you live in the county, please come and see our beautiful Fenwick Plaza and rejoice for and with us. And while you are there—don't forget to look at the map . . .

Today's Sunbeam, Salem, N.J., Sunday, July 15, 1990

Centuries of Tradition Make Food Preparation an Art

B etween those wonderful and magical times when my mind, as artist and writer, is creating pictures colored by words or paints, I can find a million other delightful things to muse over.

The very least of these is my love of food. Food to me is very expressive and I approach the experience in a very sensual and poetic state of mind.

While I love all kinds of food from many different traditions, my very favorite is Oriental cooking. The only thing better than Chinese food two nights a week, is Chinese food six nights a week! Perhaps the seventh being given over to Mexican cooking!

A few years ago I was facing a very serious surgical procedure and my doctors alluded to the possibility of certain dietary restrictions for the rest of my life.

When I meekly asked, "Like what?" They replied, "Like Chinese food." Devastation! Ruination! Desolation! It seems the problem involved the light cooking and the coarse cutting of the vegetables.

Laying aside all thoughts of my family, my friends, and my career, I suggested to God, during a very frenzied and frantic round of prayers, that if I had to go through life without Chinese food, perhaps I should just "call it a day" right then and there!

Well, God, in his infinite love and wisdom, answered my prayers with something just short of thunder claps and lightening bolts by a parting of the clouds to reveal a golden table of egg rolls, wontons and Moo Goo Gai Pan!

A wonderful and loving hospital chaplain at Johns Hopkins had to admit that it was the first time he had ever prayed for someone's culinary hang-ups!

Prior to that time in the mid-1980s, you had to travel to Wilmington or Philadelphia in order to have Chinese food. Well, I want you to know that due to a very loving God, and possibly the prayers of Ron LeHew, the southern end of Salem County has five Chinese restaurants in a 10.4-mile stretch of Route 49!

This "Egg Roll Alley" runs from Chow's in the Salem Plaza to the Dragon Pearl in Deepwater. Welcome, The Orient, and the China Inn are located between these two points.

The Chinese people who own and operate these havens of culinary magic and delight bring to and share with Salem County the ancient traditions of the Chinese reverence for food.

The art of fine cooking is considered to be a moral virtue to the average Chinese. Getting the best and the most out of what you have is a basic tenet of Chinese thought. Food is treated with great honor and respect by the Chinese and thus it has always been so.

Four thousand years ago the ancient sage I Ya had written a treatise on cooking and to this day remains a sort of patron saint for Chinese chefs.

Some of the precepts of Confucius deal with the preparation and eating of food and legend has it that he left his wife because she could not attain his high standards in the kitchen!

If ever there was a transfer of values, it would be to equate the principles of the visual arts to the preparation and serving of a fine feast.

The Orientals have so truly turned food and its preparation into a high and fine art form.

Chinese food is intended to stimulate and excite more of the senses than just that of taste. The lovely color of the dish is a delight visually, the ingredients are of a uniform size, and the dish must have a fragrance.

With several dishes to a meal there is always to be the contrast between tastes and textures. A spicy dish is contrasted to one of delicate flavors, a crispy dish to a smooth one. In their cooking, as in their philosophy, always apparent is the striving for balance.

I have sampled and gorged at all five of our local restaurants and can honestly say that they all are wonderful and you couldn't go wrong at any one of them.

Four of the five are conducive to take-out orders. They do have a few tables and chairs in the event you wish to eat on the premises.

The Orient in Pennsville is a restaurant in the sense to which we are most accustomed.

My special favorite is the Welcome on West Broadway in mid-town Salem. I live a mere two blocks away and can almost smell the egg rolls from my studio.

Along with delicious food, I think Mr. Cheung and his family are about the nicest people you'd every want to meet! I find that their food has all the wonderful qualities I have come to expect in Oriental food.

I especially love their ability to have sauces that are clear and delicate with an aroma that I find just short of poetic! The vegetables retain their crispness and beautiful color. Ah! Love it!

The Orient has wonderfully friendly hostesses and dining room help also. Their food is wonderful and just a bit higher priced than the take-out restaurants, which is to be expected.

When I need a special treat or reward, I go to The Orient. I especially love the little cubes of layered, colored gelatin they give out with fortune cookies when the dinner dishes are cleared.

Their dining room provides a very pleasant and relaxed mood and a nice light and airy feeling is created by the décor.

Along with excellent dishes at Chow's, located at the Salem Plaza on East Broadway, and the China Inn, down from the K-mart in Pennsville, is the special fun of watching your dinner being cooked a la Oriental!

The open kitchen area is just beyond the front counter in each place. Both offer a wonderful arena of flying spatulas and darting arms. Great fragrant clouds of steam momentarily obscure the area as raw meat and vegetables come into contact with flavored hot oils.

There is the wonderful din of utensils banging against iron woks as your selection is stir-fried.

Deepwater's Dragon Pearl was the first restaurant in the area and was the vanguard to break the barrier created by fast food chains and pizza parlors.

I especially love the look of the two-story high dragon that adorns the outside wall of their building.

The Chinese have always been aware of the direct correlation between physical health and the food you eat. We in the western world, in the last few years, have discovered what they knew and practiced for centuries.

Oriental cooking methods and foodstuffs are the premise for so much of today's thoughts on healthier eating habits. Quick-fry or stir-fry cooking techniques retain flavor and the nutrients of the meats and vegetables.

It is all cooked in a very small amount of oil and leaves your food with gorgeous eye appeal as the colors shimmer from under a glaze of a variety of sauces and cooking mediums.

Chinese food is a wonderful adventure in eating and I hope you are now a bit more cognizant of the wonderful restaurants in our area.

A very good friend of mine, whom I am trying to enlighten on the joys of Chinese food, says why spend good money on eating Chinese when you can simply graze in your yard on various weeds and other broadleaf forms of vegetation.

He goes to Chinese restaurants and orders T-bones and French fries!

The latest proof of my good fortune at being able to eat Oriental food is that about three years ago I had new neighbors move in next door and the wife is from the Philippines and she cooks the best Oriental food in the world!!

She also has a passion for entertaining which allows us many opportunities to enjoy her wonderful cooking.

Do I have a charmed life or what? Now if only a Mexican family would move in on the other side . . .

Today's Sunbeam, Salem, N. J., Sunday, July 29, 1990

Two Men that Have Enriched the Lives of Many

The streets of Salem, on this quiet, summer Sunday afternoon seem to hold one in an entrancing and spellbound sort of way. So quiet, so empty—a sense of timelessness prevails and abounds.

Your senses seem to beg to feel and hear the echoes of bygone days and events and to see the myriad characters who have made up the life and lifeblood of this small town.

My heart and being rejoice that we have a town to call our own. We have our past, our collective histories; we have tales and legends and stories.

Our community was not "developed" in six months' time by contractors and bulldozers and slapped together houses.

Our streets and homes and stores and schools have given birth and nurtured and sheltered wonderful, colorful, caring, giving, sharing multitudes of people.

So many have contributed; so many have inspired; so many have kept a love of community alive and aflame for the others of a next generation down through the great pathway of time.

There were so many whose memory is lost to the ages, yet their efforts and inspiration echo and tremor through us all to this time and this moment. Their spirits seem to watch and whisper to us, this day, out of shadows cast by a hazy, misty mid-afternoon sun.

In this quiet setting of last Sunday afternoon, many folks cared enough and loved enough to celebrate the lives of two wonderful men. I refer to them both, with loving and respectful intent, as two real town characters.

Donald Smith passed away a few weeks ago and his life and career were celebrated at a memorial service at the Friends Meeting House. Mr. Smith was a teacher of history and government studies at Salem High School for many, many years and was very beloved by faculty and students alike.

Behind his back we reverently called him "Smitty" and held his wisdom, his knowledge, and his humor in high admiration and awe. Our parents would whisper behind his back that such a scholarly mind should be teaching in a great university and not in some small town South Jersey school system, but weren't we lucky and priviledged to have him anyway?

In his classrooms the students were addressed as "Mr." and "Miss" and he went about it in such a way as to add a wonderful touch of dignity to your being called on, always you felt the sincerity and caring of a true teacher to his student.

Mr. Smith always looked for and found the best in all of his students. He was always quick to acknowledge their special talents and abilities and to make them aware of their unique value and worth as individuals.

His knowledge of world affairs was legend. We were totally convinced that Mr. Smith could have been a presidential advisor if only the president had had the good sense to call on him.

During the Cuban Missile Crisis of 1962, I was convinced of the utter futility of doing my homework. I was positive that by the next morning me, my homework, and my school were going to be reduced to a pile of atomic ash! I expressed genuine fear to him for the situation that our world appeared to be in.

He spoke very seriously, yet gently, to me of what he thought would happen and explained all of the "whys" and "wherefores" of the crisis and then with a big smile and unique Don Smith laugh assured me that I should go home and finish my homework, especially his!

I have many memories of seeing him walk to or from school with his briefcase and newspaper (The New York Times, of course!) and thinking that he looked the very epitome of a teacher, a professor, a real educator.

He was so very truly all of these images in the best and most honorable sense. To his classroom he brought a brilliant mind and a great sense of dedication.

Whatever your feelings for the subject, "Smitty" never failed to impress you and win you over by his vast knowledge that was tinted and tempered by his great wit. He endeared himself to his students who considered it a privilege to sit in his classroom.

In the movie "Good-bye, Mr. Chips" all of the generations of students file by their beloved teacher and bid him adieu. You were a good man, a fine teacher, and you left a mark. So good-bye, Mr. Smith. Thank you for the honor of your presence in my life.

As quiet and peaceful as the streets appeared last Sunday, the serenity was broken briefly as fire engines from all sectors of town roared and rolled through the streets in procession to pay tribute to Carleton "Slats" Plasket on his 100th birthday!

Slats, now a resident at the Salem County Nursing Home, held court at his son's home in Elsinboro where a wonderfully festive and joyous open house was held for this most special birthday party.

My son and I got to ride out on the Washington Fire Company truck. What a thrill! If I live to be 100, I'm sure that ride will be one of the highlights of my life!

Jack Plasket's yard overflowed with the outpouring of love and friendship shown his father last Sunday. In between huge, shiny fire engines and surrounded by balloons, streamers and banners was a wonderful, laughing and happy crowd of well-wishers from all age groups and affiliations.

I spoke with several people about their feelings for Slats and the answers were as varied as the people polled.

Young firefighters wanted it known that being in the same company with a man who fought fires for 75 years was to see him as a great inspiration and role model.

All the men at Washington Fire Company are so proud to call him their own, yet all firefighters throughout the city and county are proud of the example he has set for them as a measure for their own sense of dedication.

His dedication and devotion for 75 years of active duty show that to be a card carrying member is just not enough.

Bob and Barbara McAllister of the Salem Oak Diner seemed not to have enough adjectives to describe how truly loved Mr. Plasket is by everyone around him.

Barbara, describing him as a "sweetheart of a gentleman," opened out her arms and asked that one just look around at all the obvious signs of care and love being expressed as evidenced by the crowd of people, fire engines and other trappings of this very special celebration.

Ducky Steelman, who worked for 30 years with Slats at Anchor Hocking, spoke of his straight-forwardness and his no nonsense mannerisms. His great ability at solving problems within the machinist trade was considered to be no small talent either.

Honesty and fair dealings seemed to be watchwords of the day when describing "Slats," along with several anecdotes concerning his dry sense of humor that is so wonderfully disarming!

Mr. Plasket has spent the last year or two being on the mend from surgery and a fall, but prior to that he had been a very active golfer and card player. It appears that his ability as a card shark and story teller are legendary whether you talk to the guys from the fire house or the folks from the country club!

People just all seem so truly happy to know him and are so grateful that they have had him as part of their lives for these many years. His 100th birthday wish was that all the people at his party would have their own birthday be as nice as his was.

His most memorable event of the past 100 years was to hear the crowds cheering and see the bright lights come on during the Armistice celebration in Paris in 1919, marking the end of World War I. I might add that Slats and Rose Kennedy shared the same birth date 100 years ago.

Mr. Smith and Slats Plasket, each in their own ways, have added wonderful things to life here in our small town. They have enriched and enhanced our lives here and have added their own special lustre to that patina of time and memories that bind our town together.

It has been said that life is God's gift to us and what we do with that life is our gift back to God. In the case of the lives of these two men, I am sure that God is very happy with the return on His investment.

Today's Sunbeam, Salem, N. J., Sunday, August 12, 1990

Right Around the Corner, the Magic of the Old West

> *"I'm a roving cowboy*
> *Far away from home,*
> *Far from the prairies*
> *Where I used to roam,*
> *Where the dogies wander*
> *And the wind blows free.*
> *Oh, my heart is yonder*
> *On the lone prairie."*

The words of this mournful old cowboy lament seem the perfect narrative when we dream about the lore and legend of the Old West and those wide open spaces of another era. Those bygone days are now forever lost, to return only amid our romantic fantasies of how it must have been.

Because of Cowtown Rodeo, that great local institution and tradition, the opportunity has been given to us, for a couple of hours, to rekindle some of the romantic rapture that used to make all little boys want cowboy hats and six-shooters on long ago Christmas mornings. Cowtown Rodeo helps us cling to a bit of unbroken historic lineage that starts somewhere back in the early 1800s on the still unsettled plains of our young, new republic.

Sitting in the stands, emerging a bit from our reverie, our eyes come to focus on a calmer, quieter corner of the rodeo arena; a calf-roping contestant sits astride a dappled horse, a picture-perfect cowboy. Amid all the clamor of the crowds and the bustling of arena activity, he sits as though deep in thought, fingering and playing out the coils of rope that make up his lariat.

A few small loops of cord, called a "pigging" rope, is clenched in his teeth and will be used to tie up the calf's legs if he is able to bring one down. Such scenes as this and a hundred others this evening would have inspired heroic canvases by the great cowboy artists Charles Russell and Frederic Remington. Both of these artists recorded forever the real world of the cowboy in his heyday of the latter 1800s.

This calf roper sits in partial silhouette against an evening sky of pale, golden yellow along the horizon evolving into a deep, dark blue at its zenith. A few streaks of dusty rose colored clouds tinged with gold laze across the sky. Above the timbers of corrals and chute gates, all we can see is sky. It looks vast and expansive and forever.

We know different, but could this be like the big skies of Montana or Wyoming or Texas? Our calf roper, while still lost in soft gray-blue tones, appears to be backlit from the glow of the ebbing evening light. His hat, his ropes, and the high edges of his horse now pick up the glow; and as he nudges his horse forward he becomes the look and romance of every cowboy who ever was.

Artists always yearn to paint the world closer to their heart's desire, and for just a little while this night I want cowboys and campfires and and cattle lowing from out of the darkness. If the girl in front of me will stop rattling her potato chip bag, and if the guy behind me will quit complaining about the price of a hot dog, then perhaps I will be able to resurrect Bronco Jim, Wyoming Pete, Snortin' Tom, or Bad Bull Bob, all legendary cowpokes from the Old West.

Cowtown Rodeo, while to all appearances an anachronism as it exists here in the Delaware Valley of the 1990s, gives and shares with us a real flavor of Western life and we love it as it brings out the "buckaroo" in all of us. This fun word buckaroo is a derivation of the Spanish word vaca meaning cow. Spanish cowhands were called vaqueros.

Cowtown Rodeo brings to us a wonderfully fun and thrill-filled evening composed of sights and sounds that belong only to the rodeo. There is creaking and slapping of leather against horse flesh. You can hear and feel the pounding of horse and cattle hooves as they send up dust and dirt clouds that haze the brightly lit summer night.

Corral and chute gates slam and bang as bucking broncos kick and leap, trying to upset their unwanted riders! We hear the metallic banging and clanging of cow bells being riotously rung by a leaping, thrashing, hump-backed Brahma bull! There is the raspy sound of the time keeper's buzzer marking the end of a ride, sometimes adding insult to injury.

There are the crowds cheering and clapping, oohing and aahing. An electric guitar twangs out background music over the loud speakers to add an audible excitement to that of the visual. We have an announcer with his "Bartles and James" country cowboy drawl. There is the faint country odor of manure wafted along on a cooling night breeze.

All of these images and many, many more add a wonderful sense of color and contrast and form to these special few hours of excitement.

Barrel racing is the female area of competition at the rodeo. The women ride with great agility and speed as they race the clock around the clover leaf circuit of barrels. How they seem to recall the look and dash of the Pony Express riders as they ride "hell bent for leather" down the homestretch with the riders bent low over their horses' necks urging them on; manes and tails and whips flowing and flailing in the night air; cowgirl hats fly off as the crowd cheers and claps and roars! So exciting!

Two of the most important and thrill-encountering participants of this evening never ride a horse or bull or rope a calf, for they are the rodeo clowns. One never doubts the dangers faced by the competing cowboys but often it is brought graphically home when you see a clown chase or distract a bull or bronc from the still form of a downed and injured rider.

Most of the night Beaver Carter and T. J. Hawkins play the clown's game of entertaining the audience between events and the crowd loves them, but it is in the heat of competition that their real value is felt. A rider has barely hit the ground when dumped by bull or horse before the clowns run their dangerous games of interference. Shooing or distracting a 1,700-pound bull must look like a thrashing three-story building with horns!

The evening is over now, the tallies are in. The score is something like animals 75, cowboys 2. Like the announcer had said way back at the beginning, "Folks, be sure to give 'em your applause 'cause that's all some of them will take home tonight." He sure wasn't kidding. My sense of romance leaves me briefly as I ponder the fact that each participant paid good money to be hurled from a bucking bronco, or to be twisted six ways from Sunday on a Brahma bull, or to receive a cracked rib from a calf's flying hoof!

As the rodeo comes to an end and crowds noisily depart, one notices a beautiful full moon silently and serenely crossing the night sky. It was a quiet observer to all of this evening's fun and excitement. This is the very same moon which, all those long misty years ago, reflected off the canvas cover and tin pots of a trail drive's chuck wagon. It reflected off the metal of gun barrels and the flint of arrowheads as a herd was driven through Indian Territory on its way up the Shawnee or the Chisholm Trail to Abilene and Kansas City.

We see the North Star and the Big Dipper. Both were nature's clock to the cowpoke riding guard duty on the night herd, for by the Dipper's rotation around the North Star he knew when his shift was complete.

The reality of life as a cowboy is that it was a dirty, overworked, laborious way of life. A life lived out in all sorts of terrible weather conditions and occupational hazards. Aahh . . . but when you see the old tintype photographs and drawings, you see by their expressions and poses and props that cowboys had a noble and heroic image of their role in life. And all of this nation came to believe and share in the sense of their heroism and the colorful myths and lore that surrounded them.

To the cowboys who came here tonight from places as divergent as Bowlegs, Okla.; Billings, Mont.; Carneys Point and Alloway; thanks for adding to the lore and legends and that long, unbroken cord that binds a white-washed rodeo arena in Sharptown to such legendary places as Abilene, Cheyenne, and Dodge City.

"When I die
Take my saddle from the wall;
Just put it on my pony
And lead'im from the stall.
Tie my bones to his back;
Turn our faces to the West;
And we'll ride the prairie
That we love the best."

Today's Sunbeam, Salem, N. J., Sunday, August 26, 1990

Fond Memories of Nights at Riverview Beach Park

Oh, no! Those joggers just ran smack into the wall of the Laughing Castle! Gee whiz! Some guy just backed his car into the Tumble Bug and he side-swiped the Donkey Ride as he pulled out! Come on, lady!! Watch it! You just slammed your car door into the Flying

Scooters' ticket booth and that dumb kid just skate-boarded through the middle of the merry-go-round and almost hit the Ferris wheel!

Those folks are having their picnic right in the midddle of the Tilt-A-Whirl and they're gonna get potato salad all over the ride!! Geez!! Isn't anything sacred?

Do any of these amusement ride names ring a bell with you? Does your heart leap a bit and your eyes grow wide and bright at the very sound of them? If you are a bit over 30 years of age and older, you know I'm not talking rides at Hershey Park or Great Adventure.

I'm talking about a period when Disney World was just swamp, bugs and alligators and merely a gleam in Walt Disney's eye.

Can you walk through the lattice-work gate in Pennsville that says "Riverview Beach Park" and blink your eyes and see the Wildcat roller coaster? Can you see the timbers shake as it roars and thunders along its ribbon of track?

Can you see the red and yellow cars of the Tilt-A-Whirl flash under the glow of naked light bulbs on a summer's night?

If you can hear the music drifting over from the carousel, and if you can feel the slam of the Spook House doors and if you can hear and see and smell and taste a thousand other pieces of magic that make you feel ten years old again—then you know, my friend, that you stand on sacred ground.

A patch of earth that has been dedicated and hallowed by the joy and laughter and merriment of thousands of children and their families all these many years.

A once-a-season trip to Riverview Beach Park—now this was "Christmas in July!"

On the Fourth of July, about six seconds after the glow and sound of the last sparkler and fire cracker died out, I'd start to beg and plead for some hint of commitment from Mom and Dad as to when we could spend an evening at Riverview Beach Park. Being from Salem, I always thought of it as Pennsville Park.

This question was asked with the same hopeful expectancy as when on a 500 mile trip and yet a mere 16 miles from home you'd ask, "Are we there yet?"

After hearing Dad answer, "We'll see" 400 times in three weeks, the pronouncement would be made, the prayers were answered, the manna was delivered: we were going to the park TOMORROW NIGHT!

I would awaken on the morrow to greet a day that could not be any more exciting than if Christmas, Easter, my birthday, the last day of school, a visit from Aunt Clara and falling in love were all rolled into one!

All day long as I played with friends, or ran errands, or hung around the car (they ain't leaving without me!), always on my mind was the thought of going this night to Pennsville Park!

Dinner was always something quick yet special, like barbecue sandwiches and iced tea. For some reason my mom only made iced tea about three times a summer so it became this incredibly special treat because I loved it so much!

So on this special night, you could bet we'd have iced tea! The combination of seeing the steeping tea in the pitcher on the countertop and knowing that this was our special night for Pennsville Park drove me to great bouts of anxiety all day long.

I later learned, as I grew older, that my sense of excitement was in direct proportion to how many times I gagged in the hours preceding a special event.

At last! As our car drove through that latticework gate I'd be half hanging out of the window trying to take it all in!

The park was such a wonderful assemblage of sights and sounds and they all blended to raise a kid's excitement level to a fever pitch!

Everything seemed to have its own unique sound: the ratchety sound made by the roller coaster as the cars were pulled to the top, the canned laughter of the Laughing Castle which seemed to form a back-drop to all the other park sounds, the swoosh of the Bubble Bounce careening on its circular journey, staccato sounds of the Tilt-A-Whirl as its wheels rolled over the wooden floor, the chug-chugging of the miniature train, and the scraping and scrunching of the Donkey Cars as they traversed the iron rails.

The ultimate sensual high had to be the beautiful and classic carousel that was created by the renowned Dentzel Company of Germantown, Pa.

The carousel was housed in a beautiful building composed of hundreds of panes of glass and a great domed roof. It had a mechanical "military band organ" that played the wonderful carousel music that added so much to the magic.

The music's melodious tones were punctuated by a clanging bell that marked the beginning and end of each ride. In reminiscing with friends, I seem to be the only one who remembers that once inside the carousel building, there was a special odor that had an acrid and pungent quality about it.

While I have no idea as to its cause, I can still recall it. Via a friend who restores carousel animals, I learned that one of the lions from Riverview's carousel brought $50,000 at auction about five years ago! This spectacular carousel's beauty was beyond words and I only hope that many of you have your own vivid memory of its majestic quality.

A facet of the park that I failed to remember until my memory was jogged by some old post cards was the special architectural features that several park buildings possessed.

The park's high point of development occurred during the late 1920s and early 1930s during what is referred to in design terms as the Art Deco period.

Several of the park's arcades, eateries and ticket booths reflected this style. The Whip was the only ride I remember as having this type of structure. I can best describe Art Deco by referring to it as a modernistic, streamlined kind of look.

My special night at the park allowed me to ride each amusement about 100 times, or so it seemed. The Aerial Rocket ride was always saved till last.

This quiet and graceful ride, set off to one side and sort of in the background of things, had fewer lights and thus was less showy than the other amusement rides.

This ride had sleek, gleaming, open rockets suspended by cables from a tall structure. The only sound that you heard while riding it was the soft sound of the wind as you went around in wide gentle circles. I loved watching all the lights from the rest of the park reflecting off the chrome-like sides of the rockets.

The quiet, gentle quality of this ride acted as a sort of elixir on the spirits of young children. It seemed to gently ease them off their amusement park high.

They yawned a lot after this ride. They were able to walk past the Flying Scooters and the Tumblebug without "Just one more turn! Huh? Pleeze, Dad!" Perhaps some magical fairy godmother whispered little secrets in their ears, patted their cheeks and blew them good-bye kisses to close out their special night.

In 1922, W.D. Acton, Riverview's founding father, wanted to expand his Silver Grove Hotel, dance hall and picnic grove area into a full-fledged amusement park by buying up some adjoining farm land. His lawyer's advice was, "Damn it, Bill, you're crazy if you put a roller coaster in a cornfield! You'll lose your pants! Why, the sheriff will get you, sure as the devil!"

Well, W.D., thanks for all the beautiful memories you created for hundreds of thousands of people. I'd trade eight days and seven nights in Disney World for about one hour in your park. Lawyers sure don't know much about having fun, do they?

Thanks to Grace and Joe Alliegro for the fun afternoon of molasses cakes, iced tea and swapping memories of Riverview Beach Park.

Today's Sunbeam, Salem, N.J., Sunday, September 9, 1990

Labor Day Brings Back Memories of School's Return

Labor Day marks for me the beginnings of autumn. The signs start appearing on Tuesday morning. The early light on the trees suggests that the green leaves are not the same lush, deep, verdant hue of only just a week or so ago, the blue of the sky is more intense, tonight's sunset will reveal colors that have a clarity and purity unseen all summer long. Nature gently begins to hum all those delicate rhythms and harmonies that tug at the souls of the dreamers.

As a kid, this holiday was approached with anxiety and trepidation. It marked the beginning of school for another year. The only music tugging at my soul was a screeching television clothing store jingle that exclaimed irritatingly "school bells ringing, children singing, it's back to Robert Hall's again!" Believe me, no kids were singing in my neighborhood!

It wasn't so much that I hated school, I just couldn't see forsaking a gloriously lovely day by spending it inside! Socrates, with his students gathered all around and sitting under an olive tree on a Grecian hillside, was my idea of a classroom.

The seasonal ritual of the return to school was brought home to this "autumnal dreamer" in a most touching way last Tuesday morning. While driving I had noticed a woman and a small child walking down the street and I had to wait for them to cross the intersection. The little boy was obviously in joyful deliriums, the mother was having an anxiety attack of major proportions!

By listening in on the ensuing conversation I discovered that they were out "practicing" the route the little boy was to take to kindergarten a day or so later. This little blond haired boy was all caught up in what was obviously his first and brand new lunch box and book bag, while his mother was begging him to remember what the intersection looked like and which way to turn!

What truer image would we want of the old Jewish adage "God could not be everywhere that's why He made mothers."

Let us now praise mothers. This past week I was on the sniffling, tear ladened, anxiety end of phone conversations with two friends of mine. Both of these friends are mothers with children in college. Both were in the same dilemma of having children leave for school. My one friend's son will be studying in England this year, 5,000 miles and an ocean away; and the other has a daughter moving 10 minutes from the toll booth of the Delaware Memorial Bridge and both mothers are equally heart-broken!

Watching and listening to these three mothers in operation flooded me with memories of my own mother. I came to the realization that mothers often play an unsung and overlooked role in our educational experiences.

One of many enduring memories I have of my mother was my being the unwilling participant in the "new shoes/corduroy pants/flannel shirt" back to school routine. Mom had a screwed up internal alarm clock that caused her to think that the division between summer's heat and winter's chill was ordained by Labor Day! She always expected that the Thursday after Labor Day, the first day of school, would find the temperature to be around 38 degrees!

So Wednesday we would head off to J.C. Penny's or Jack's to buy corduroy pants and flannel shirts so that I would be prepared for one of those "snap blizzards" that are so prevalent in early September here in South Jersey.

We never bought shoes a few weeks before school so that I could break them in slowly; they had to be purchased no earlier than 24 hours before school started. Mom thought they might go bad or spoil or something if they sat around unused for a few days.

Salem had about five stores that sold shoes back in the 1950s and mom selected a new store each year so as not to hurt anyone's feelings by shopping at the same store two years in a row! You would pray fervently that the style of shoe you had your heart set on was available at this year's selected store.

I loved the smell of new school shoes! In that 24 hour period I could almost sniff them down to bare leather in spots!

School would open, temps in the high 80's to low 90's and I'd start perspiring at about 8:45. By 3 p.m. I'd have lost seven pounds and be in the third stage of chronic dehydration.

The memory of staggering home in my soggy corduroys and drenched flannel shirts can still reduce me to blubbering! I'm not sure if the blisters came from the new shoes or just the sweat pouring off my legs and making my socks soggy! Those corduroys would shrivel my legs so that they looked like two sticks of pink beef jerky. What I know about prickly heat would astound you!

Good old mom saw me through hundreds of homework assignments, science projects, plays, catastrophes with friends, girls, and other assorted aches and pains over the ensuing school years.

By the time I was to start art school I figured mom's involvement in my education was over for the most part. I was going to live at home and commute to Philadelphia each day on the bus.

Well, the first day of art school arrived! Over night I had now become a mature, confident young man. Got my goals, got my life under control, going to go out into the world and knock'em dead!

Filled with gusto, I leaped aboard the 6:30 a.m. bus for Philadelphia, art school, and new horizons! Passing through Woodstown, I decided for the thousandth time to check over my art supplies needed for that first day's class. To my intense horror I discovered I had forgotten my box of water colors. This wouldn't have been any big problem if your first day of knocking'em dead on new horizons wasn't to be spent in a water color studio!

I screamed for the driver to stop, scrambled off the bus, and frantically called home from the bar of the Woodstown Hotel. At 7 a.m., in the middle of Woodstown, my mom arrived to find me crying, cussing, and stomping on the steps of the Woodstown Hotel!

By now I had missed the next bus, so Mom, with lots of love and her Catholic School philosophy, and I with my paint box headed off to my new horizons. I was the only college freshman in the entire world that September day in 1963 whose mother brought him to school on the first day!

Those steps at the Woodstown Hotel never fail to give me cause to reflect that perhaps this is where my career really began. It is at the very least a reminder for me of one more endearing memory I have of a mother's love.

And so little man, whoever you are, when that school door opens to you, so do wonderful new dimensions and spheres of your mother's love—the sweetest, purest, most unconditional love you shall ever know. You are most truly a lucky little boy. I wish you well.

Today's Sunbeam, Salem, N.J., Sunday, September 23, 1990

Magazine's Staffers Appreciate the Small Towns

As the 10 cartons that had been delivered by the UPS man were stacked in the office of Alloway Elementary School, it was assumed that more text books had arrived to mark the beginning of a new school year.

As they were opened by the office staff, it was to everyone's delight and surprise to discover that the boxes contained 500 copies of the October issue of *Highlights For Children* magazine!

Of all things, featured on the cover design was a typical scene, complete with float, costumed children, and a twilight sky, from none other than the Alloway Halloween Parade! A banner hanging from the side of the float verified that fact! The old Alloway Hotel was painted into the background and there was a portrait of township clerk Bill Haskett as the driver of the float. A certain local artist appeared in a crowd scene on the back cover.

The fact that the Alloway Parade now appeared on the front and back cover of the world's largest children's magazine and would appear in the homes of 3 million children, seemed to cause a bit of excitement in the usually serene and lovely small crossroads town of Alloway, N.J.

Last winter, when I received the assignment to design the October cover, it was only natural that visions and memories of this wonderful parade would start nipping away at the old creative process. Designing projects of Halloween in February and Christmas in July are standard fare for illustrators.

When sketches were sent to *Highlights* for approval, the editor's and art director's only comment was that I change the name of Alloway to that of a real town! I laughingly exclaimed over the phone, "This is a real town!" I then went on to explain in glowing detail my love affair for this parade and the magical and special night that turns a beautiful little country town into the Halloween capital of the world!

The folks at *Highlights* can really appreciate small towns. The editorial offices for HFC are located in the small rural town of Honesdale, Pa. Honesdale sits amid the beautiful Pocono mountains about an hour east of Scranton.

Highlights and Honesdale have been together since 1946, the year of the company's founding. Shortly after 1946 it was decided that the magazine needed to be closer to the paper and printing industry of postwar America. The chosen location was Columbus, Ohio, where the business end of the publishing is still located. The more sensitive, gentler and nature-loving sides of the "powers that be" decided that the editorial part of the company would remain in Honesdale.

Honesdale would not be foreign to anyone of us from the small towns found here in Salem County. Even though the roads have a lot of curves and hills, and the roadsides are loaded with what seems like endless varieties of delicate mountain wildflowers, it is the ambiance and attitudes and values that appear the same as found here amid the marshes, meadows and farmlands of home.

Time magazine, a few months ago, carried a report on the state of the corporate world as it appears in America today. The article was not a report on products or production or other businesslike concerns, but a report on the human element within companies. What state was middle management in? How fared those "up and coming" young executives?

The answers, sadly enough, were depressing. A sense of isolation, insensitivity, distrust, fear, greed and many other terms seem to identify the climb up the ladder of success and it's killing the human value system in corporate America. Forecasts for the 1990s indicate a backlash to the past two decades of greed, materialism and "me first" attitudes. I sure hope so.

Because I freelance and conduct most of my business from home and over the phone and via the postal service, I have hardly any "perks" (corporate jargon for free lunches, trips, monetary rewards, etc.). In 20 years I've been invited to lunch only three times! Is it my table manners? The way I dress?

Highlights has changed all that. My son, Christian, and I just spent a warm, friendly, loving and wonderful two days amid the corporate world as run by *Highlights* magazine. Every fall they have a great get-together for all of their freelance illustrators. For the last two years I have been able to attend and it's wonderful! They always have a theme for their annual party. (They know illustrators are big into costumes!) Last year the theme was the circus and this year it was a Wild West/Rodeo scenario. Staff and guests alike get very involved in the various themes.

Posh and class are not the catchwords of the day at a Highlights party. But words like happy, caring, warmth, affection all seem to spring to the fore.

It is in the lovely old mansion that houses the editorial offices that one is first welcomed to the festivities. All the art work done by the illustrators for the magazine is on display which gives one a great chance to see what the competition is doing! Finger food and refreshments that reflect the party's theme appears to cover every flat surface available.

After a jubilant and animated couple of hours of greeting old friends and making new ones, we all head off to dinner at a marvelous old Victorian-looking fire hall.

Throughout all of the partying and merrymaking, the folks from *Highlights*, be they the CEO, a secretary, an editor or art director, the founder's grandson or a receptionist, all seem to be thrilled that you are there. They all seem to be happy that they are together with each other. It is so obvious how hard they work to make such a fine time for all of us. My son was thrilled over all the attention he received from everyone and I loved them all for it.

This year, Saturday dawned as a glorious autumn-in-the-mountains type of morning! This part of our time in Honesdale is spent at a beautiful, typical Pennsylvania country home which was the home place for the founders of *Highlights*. It is here where we all socialize over a country breakfast that dreams are made of! It is the best breakfast I have all year! No offense intended to the No. 1 Special on the breakfast menu at the Salem Oak Diner, but it sure is great!

Everyone gathers in the living room or sits on the porch or outside on the grassy slopes enjoying the surrounding woods and fields. I am content to wolf down four helpings of everything and still keep a steady dialogue going with any available ear!

In the business scheme of things, I am the one selling the product (artwork) to a buyer (HFC), so if anybody should be taking folks out for a great time, it should be me buying them breakfast! I sure hope they never realize they got it backwards!

This year's party was joined by eight visitors from the Soviet Union who are here observing how *Highlights* is structured. These visitors are very involved with education and children's literature back home in the Soviet Union. Not one to stand on formalities, the folks from *Highlights* dressed them in blue jeans and cowboy hats, taught them to yell "yehaw!" and "yahoo!" and they joined right in on all the fun!

Heading on home down the curving roads along the mountainsides, the day was so beautiful under a brilliant blue sky filled with wonderful, powerful banks of clouds that foretell that it will soon be truly autumn. On the roadsides one sees delicate soft passages of varied white and blue and yellow wildflowers played against the rich earth tones of dried grasses, and all appear in sparkling contrast to the deep, dark stands of trees.

I leave Honesdale and *Highlights* in a mood mixed with joy and melancholy. I am so happy for the friendships established here, and yet a bit sad because it will be a whole year before we shall all be together again.

Freelancing has its pitfalls at times, yet my career abounds and overflows with a myriad of blessings. Blessings to me, while perhaps being poor theology, are sort of like hugs and kisses from God. *Highlights* and the folks who work there are some of the very best and sweetest of all.

When I asked Kent Brown, *Highlights* editor, about sending 500 copies of the magazine with my cover design to Alloway children for its promotional value, his reply was "No. We'll send 500 copies because it will be a lot of fun for the kids."

The drift of today's writing was to try to let the kids in Alloway, and the others in Salem County who receive *Highlights*, know that behind every issue are some very real and very special people.

On the night of Oct. 27, as we are all caught up in the revery and excitement and tradition of this marvelous parade, I hope some kid will pause, take a bite from a glazed donut, link arms with a ghost or a goblin, lift high a paper cup of cider or hot chocolate, look northward and yell, "Thanks! Wish you were here!" to Kent Brown and all the other fun people at Highlights. They'd love it!

Today's Sunbeam, Salem, N.J., Sunday, October 7, 1990

The Silent Majesty of Trees an Inspiring Sight

An artist friend of mine who originates from Iowa and now lives and paints in Philadelphia, claims that he finds it necessary to return to his home state at least once a year to give his eyes a rest!

When you inquire as to what he means, he grins and explains that Iowa is so flat you can see for miles and miles and that nothing vertical hinders your view! There are just miles of grassy plains and open sky, great expanses of flatland without benefit of trees or even a large bush! As a result, he returns to his studio in the Delaware Valley visually rested and relaxed.

While I find this approach a real "hoot" (Iowa talk for funny), I just can't imagine that a landscape devoid of trees as something I could deal with artistically, visually or otherwise for very long.

One of our biggest blessings in Salem County is that almost anywhere you look, wherever you are, there always seems to be a tree or trees as part of your view. Out in the countryside, many times we see broad ranges of woods that become a wonderful backdrop effect to scenes played out across the fields.

As part of our daily comings and goings we are so fortunate to have such an abundance and variety of trees in our existence. To our daily world they bring contrast, texture, movement, color and sound.

They are a part of our world and can be numbered among our most faithful and beloved friends. Like friends, I have certain special trees that live here in Salem County and others who live in other parts of the country. And as is the way of friendship, some I am close to and see often, and others I have not seen for many, many years, but the memory of them is still alive within my heart.

Trees can be touchstones in our lives and can become part of the unwritten record of that life. Our hearts whisper the various recollections that this tree or that tree may hold for us: it was within these limbs I played as a child; or it was from under these boughs we last said good-bye; how well I remember "slooshing and swishing" through the beautiful piles of autumn leaves created by this row of maples; and the beauty this holly tree gave to our home all these Christmases.

Some trees that I love are special for no certain reason except they are just so lovely to look at, so visually exciting to see. A whole combination of elements are orchestrated to allow it to appear magnificent regardless of the season or the weather or the time of day. It is perhaps this kind of sensing and seeing that brings to us the realization that nature can and does provide lessons for us on how to get on in life. Nature can help us see how we relate not only to ourselves but to others in the world around us.

Trees can become but one example of these lessons. We all know someone who, despite how he is clothed or the condition of his health or how the vicissitudes of life have dealt with him, he has never lost a beauty of character. He has kept a strength and a durability. He has remained deeprooted in his faith and belief, bent, twisted but still reaching upwards.

How deeply and how reverently the American Indians respected nature and allowed their lives to be conducted by the lessons learned from this deeprooted love and respect.

It is an unforgivable sacrilege that nature often becomes something that is only "in the way" and becomes overruled in the name of progress.

How fortunate we are to still have so much open land and trees as part of the county. On almost any road I have a favorite tree or stand of trees. I enjoy, so very much, seeing them in the various lights of the day as dictated by the seasons.

A tree that in one light and atmosphere and weather condition would appear delicate and gentle can become strong, rugged and forceful under other conditions. Could any scene be any more poetic or wistful than to see the hedgerows of trees in an autumn field of late afternoon light as we drive down Acton Station Road? How deep and lush is the tunnel-like effect of arched trees in Muttontown Woods.

Have you ever seen the beautiful rosepink glow created by the 7 a.m. sun shining on any of the winter woods along Slapes Corner Road? Huge buttonwood trees (sycamores) surround, with splendid and majestic grace, the Friends Meeting House in Hancock's Bridge. The wind through their branches and the dappled sunlight they cast over the lawn could break your heart with its serene beauty.

A large wild cherry tree stands atop a small rise on Auburn Road and is at its heroic best with windswept snow piled against it as its bare branches create lacelike patterns against the grays and blues of the February sky.

My son and I, when he was very little, would lay atop our picnic table and stare upward into the branches and foliage of a huge maple tree that almost covered our entire yard. It was so large that your total field of vision was filled with only flickering pinpoints of sunlight and the only sound you would hear was the swishing and rustling of its leaves. The whole experience became magical, almost transcendental and, at times, very spiritual.

To view one tree or a stand of trees in a subjective way, to see the mood and the subtleties created by sunlight and season, to see them with real intent and to allow them to speak to your soul is to see them as much more than just green 80-foot plants. To sense this poetry is to open yourself to the spirit of the land that surrounds you. The spirit will lead you to know the grandeur, the magic, the majesty and even the melancholy an awareness of nature can bring to our souls.

We can come to feel this spirit whether we are seeing a white church steeple rising amid soft, dusky foliage along Salem's busy Market Street; we will feel it as we see a grove of trees shining in a frosty moonlit field in Mannington; and, yes, the poetry and magic is and can be in our own backyards.

It will soon be so easy to be "tree conscious" as the trees take on their fall colors. Soon our breath shall be taken away by sheer delight and visual excitement of this most colorful of all seasons.

This winter as we see them bare and skeletal and black against the snow, it will be perhaps a bit harder to realize them for their beauty and being, but be assured that it is there in a myriad of ways and is so worth the effort of the search.

So many of us "look" but so few of us truly "see" what is in this wonderful world around us.

I end with words of Walking Buffalo: "Did you know that trees talk? Well they do. They talk to each other, and they'll talk to you if you listen. Trouble is, white people don't listen. They never learned to listen to the Indians so I don't suppose they'll listen to other voices in nature. But I have learned a lot from trees: sometimes about the weather, sometimes about animals, sometimes about the Great Spirit."

Today's Sunbeam, Salem, N.J., Sunday, October 21, 1990

Reach Out to Others. The Responses Will Surprise You

One of the great joys of my life and career is that I get to go out and speak to many groups of young school-age children. I get to interact with them in many ways.

Children give of themselves so readily and are so willing to take you at face value. I love receiving huge envelopes of their artwork and thank you notes after I have been to their schools. Children offer up such wonderful open feelings of love and praise. I feel truly blessed and transformed for this outpouring of emotions into my life and work.

Sadly enough we grow up, and what happens to this loving feeling we have for others? As children, and rightfully so, we are told to beware of strangers. But why is it that we seem to obey this parental message to a fault as we live out the rest of our lives?

Perhaps it is idealistic, or simplistic or romantic to suggest that the human condition could be altered and changed if only we would extend ourselves beyond ourselves! But isn't it worth a try?

In every situation of every day we are confronted with choices we need to make. These choices manifest themselves into attitudes: me first, my mind's made up, keep your distance, I'm right/you're wrong, and so on. Unless it deals with the intimate circle of our family and friends, do we ever consider love as a choice?

Love? Are you nuts!?! Show a little compassion and people will walk right over ya! They'll stand in line to kick your teeth down your throat!

What is so hard and so fearful about the effort it takes to extend ourselves emotionally to each other? We need to start closing some gaps, building some bridges between ourselves and the next person. It matters so little whether we know them or not.

A friend of mine once designed a book entitled *I Don't Have To Know Your Name To Be Your Friend*. I never got to read the text but the title alone tells us the story.

Living here in Salem County we are not lost to each other in "teeming masses" of people. It is very possible to see the same unknown people we saw last week, or yesterday, or last month, etc. We will often ask someone, "Who is that person? I keep seeing them here or there and I don't know who they are."

We don't need to know someone to make the reasonable assumption that we all share a lot of the some feelings. When we make the choice to look beyond color, nationality, creed, age, and gender, we find we are not all that different. Most of us want to be accepted; we feel loneliness; we want a sense of self-worth and dignity. We are all capable of giving love, and most of all we want to feel loved!

When we look within ourselves, and think about all the acts of human kindness and love that we could show and do for others, then we see the potential vastness of the riches we possess. The more of it we give away, the more replenished our wealth becomes.

Within this potential storehouse that we possess, how much of a strain on our love budget is it to say a sincere, "Hi ya!" or "Hello" or "How are you??!" to a stranger? I don't find it a very threatening situation to say hello to someone digging through the

TV dinner section of a supermarket, or on the front steps of the post office, or in a bank lobby.

Of course some people wouldn't respond if you stood on your head and spit nickels, but we just have to try.

Ah! The responses you get can be just marvelous. They can make your day as bright and wonderful as Christmas morning. I've greeted people who were so shocked that someone said a cheery greeting to them that they ran into someone else! This is the best kind of reaction because now they have to deal with another person and you got them talking! Two birds with one stone, eh?

Other responses are simple, quiet and sweet. Others can tell you how lonely some folks are for any form of acknowledgement from another human being. Perhaps, these are the very best of all.

We may never know what we have accomplished in the giving of ourselves to another. Its ripple effect could be boundless. Think about it.

There is a wonderful fable about a field mouse who asks a wild dove the weight of a single snowflake. "Nothing more than nothing," was the dove's answer. "In that case," said the mouse, "let me tell you a story."

The mouse goes on to relate how one wintry day, as he sat on a pine branch, he counted all the snowflakes that fell and covered the branch. The total number was 3,748,956 flakes of snow. Yet when the 3,748,957th flake fell, its weight, which was "nothing more than nothing" as the dove had said, caused the branch to break off!

Having finished his story, the mouse scurried off. The dove began to think on the story and said to herself, "Perhaps, there is only one person's voice lacking, for peace to come to the world."

We could fill a hundred editions of this paper and more with all the little one-and-two-line quotes that have been said about giving and sharing love. We all know some of them and probably we have a couple favorites tacked about our work place, or taped to the refrigerator door. But do we just admire them, or do we make the choice to love and to live them out in the everyday world that we are a part of?

I spent two days last week consciously greeting as many folks as I could without getting ridiculous about it and I had some wonderful success. I figured about five people in 75 ignored me. I believe only about 10 people did not smile. It was heartwarming and uplifting.

Three guys I am aware of who really know how to greet folks on the street are Rusty Mitchell, "Knot" Smith, and George Pappas. These men have turned saying "hello" into an art form!

They really are my heroes in their style and manner and technique. As a young boy, I always admired the mannerisms of Clara Slick (don't you love the name?!) who, when you asked her "How are you?", she would always say, "Ah, my dear, I am so much the better for seeing you!" Now is that style or what?!

I'll say hello to anything with ears and two legs and wave to every car that honks its horn. Friends will tease me and ask how I knew the car was honking to me. I don't know. I don't even care! I'd rather wave and shout "Hi!" 10 times and be wrong, than to miss the one meant for me!

In my going about the county and in its stores, banks, corporate offices, businesses, etc., I see so many people, for the most part, living within themselves and going through their daily world lost in a sense of isolation. I just can't help but feel and believe that it's our role in God's world to try to correct this.

How sweet and lovely and yet profound are the words of Emily Dickinson when she writes, "All I know of love is that love is all there is." Amen.

Today's Sunbeam, Salem, N.J., November 4, 1990

Long After Graduation, Teachers Still Have an Impact

The week of November 11th to the 17th marks National Education Week which is the inspiration behind today's column. This morning as I write, I am aware that today is All Saints Day and I cannot help but realize the heart's connection between these two special times.

Lehigh University English professor Peter Beidler says of teachers, "Most human beings are as good as they are because some unsung teacher was there when needed."

If we sit back and reflect on our lives, jobs and careers, friendships and accomplishments, I wonder how wont we are to offer up any credit to the men and women in our lives, the teachers who were there "when needed?"

Of the many and great loves that I have had in my life, very few rise beyond those feelings which I have had and held for the people I have called "teacher."

In almost every instance, I could and would equate these giving and unselfish people to be truly saints dwelling here among us. Since that first tearful day of kindergarten in Salem's R.M. Acton school 40 years ago, there have been so many great teachers and so many different schools and institutions that I have been privileged to be a part of.

My memories of each are as sharp and focused as ever, from remembering the perfume and chuckle of my first teacher to the bizarre neckties and riotous laughter of my art history lecturer of just last spring at the Barnes Foundation in Philadelphia. Each and every teacher brought and offered to me wonderful and divergent areas of learning and development and values for my life and my work.

In my first eight years of school I had a severe visual handicap and I owe my life to school superintendent Granville "Granny" Thomas and all of my grade school teachers who knocked themselves out to help get me through school.

I often think about all the special things that are so meaningful today that came out of those early years. I am amazed at their direct influence on my life as it is now.

I remember the afternoon in first grade when I was taught my first lesson in perspective drawing. We learned how railroad tracks come to a point as they go away from you and why trees get smaller the farther away they are. Twenty-five years later I was teaching the same subject in a year-long course to art school freshmen.

In the third grade we would read a story and then in the four quarters of a folded sheet of paper we would have to draw four pictures to tell the story. The biggest project of my career was to do a seventy-five page phonics book in which the pages were divided into quarters and on each page I had to draw four pictures to illustrate the accompanying story!

A fourth-grade school teacher doomed me to being a horrid romantic and idealist by having me read aloud the death scene from the story of "Joan of Arc."

In the fifth and sixth grades I was encouraged and nurtured into combining my attempts at poetry and writing with my love of making pictures.

Doris Bryant, my art teacher in high school, made it her mission to set me on my way to art school. To this day, depending on how my career is going on any given day, I still maintain a "love/hate" relationship with her! I have my moments when I wish she had had more of a propensity toward law or accounting!

Mae Allen, English Teacher Emeritus To The World, is plagued by her former student for editorial advice and grammar rules every other day as he tries to write a newspaper column.

The list could go on and on and on. Each teacher in my heart and memory could be verified by some aspect of my life today. Some of my teachers from art school are part of a close and special circle of friends. Some still retain their hero status as I strive and aspire to get good at what I do. One has become like a brother, one like a loving father. All of them shared and gave to me the very best of their efforts and talents and the emotional content that made them the artists that they are.

It was the love and care shown to me over the years "when needed" that caused me to want to give something back to the students coming behind me. I spent 20 years teaching part-time at my alma mater, the Hussian School of Art in Philadelphia.

We never realize how demanding the job of teaching is until we do it ourselves. The weariness at the end of a day of teaching is unlike any other form of exhaustion that I've experienced. A beloved teacher once told me when I first started teaching that unless I was willing to crawl out of the classroom at three o'clock, tired to the bone then I had no business being in there in the first place.

Those 20 years teaching part-time taught me a lot about the teachers who do it full-time. Professional teachers have to be the most devoted and dedicated people in our society. Thank God for school teachers!

It is so unfortunate, in so many ways, that many parents do not and will not take a supportive role in their child's education, and especially when it comes to supporting the efforts of the teacher.

Every year I get to go out and lecture about my work to several schools here in South Jersey, and I love being with the teachers and their students. I get to see first-hand the wonderful role that teachers play in the lives of our children.

I see how much teachers and administrators want for the kids and how frustrated they are if they can't get it. I see their eyes light up when we discuss special things to help them out in the classrooms. Their love for their work is so evident and so obvious.

It is exciting and inspiring to see the excitement teachers can generate in a classroom, but it is also the relationships between teachers and their students I most like to experience. It is the personal and human touches I believe will endure long after spelling tests and the foibles of fractions.

I see teachers touching and holding and hugging their students in special moments. I see them giving a student a feeling of self-worth by bragging to me about what a great artist he or she is. I see wonderful, happy, humorous, spontaneous moments happen between students and teachers. I see quiet and tender and emotionally charged times that thrill and move me. In this world of "high-tech and low-touch" it's nice to know that a loving and caring attitude still exists somewhere among the professions.

In tribute to all of those who teach, I hope that today's column will give us cause to reflect on all of those who gave so selflessly and so generously of their talents and love. We should all offer up a prayer of praise and thanks for those "unsung teachers who were there when needed."

For any of today's readers who ever found my name in their roll books, know that this column is dedicated to you and signed with love.

Today's Sunbeam, Salem, N.J., Sunday, November 18, 1990

Give Thanks for Your Beautiful Surroundings, Friends

I think November must be just about the nicest month of the whole year. November seems to bring to me so many deep feelings and longings about so many things.

Artists are very sensitive to light and the effect it has on creating a mood and atmosphere in the world around them. It must be that special light of November that affects me in such poignant and impassioned ways.

How beautiful the world becomes as it basks in the soft warm glow of the autumnal sunlight. November's light seems to envelope and enfold all objects upon which it falls. Trees and fields and earth and buildings seem to glow suspended, bathed in this magical light.

How pure and rich are the hues of reds and golds and rich browns and warm grays when we see them set against the deep, cold blue of the November sky. This free lesson in art theory about placing warm colors against cool colors for contrast is brought to you lovingly and most abundantly by God and Mother Nature.

Since we are speaking of sunlight on autumn trees, I have to tell you my latest idea on a bit of Biblical theory. Would you believe that the one true Garden of Eden just might well be Muttontown Woods in November? The other afternoon, while driving down Acton Station Road and gazing out over the gray and tan fields, this familiar patch of woods appeared bathed in a golden glow of shining and shimmering light that was breathtakingly beautiful!

As I got closer and closer the golden glow broke down into rich, vibrant colors of deep plum and ruby reds, oranges and yellows, and sienna browns. The vivid brightness of the leaves cast the tree trunks into dark, black silhouette shapes. As if this scenario wasn't enough, the entire woods was shot through and through with wonderful, hazy shafts of sunlight!

Feeling that it would be almost sinful not to take the time to stop for a few moments, I parked the car and walked over to sit awhile on a piece of fallen tree limb. To be surrounded by all this beauty and to try to absorb and take it all in was almost too much to do. When, and if, we allow ourselves to respond to something beautiful, we each react in our own special way. I am doubly blessed that my response can be expressed both with the brush of the artist and the pen of a writer. But my first response, before anything is committed to paper, is to just be so thankful that God has given me the senses and faculties to realize the beauty that is before me; and that I sense the need to make it a part of the collective memory of my heart and soul.

Before I leave these woods I must tell you about the oak leaves. As I look upwards I see several branches of red oak leaves hidden in the shadows of other foliage. As long as they remain in the shadows their color is a deep, dark red but suddenly the wind pushes them into a stream of sunlight and they glow with a wonderful, rich and delicious color of ruby-red stained glass as the light illumines them from behind! And they all dance to the tune played by rushing wind through the tree tops!

Other spots of jewel-like color flash and dance yellow, orange, red and green and give to these woods the appearance of stained glass high on a dark cathedral wall. It is like the effect of light reflecting off the mirrors and colored glass baubles of a carousel. Whatever transfer of values you wish to give to it or call it, it was beautiful and lovely and it contained a real sense of God's presence.

In harmony with the subtle and tender nuances of this month of November, how very right it seems that its special holiday should be Thanksgiving. Steal away for a quiet moment or two alone amid all the festivities and social gatherings, the spirit of this day lends itself to reflecting upon those things in our lives that we deem as blessings and thank God for them.

The very nature of the month, with its quiet, settled-down, snuggled-in kind of feeling, creates for us moments of musing and thumbing through the emotional scrapbooks of our hearts and minds. It is the "gathering in" symbolism of Thanksgiving that always causes me to find some time to reflect and recall family and friends and other Thanksgiving Days long since gone. These recollections, though some be tinged with sadness, cause warm, good, loving and fulfilled feelings to well up within.

This is a marvelous holiday! A day ordained and designed to wrap ourselves in wonderful, warm memories of all those blessings for which we should be so thankful. As I have written before in this column, I think of blessings as hugs and kisses from God. He must really love His artists because I feel so truly blessed to be able to live the kind of life that I have here in Salem County. As I write these words, thoughts of so many of you come, first, into my mind, and then settle down so very sweetly into my heart.

In my special quiet moments of this Thanksgiving Day I will think of you and me and the special love and warmth that this column has generated between us over the last year and a half, and I will feel blessed.

I will recall walks through downtown Salem, and that will give me cause to think of the folks who deal with me in such fun ways at the Post Office. I will remember and fall in love all over again with the ladies who work at Security Bank. I buy paper clips one at a time just so I have plenty of excuses to drop into BYCO where Barbara and Bonnie are special new found friends. The love and friendliness dispensed by everyone at McCoubrie's is as therapeutic as any prescription they might sell. Hilda and company at the Acme, Becky and Sue at United Way, everyone at the newspaper, the Oak Diner, all are so very special. I will think of all of you, and so many of the others who live and work here in town, and I will feel again the joy and happiness just seeing you brings to me everyday and I will feel blessed.

I will remember, and give thanks, for all the tireless and unsung workers who bring to Salem County such things as Septemberfests, Carneys Point Pride Days, Alloway Halloween Parades, historic Christmas tours in Woodstown and Salem, Salem's Magic of Christmas Parade, county fairs and so much more. I will recall the fun and merriment of it all, and I will feel blessed.

I will think of all the beautiful landscapes that I know and love here in the area. I will recall each one's special look at any hour of the day or during any season of the year. Once again, their beauty will return to me and tug at my heartstrings, and I will feel blessed.

For the 15 years or so of my career that my mother lived through, she would always tell me that someday I would be "rich and famous." Well, the last few years it occurred to me that good old Mom was maybe "pullin' my leg!"

When I get to thinking that I'll most likely never be rich or that my fame will never get much past Woodstown or Pennsville, I take a walk through Salem. My friend Tom Purchase says I "schmooze" through Salem. "Schmooze" is a Yiddish word which means you chat a little, you flirt a little, you laugh a little, you joke a little, and you love a little. After a while I return home to my studio and my work, but I return feeling loved and cared about and knowing that I am deeply and truly blessed.

I now know where my riches lie, and my life is as lovely as a shiny red apple. Everything is as it should be and I have all the wealth and fame that I shall ever, ever need.

Happy Thanksgiving!

Today's Sunbeam, Salem, N.J., Sunday, December 2, 1990

As the Great Day Nears, Christmas Memories Abound

To all appearances, if someone walked into our foyer, he or she would assume that we were moving.

Boxes and bags are scattered here and there; furniture askew or simply moved to other rooms. Huddled amidst the turmoil, we are enjoying (?) our eighth consecutive meal of Thanksgiving leftovers!

"I swear, Honey, this turkey just keeps on getting better and better, hmmm?!?"

Someone once defined eternity as two people and a ham. Well, believe me, a family of three could live off a 20-pound Thanksgiving turkey and its various caloric accoutrements 'til about Groundhog's Day. The last piece of dried out pumpkin pie went sometime between Tuesday breakfast and Wednesday lunch.

The coleslaw is down a quart and the fresh fruit salad seems to be subdividing every two hours! While many of us are quite guilty 365 days of the year of not keeping the spirit of Thanksgiving alive in our hearts, it is quite possible to keep its memory a part of us for a good 10 days, and even longer if the sweet potatoes and succotash hold out.

One year we even had little heart-shaped turkey croquettes for Valentine's Day dinner. Hey, what's a little food poisoning when you know you've gotten every last penny's worth of your turkey dollar?

Well now that I've fought one more pitched battle to decimate a huge dead bird, I turn my thoughts to the piles of cardboard boxes in the foyer.

The sides of these large brown boxes indicate to the casual observer via the printed words on their sides that they once contained bottles of fabric softener or boxes of breakfast cereal, perhaps cans of motor oil or Hershey bars, or a hundred different items of supermarket merchandise.

Ah, but I assure you, dear and gentle reader, they are treasure chests extraordinaire, except they are in the guise of common everyday cardboard boxes!

The family fortune? No, that's tucked safely away in an empty corner of my wallet just waiting for the next big sale day at Ames or Kmart!

The valuables contained within these boxes are our Christmas decorations that have been collected over the years. Each and every one of them plays its own special part in orchestrating and making our Christmas uniquely ours, as I am sure your decorations give a special look all their own to your home.

When growing up at home, we would bring down from the attic rafters a certain long wooden box that contained most of the ornaments that I grew up with. On a hot July day while making a quick trip to the stifling attic for something, the mere sight of that wooden box brought a special thrill and excitement to the heart because it just glowed with a feel that said—Christmas.

Our ornaments at home weren't much more than just plain colored glass balls and tinsel, nevertheless, it was our way of doing Christmas. That box held tangled strings of large colored lights, dozens of colored glass balls, and everything locked within the grasp of shiny, prickly tentacles of gold garlands!

When it came to doing the tree, my mother believed that spray cans of artificial snow were the greatest thing added to Christmas since pre-tied bows! Instead of spraying the tree beforehand, my wonderful, slightly eccentric mother would wait till after it was trimmed.

In the finest tradition of Old Man Winter and Jack Frost combined, and with great, dramatic, sweeping gestures, she would commence to spray the tree. In the process, at least a third of the living room was covered with artificial snow!

It smells like the same chemicals in model airplane glue are contained in artificial snow. It's no wonder our family was so happy and joyous throughout the season, we were all probably "tripping out" on an artificial snow "high!"

As kids, my brother and I saw more than just visions of sugar plums dancing in our wee little heads, believe me! After all those years of built up layers of artificial snow on the round ornaments, Mom's tree took on the look of being decorated in either large marshmallows or small baseballs.

Although she may have had strange ideas on decorating, my mother most assuredly kept Christmas in her heart every day of the year.

In spite of the fact that my sense of decoration came out of that tradition, I like our decorations to be a bit more hand-crafted and individual. Most of our ornaments are made from wood or straw, corn husks, feathers, salt dough, or any of several other natural mediums.

I like to have our tree appear like something I would draw for one of my illustrations. For 20 years we took three days each Christmas season just to string popcorn and cranberry chains. That effort has since been replaced by purchasing strings of pearl-like beads.

We use the little star-like white lights and the whole effect has a nice old-fashioned look to it. My son can't wait to be living on his own someday as he has always felt deprived that our lights aren't colored and flashing in time with some Christmas melody.

His sense of beauty yearns for glass balls and tons of shiny tinsel and the crowning glory would be a revolving and flashing star atop it all! Thank goodness he's not aware of spray cans of artificial snow!

I love unpacking our decorations one at a time and ooohing and aaahing over each and every one. Each ornament always seems to be someone's "favorite one." Each one offers up its own special memory or feeling to our sense of holiday spirit.

An old favorite is a turkey wish-bone coated in gold glitter that came from our first Thanksgiving turkey after we were married. It is a bit glitzy to look at but makes us very sentimental! We have beautifully delicate straw ornaments from a dear friend in Germany. Other special favorites were handmade by friends and are poignant reminders of cherished friendships over the years.

We aren't into collecting anything in the way of plates, figurines, or the like, but throughout the year we always have our eyes open for tree decorations. Everything is looked at as a potential tree ornament. It takes us about eight hours to do our tree.

One Christmas season, a Jewish friend of ours had stopped by to see the tree and his response to it was, "It's so beautiful! I've never decorated a Christmas tree, but aren't you supposed to let some of the tree show through?"

About mid-November I start to get excited knowing that I will soon be unpacking a wonderful cross-stitched Christmas sampler that a friend made for me a few years ago.

Another friend gave me a fragile copy of St. Nicholas Magazine, which was one of the first magazines ever published for children and it is a Christmas issue dated December 1875. This special gift becomes the focal point of a still-life I create each year using old antique photos of children and other nostalgic items.

A friend who does lace-like silhouette paper cutting gave me a beautiful piece that depicts a German-style Christmas tree with candles and other decorations. It has become a real jewel in my collection.

I have so many other decorations and memorabilia from friends that I did not take the space to mention. These pieces are all beautiful and mostly handmade and are so lovely sitting about. Their real loveliness, their special charm, and their endearing sweetness comes from the fact that they were given out of a sense of love and caring.

I'm at that point in life where the receiving of gifts has gone somewhat by the wayside in favor of just wanting to enjoy the beauty and spirit of this great season with as much intensity as I can muster.

Over the next four weeks I will be in my own little world that is half fantasy and half reality and all wrapped in the wonderful spirit of Christmas! I have a marvelously bright, showy, seven-foot long scarf of red and green wool that makes me feel like a character out of a Charles Dickens' Christmas story. I love how it causes conversation with strangers who just have to comment on its obvious Christmas appeal!

Part of the spirit of this wonderful season is generated by the historic Christmas open house tours in Woodstown and Salem. In addition, there is always the excitement of Salem's Magic of Christmas Parade.

I just returned from a beautiful concert of seasonal music in Salem's Old Courthouse presented by the Salem City Singers and The Johannes Brass. It was wonderful, but I missed you. See, I now have a head start on you because I was there and you weren't.

Before this season is over, there will be candlelit churches with old, sweet, familiar carols; running into friends shopping at area stores (I detest malls at Christmas. Actually, I detest malls at almost any time!) Time will be spent looking at brilliant, starry skies over Elsinboro where it seems that if you wait and watch just a little longer, you just might see a very special star.

Area churches hold soup and sandwich lunches as part of their Christmas bazaars and they are excellent sources of Christmas merriment. On and on and on the list could go if I wished it to, but it is better for you to seek out and discover your own favorite Christmas memories.

As long as Salem County has churches, Christmas tree lots, a chance of snow, and folks willing to go out and be with others, Christmas spirit and merriment will be abounding in great magical swirls.

If you run across a rather bizarre character with a seven-foot red and green striped scarf and a spring of holly in his hat, a carol on his lips and Christmas in his heart, remember, you read about him here first!

Today's Sunbeam, Salem, N.J., Sunday, December 16, 1990

Memories of Christmases Past Provide an Inner Glow

Well, it is now about eight or nine days until Christmas and I am beginning to wonder if I have the strength and energy to make it to the big day. Between parties, decorating, and historic open house tours, I am about worn out!

I remember one rather exhausting Christmas season a few years ago. In a frenzied fit, I asked my wife why Christmas never seemed like this much hassle when I was growing up?

Her reply was quite simple and very obvious: My parents did all the work and all I had to do was sit back and watch it all happen around me! Yep! That explained it alright!

Even though I sometimes complain, I do so love all the outward trappings of this wonderful season. Yet, it is very important to me that I start to focus on the lovelier and quieter and more spiritual aspects of what Christmas is all about.

It is important for me to know that I experienced and sensed Christmas in a deeper way than just to have laughed and partied my way through it. January can be a very cold and lonely month if I feel like I hurried and harried my way through the holidays.

The realization that it's time to start shifting gears comes sometimes from within, sometimes from without.

Inspiration works its magic in many forms and guises. At a wonderful party, filled with happy and interesting people, great food, fun times, and wonderful holiday spirit, the piece of inspiration I had sought was provided.

In a small alcove, off the living room, sat a woman playing Christmas carols on a lovely, plain wooden harp.

To be able to sit two feet away and hear "Lo, How A Rose Ere Blooming" or "What Child Is This" being played so sweetly is to have a foretaste of angels celebrating Christmas in heaven.

To be able to see the beautiful and poetic flow of her arms, and the way she closed her eyes as her fingers made the runs across the strings, to experience all of this was to receive a wonderful gift of Christmas.

As an adult celebrating Christmas, I have allowed so many of my childhood memories of this special time to add their sense of form and feelings and color to all of my attitudes of today. Like all children, I felt that December 25th was the all and everything of the entire year!

I was blessed with a mother who waited for Christmas with all the anticipation and sense of wonder of any child. Existing side by side with her love of the merriment of the season was a wonderfully deep and abiding sense of the glory and beauty and spirit of Christmas.

No matter how hectic and frantic the days would become she could always find the time to reflect on the meaning and loveliness of it all.

To her, every event and aspect of the season, regardless of its importance, was enacted to create for her children a special, bright, life-long memory.

At least once during the season, we would all walk downtown in the late afternoon just so we could see all the Christmas lights in the business district turn on at the same time!

While lacking snow and a sleigh, we would walk to the local Christmas tree lot to get a tree which was then laid on my red express wagon. By singing carols the whole time, Mom felt this added to the Christmas card scenario of "bringin' home the tree!"

My mother judged the worth of a tree by how much sympathy it elicited from her. The skinnier it was, the better. After all, it gave up its life for Christmas, someone had to take it home and make it beautiful.

Why not us? If you read my last column, you will remember that Mom's Christmas credo was that there was no tree so scrawny that two spray cans of artificial snow couldn't make it beautiful!

At last, Christmas Eve Day would dawn. This day was as special to me as Christmas Day itself. It was on this day that I felt the magic, sensed the glory, faintly heard the music, and knew with all my soul that Christmas had truly arrived.

I would awake to the sounds of snipping scissors and the rustling of wrapping paper from my mother's bedroom. All deep, ethereal feelings for the spirituality of the day fell, momentarily, under the onslaught of pure greed as to what might be getting wrapped this very instant with my name on it!

Yearning to envelope myself fully in the spirit of this day, I would scramble out of bed and be dressed in mere seconds. My mother would give me five dollars so that I could go downtown all by myself and buy presents for the family.

There was always extra money so that I could buy my lunch out! If Donald Trump gave me unlimited use of his MasterCard, nothing I could buy would equal the thrill of those Christmas Eve shopping sprees I had as a kid.

For six years in a row, or so it seems, I bought Mom egg enriched shampoo from McCoubries. She made such a wonderful fuss every year over it that I was afraid to disappoint her by not buying it each Christmas!

I would be home by early afternoon and would wrap my presents next to the tree just so I could be near it. How well I can still see the afternoon sun pouring in through the windows and making sunbeams through the tree. The tree would be sparkling with the sunlight shining on the tinsel and ornaments.

It seemed I was always the only one around during the afternoon and I loved just being by myself near the tree. My mother would appear occasionally to put on more Christmas music or to get more tape or something, but for the most part, I got to enjoy quiet, peaceful moments lost in my own Christmas dreams on this special afternoon.

It was my job to set up the manger scene under the tree and I loved the "pretend" that it allowed me as I arranged the chipped plaster figures. After an hour or so of positioning the figures I would decide that this is how it must have really looked in Bethlehem.

We also had some little cardboard houses and a few metal or plastic figures that I just loved to and play with. They provided all the props I needed to live out my Christmas Eve fantasies. I would pretend they were visiting each other, or were peeking into the manger scene, perhaps they were running out for one last gift, or were gathering together for midnight mass.

After awhile I would realize that the sun was going down and the room would take on a serene and quiet beauty. For me, the closing of the day on Christmas Eve brings a sense of peace and profound beauty that makes wonderful, illustrative images happen within my heart and soul.

Even as a child I would see Mary and Joseph arriving at the inn against a twilight sky. Golden clouds streaking across the heavens allowed me to wonder what the shepherds on the hillsides would have for their dinner. As the sky turned from yellow-green into dark blues and violets, the Wise Men would spot once again a single, bright star.

They would know that the journey would soon be over, and they would arrive at a small stable at about the same time we would be having communion at midnight Mass.

We always ate supper out because Mom would be too busy to bother or even to come along with Dad and us. All through dinner Dad would be adding his efforts to heighten our anticipation of the coming hours.

After dinner we would ride around and look at everyone's Christmas lights. I always wanted to get back home because I knew that while we were out my mother was putting the final touches on what would be our Christmas.

We would return to find the presents pouring out from under the tree. Candles would be aglow from every available flat surface, and carols were playing as a background to it all! Long after we had quit believing in Santa Claus, we were never allowed to doubt his existence.

My mother felt that to give up on the spirit and romance and fantasy of this legend was to deny yourself the magic and mystery that was a special part of Christmas.

Then, as now, I am willing to believe that the most beautiful and meaningful part of all of Christmas is to be at the midnight service at St. John's Church. I spent two Christmas Eves away from home and it was the beauty of St. John's Church that I longed for the most.

The meld of hundreds of candles, poinsettias all about the altar, and the singing of the carols makes for a beauty that always brings tears to my eyes.

Afterwards we would return home to a midnight snack and then the opening of the presents! My older brother, home on leave from the Army, would always be the one to hand out the presents. Around four o'clock we'd all head to bed only to reappear at staggered times over the next few hours to see how our neighbors fared from old St. Nick!

Several times throughout Christmas Day Mom would tell me how happy she was to have her supply of egg shampoo replenished. That always made me happy.

One of the greatest truths ever written says that "memories allow us to have roses in December." I rely so much on the memories of Christmas that I have as a child to help keep my sense of its awe and magic fervently alive.

I still cherish my time on Christmas Eve afternoons as being very special and reflective. And as always, come the vesper hour, the sunset time, I will worry for Mary, wonder about the shepherds, and gaze out over a gold and purple landscape made of clouds and will watch and wait for a kingly caravan to appear.

This columnist wishes for you fantasy, love, serenity, and peace this Christmas.

Today's Sunbeam, Salem, N.J., Sunday, December 30, 1990

A New Year Celebrated in Salem County Must Be Good

New Year's Eve is about the most overrated event that I can think of. I have a hard time dealing with huge doses of loud people, even louder music, and social graces thrown out the window all in the name of "it's New Year's Eve!"

On this night everybody wants to be your long lost friend and when not extolling your virtues, they try to give you advice on the course your life should take!

When it appears that you have, (1) spurned their offers of becoming blood brothers on the spot and (2) ignored their advice as the ramblings of a rum-sotted idiot, they turn violent and want to punch you in the nose! I guess I just can't deal with such a wide range of choices or emotions that this night's merry-making has to offer.

Unfortunately, I think a lot of people approach this evening with a bad attitude. Their attitude is that the coming new year has to be better than the last! Many people, I think, decide that they had such a rotten year that they now have a wonderful excuse to get "smashed" and dance with their host's Christmas tree or to put mushroom caps and clam dip down someone's dress!

At these types of parties I am usually suspicious of people who hang off your shoulder and blubber away in your ear. At one such New Year's gathering a guy draped his arm around me and with eyes askance said "See that good lookin' girl over there? Oh, Man! She does my teeth!" A bit puzzled, I said, "She does what?" He answered back, twice as loud, "She does my teeth!!!"

I thought this was some term, unknown to me, that perhaps meant that she excited him or "turned him on" as the phrase goes. So I said, "What do you mean she does your teeth?!?" At this point his eyes rolled in two different directions and he fairly screamed, "She works for my dentist!!!"

As he muttered some profanity and staggered away, I decided that I needed to spend New Year's Eve in calmer and more reflective surroundings.

I really enjoy being with just a few good friends and contemplating the old and the new year over huge quantities of Chinese food. To me, no year was ever as bad as it seemed, or as fearful as it may be, when your senses are being caressed and cajoled and comforted by Oriental cooking! Any year that was plotted and planned over an exquisite Chinese dish called "Seven Stars Around the Moon" is a year you just know is going to turn out great!

I love the symbolism of a brand new year. A new set of opportunities that are opened to us; new chances to find in our lives that which we feel we need to make life more complete.

Going through life in the uncertain and insecure role of being an artist and a writer is to pass through the days of the year filled with hope and faith. The carrot is always dangling just a bit out of reach, yet, I find that it is in the reaching and the stretching that life takes on a great deal of meaning and fulfillment.

Ben Franklin once said that he who lives on hope will die fasting, yet, to live a life based on hope and faith allows me to live in a realm of expectation and excitement. My creative existence depends on my remaining open and fluid to all of life going on around me.

I can never be sure what impact the next moment, or event, or person might have on my life and my work. To know and realize this interdependency between life and work is to truly feel that it is all being lived as one huge blessing and gift from God.

As a reader of this column, you all know that I would consider any year, an old one or a brand new one, as "good" provided that it is lived out among the people and the landscape of Salem County.

One of my richest blessings is the readership of this column! Many of you folks, some I know and many I don't, will call, or write notes or stop me on the street and say how much you enjoy reading my column. The best part about all your comments is the fact that so many of you agree with my sense of excitement over living in Salem County!

There is a reader who lives in Mannington who will call me on the phone to alert me to the evening's sunset, if particularly beautiful, just in case I wasn't looking! God bless her, Kay and about

500 cranes can be seen on any given evening standing around the causeway on Route 540 enjoying the view!

I recently spoke with a couple who moved to Salem from Camden County and purchased a home on Market Street. They smile and their eyes glow when describing how wonderful they feel Salem and its people have been to them. They feel that our area is a touch of heaven when compared to other parts of New Jersey.

Speaking of heaven, a minister friend disclosed to me that he always takes a drive through the countryside when trying to get his thoughts together for his next sermon. He especially loves being by the river and watching it through the marsh reeds in Elsinboro.

A lady wrote to me from Cape May. In her note she said that at least once a week she will drive up to Salem County just for the landscape! I might mention that she scored a thousand points with me by saying that when she reads my column it is like a second trip! I wonder if she could have meant that reading my column was as tiring as a 120-mile, round-trip car ride?

One can always find outsiders pulled here by historic tours or street festivals. They offer profuse accolades for the life around this area: its scenic beauty, its people, its historic heritage.

As excited as I am that you all share your thoughts with me, I hope so much in the coming new year and new decade you will share your feelings with those around you over just how green the grass is on our side of the fence!

I spent the waning weeks of 1990 being delighted almost daily by the manifold and various beautiful scenes going on around me, each being oft times lovelier than the last.

Did you see Market Street all candlelit and glowing jewel-like the night of their Christmas open house tour? To view that beautiful street as a hand bell choir from St. John's Church played softly in the background, and as bare tree branches overhead made lovely lacy patterns on the night sky was to live, for a few moments, in a fairyland. It was all the splendor, beauty, and magic one needed to feel Christmas.

We all decry the look of the nuclear plant cooling tower on the landscape of Elsinboro and LAC but even that has its moments. The other evening in concert with sunset colors and wind movements, the steam clouds appeared to have created two beautifully delicate Oriental peacocks or crane-like birds. Their slender necks and flowing, graceful tails painted gold, purple, and magenta by the dying sun, majestically strutted and danced their way across the opal streaked skies of the meadows.

On Sunday before Christmas, as part of a church pageant, I watched a pretty 12-year-old girl named Suzanne transcend into the role of the Swedish legend of Santa Lucia. Down through the center aisle of our darkened church she came dressed in a beautiful white gown. Upon her head she wore a wonderful wreath of flowers and greens with four burning white candles to complete a stirring effect. Tears still return with the memory of the sweetness of the moment.

To see the warm and welcoming candlelit glow of Abbott's Tide Mill Farm Bed and Breakfast Inn appearing across the Mannington fields on a misty December night is like looking at a scene from a Christmas card.

These past few weeks there just seemed to be so many beautiful sights to behold for the visual enjoyment of all to tuck away in the heart and mind; to help give color and form to our opinions and views on the beauty of the area we live in.

As the ending days of 1990 were filled with visual delights, so, too, were they filled with wonderful acts of caring and kindnesses. A sweet and dear friend who reads this column gave me a coupon book to use at McDonald's so I could have "lunch out" on Christmas Eve day, just as I had mentioned in my last column!

To my surprise and delight I was given a delicious tin of cookies that acknowledged my "good customer" status at a local store.

I was invited to share in the combined Christmas luncheons of two local agencies and I had a wonderful, happy time! When you work alone in a studio as I do, the annual studio Christmas party is a rather lonely affair. The boss always seems to know ahead of time what I bought him!

Only in Salem County can you return a book at the local library, be fined forty-five cents and then be invited to stay for a lovely, lovely party. It was delightful and will make for a wonderful Christmas memory. There I was, surrounded by delicious food, rows of great books, and special friends, and I rejoiced and reveled in it all!!!

For anyone who spits, stamps, and stomps about life here in the county, all I can say is, "you're just not tryin'!"

Thank you all for tolerating three columns in a row about the holiday season that I love so much. Thanks for all the nice things said about them and all the other columns throughout the year. Keep those cards and letters coming folks, they really keep me going!

In a children's book called "Love You Forever" by Robert Munsch, I would like to borrow and adapt the book's reoccurring refrain. I send it to you wrapped in heartfelt best wishes and prayers for your new year . . .

I'll love you forever
I'll like you for always
As long as I'm living
My sweet friend you'll be.

Today's Sunbeam
Columns

1991

Today's Sunbeam, Salem, N.J., Sunday, January 13, 1991

Snow Instills Magic in the Soul, Beauty in the Eyes

S now. I am wild about it!
     There have been so many times and so many memories in my life when snow has been a part of the scenario. There have been moments as bright and pure as morning sun and cobalt blue skies reflecting off new fallen snow. There have been the times when snow has been a gray and dreary companion to match my feelings of the moment.

Snow, like autumn, makes the world a bit more romantic to live in for a little while. This is quite easy for me to say–I work at home! Even on the snowiest of days I walk to work in slippers and a turtleneck sweater.

My memories of snowy days as a young boy are as clear and crisp as . . . well, as a snowy day! There will always be the memory of that first slap of cold, frosty air as I rushed outside to join the others. I would always pause spellbound for a few moments over how the world had changed between last night's bedtime and the cries of neighborhood friends who knew school had been closed for the day! As I rushed to get dressed I would have to listen to my father's diatribe on snow days when he was a kid in Ohio.

It went something like, "By God, when I was a kid, we had snow from September to June! It was 50 feet deep! You risked your life just reaching outside for the newspaper! They *never* closed school! I walked to school everyday through it all!" At this point Mom would firmly remind him that he lived right across the street from both the elementary school and the high school. This lecture was just Dad's way of showing insane jealousy!

The streets in our neighborhood were never plowed until about Easter, and only if it came early that year! Everything was covered in wonderfully rounded, soft, curving slopes and ridges of snow. Never did I make it much longer than 10 minutes before I had snow in my boots and halfway up my pant legs! Remembering

Mom's refrain, "Don't come running in here every 10 minutes tracking snow all over the floor!!" kept me sufficiently inspired to remain outside for at least the first 30 minutes.

About mid-morning, my wonderfully compassionate mother would take pity on about 800 cold neighborhood kids and dispense hot chocolate by the gallons from the back porch. Dixie cups were all that was available for disposable containers in those days and they were not meant to hold steaming liquids. The wax coating would soon melt and we were left holding, or dropping, a disintegrating cup of hot chocolate! If you kept your soggy, ice-encrusted mittens on, it kept the burns to a minimum!

I never tired of seeing how the snow changed the shape and feel of the world around me. I was fascinated, enchanted, by the moods and feelings that this wintry world seemed to stir within me. Long after the other kids would have gone home, I was content to just wander about. I loved how the snow changed in form and color as the sun started to go down. As a perfect accompaniment to all the soft, rounded forms of nature came the peace and stillness of a snow covered world that muffled and subdued all sounds.

Now, many years and snowfalls later, I am still enthralled whenever it snow. It continues to instill its magic on my soul and its beauty to my eyes.

Light creates such wonderful effects on snow. Light and shadow gives to our eye marvelous nuances of color and contrast. Colors are often in sharp and sudden contrast to the snow's bright and intense sun-lit whiteness. Almost poetically, or like an adagio in music, soft and delicate gradations of blue, violet, and rose unite light and shadow together in the half-light of early morning or late afternoon.

Snow can bring to my soul great mood swings of exhilaration and melancholy; both effects are important to my emotional needs as an artist. In literature and in music, my two favorites are the writer Dostoyevsky and the composer Tchaikovsky. The creative work of both of these great Russians is highly emotional and explores the human psyche throughout their careers. I often muse and wonder what influence the interminable Russian winters may have had on their creative spirits.

Pieter Brueghel, the whimsical 16th century Flemish painter, thought it only natural to paint his wonderful, fanciful religious and peasant scenes amid the snowy, wintry world and gray half-light of Flanders.

Snow scenes are so exciting and so much fun to draw! On cloudy, overcast days the world in snow appears very stark, and very much just black and white. When you sit outside you see that all shapes appear as gray masses against the white areas of snow. All you need is gray paper, white chalk, and a dark pencil, and the picture almost draws itself! Well, not quite, but it's pretty easy.

The other day, in the fading light of a sunless sky, the snow that lay on the surface of every tree limb and branch and twig was only a bit lighter in color than the slate-gray sky behind. If you looked carefully, you could see a faint band of rose color evolving across the gray clouds. The almost imperceptible softness of this color "brought out" the whiteness of the snow against the sky; and the total effect was as of lace, or the confectioner's filigree on a wedding cake.

Happily enough, we, here in the county, get to enjoy our snow as it blankets meadows and woods and small-town streets. We have open expanses of sky so that we can see the effects of the light of dawn, or dusk, as it sweeps over the fields. Have you ever seen a snowfall in the city? It is, especially at night, that the snow, falling on city streets amid the tall buildings, takes on its own unique and special beauty.

I remember being in Philadelphia during a real blizzard back when I was in art school. At eleven o'clock at night, two school friends and I were lying on our backs making "snow-angels" in the middle of Broad Street right by City Hall. We were the only signs of life for as far as the eye could see. In the city the snow clouds reflect the lights and give a false sort of twilight glow to the night sky. This brightly lit atmosphere allows you to see the snowflakes falling from very high in the sky! Part of that evening's fun was that one friend was experiencing snow for the very first time in his life! Scott had lived all of his life in Florida and had never seen snow. He was quite willing to freeze to death just so long as he could play in it till the end!

Usually, I feel no need to apologize for the content of my columns, but, least some of you think me entirely crazy for my feelings about snow. I have been known on occasion to say that the older I get the more I know why people spend their winters in Florida!

Until the time when I'd rather build sand castles than a snowman, I'll rally around the words of the English poet Shelly who said, "I love snow, and all forms of the radiant frost."

Well said, Old Chap!

Today's Sunbeam, Salem, N.J., Sunday, January 27, 1991

Dreams of a World Living in Peace Suddenly Shattered

I am angry. I am mad. I am frustrated. And when I am not one of the above, I feel an intense sadness and longing.

Wasn't it just a year or so ago that it appeared that "peace was breaking out all over?" What happened? What went wrong?

It seemed like a sure thing that maybe, just maybe, we were seeing a world that was going to enter the 21st century with the knowledge of how mankind could live in peace and harmony. It seemed like the world had started to discover and explore new ways of solving the old problems of aggression and greed and internal disputes.

The potential and possibilities for so much "good" to evolve seemed boundless. The Cold War was over, the Iron Curtain had risen, and the Berlin Wall came tumbling down! It was a wonderful new day for so much of the world to sow new beginnings for peace and freedom . . . and now it all must wait a little longer.

I am angry that I feel forced by world events to break with the traditions I have tried to maintain in my column, even if only for one Sunday.

I sat for two days along with the rest of the world watching and listening to this new war unfold before us. How clean and sanitized this modern, electronic, computer-aided war appeared in those opening hours. We didn't see many combatants, just the machines of war. We were given statistics and numbers and optimistic reports that this was to be a short war.

Through all the television coverage and special reports from the Gulf; through all the new terms and jargon coming out of this conflict; throughout it all, my heart and mind turned to another time and to another war. Another war that for me will never be just a matter of statistics and numbers and politics. It will always be names and emotions and memories.

I will always remember an August night in 1966, sitting in the living room and hearing, from the kitchen, my mother's cries as she was told that my brother had been killed in Vietnam. For most of my life he had held the hero status that is reserved for an older brother. He had spent 13 years in the Army and was a paratrooper, a Ranger, and a Green Beret.

I was 21 and he was 32 and it had only been the last couple of years that we related to each other as adults. He was supposed to come home and I was to work hard so that perhaps someday I could be a hero to him. I remember one of his Army buddies telling me that if it was any consolation, my brother died in one of the most beautiful parts of Vietnam. Nice try. But, no consolation whatsoever.

The image of a flag-draped casket, the physical jolt of hearing an honor-guard gun salute, and the awful, awful beauty of a bugler playing "Taps" is what I have left of my hero.

And there are other memories.

My cousin David had spent most of his young life wanting to be a priest and in spite of a devilish sense of humor, you just knew it was something he was meant to do. It was the suggestion of the parish priests at his church in Ohio that he should wait a couple of years before making any kind of religious commitment.

David joined the Marines and died in Vietnam a year after my brother. The ultimate tragedy is that my Aunt Jane, David's mother, literally died of a broken heart the day after hearing of her son's death. They were buried side by side.

If you should ever visit the Vietnam Veterans Memorial in Washington, go to where the names of the war dead begin and count down to about the 44th name. It will say Claude McBride. "Micky" and my brother Don grew up together and all they ever wanted to be were soldiers. They enlisted together and both left for boot camp the same day.

Micky died 10 years later in August of '63 serving as an advisor in Vietnam. I can remember that people had never even heard of a place called Vietnam in those early days. Micky was the first from Salem County, and one of the first in the country, to lose his life there. Ten years and 58,000 names later, the war would be over.

I sometimes find, quite by accident, that I have walked by that same place where I last said goodbye to my brother. I never realized that morning how much of my hopes and dreams and life he took with him when he left. He did not come back and neither did the part of me that went with him.

Life was never to be the same again. I still miss and yearn for what "could have been" in my life, the lives of my family, and of my brother's family, and the list could go on and on.

By the content of today's column I do not wish to imply that I have cornered the market on sorrow or suffering.

Nineteen other families in Salem County lost a loved one in Vietnam. Many, many others have losses from previous wars and conflicts. Anyone of them could have written today's column, all of them know what I am trying to say.

How many other men and women will leave from Salem County to take part in this war is anyone's guess. They will take with them the hopes and dreams of their loved ones. It is my very fervent and constant prayer that they will all safely return to see those dreams fulfilled.

Today's Sunbeam, Salem, N.J., Sunday, February 10, 1991

Why Not Celebrate the Joys of Love All Year Long?

What is it about love that makes it feel so very good. To be able to give love and to receive love, openly and unabashedly, seems to me to be the greatest blessing a person could have.

Soon, Valentine's Day will be here and we will all have the opportunity to celebrate the joys of love and get away with it! On this day we expect to participate in the giving and sharing of our love with others among our family and friends.

We will all be a bit giddy and nervous and secretive while trying to hide our gift-wrapped show of affections until just the right moment! Profusions of worry are just everywhere on this delightful day: What if he discovers it!?! I hope she doesn't suspect that I bought it for her! Mom has just gotta love this, I hope!?! I'm really scared, she doesn't even know I exist!!

The day seems filled with a wonderfully electrifying air of hopefulness for our attempts and efforts to "show and tell" our feelings for our beloved.

Valentine's Day is like a mini Christmas in many ways. It has the properties of expectations and anticipation; surprise and giving of gifts; the sharing of love and joy with others. The day is delightfully visual with an abundance of tradition-bound images: lush, flower-bordered hearts; lace trimmed ribbons and gold filigree; chubby, pink-cheeked, curly-haired cherubs flying over-head and spreading the magic and elixirs of love to all in their appointed charge.

In place of the Christmas tree of December, the icon of this February day is a heart-shaped box of chocolates! This sweet, caloric token of adoration comes in a myriad of sizes, colors, and decorative touches. Some are wrapped simply in red or pink quilted foil with a discrete little name card, and others take on the guise of Italian Baroque masterpieces of cascading plastic flowers, velvet and silk ribbons, yards of lace, nine layers of assorted chocolates, and all held together and unified in one common mass by 15 square feet of squeaky, red cellophane!! It requires a Cupid built like a football line backer to deliver one of these gems! But, alas my love, you are worth every penny invested and you are every bit as sweet as the 28 pounds of candy contained within!

Valentine's Day was always so exciting as a kid in grade school. I would start clock-watching at about 8:55 a.m. in anticipation of our party that afternoon. All week long we kept one eye on our books and the other on the red-papered, lace and heart covered box into which we put our Valentines for our teacher and classmates. At about mid-afternoon our "room-mother" would try unobtrusively to come in without disturbing the lessons. Lots of luck, lady!

I think God must have a special corner of Heaven set aside for room-mothers! I can still feel the anticipation of having to sit at your desk while all the goodies were distributed. I must have smoothed out my napkin-placemat a zillion times waiting to receive a pink, strawberry flavored cupcake with white icing and decorated with red cinnamon hearts! I loved the little nut cups filled with those sugary little pastel-colored hearts; and the seemingly endless supply of cherry soda or red Kool-Aid! In the midst of all this chaos of cupcake crumbs, red splotches of spilled drinks on school clothes, and icing mustaches, it was time to open the Valentine box!! Thirty kids tearing open envelopes and yelling "thank you" to each other across the room created a wonderful, happy din!

I would be so excited if I received a card signed only "Guess Who?" or "Your Special Valentine!" I would dream for days that perhaps one girl or maybe even four girls really were in love with me!! Wow! To be in the second grade and have secret admirers was to know life at its finest!

The party spirit continued on thanks to my mother. When you got home from school that day you were not allowed in the kitchen. The reason being that she was decorating it for our Valentine's Day supper. There were paper napkins and table cloth with Valentine motifs and crepe paper all over the place! Each paper plate had a Valentine card and I and my brother always got a dollar inside ours. We always had spaghetti because it was red. Last year I made a heart-shaped meat loaf coated in mash potatoes and decorated with ketchup. For dessert we had cherry Jell-O. Like mother, like son I guess!

As other Valentine's Day celebrations occurred through the coming years, their memories carry a special sweetness and joy.

I remember a wonderful Valentine's Day lunch with a very special and dear friend in art school. She and I were like brother and sister to each other. On this special day we decided to trade in our blue jeans and sweatshirts for "real" clothes and I took her out to lunch. It was from Marilyn that I learned that you could love a person in wonderful and special ways without romantic trappings getting in the way. To this day we are still very close and blessed by our friendship for each other.

A few years later, when I was a designer for Hallmark Cards, I decided to celebrate Valentine's Day in a big way. You have to understand that in a company where the main product is so holiday oriented, employees do not get very excited over celebrating and decorating their departments and offices for a holiday. When the rest of the world is thinking Valentines, the artists and writers at Hallmark are thinking Halloween and June graduations!

I designed and printed a rather absurd, slightly grotesque self-portrait depicting me as Cupid and made complete with an equally silly verse. I commenced to spread Valentine's Day cheer by handing out over 250 Ron LeHew Valentines to every female on the top three floors of Hallmark's corporate headquarters.

The late J.C. Hall, founder and chairman of Hallmark, discovered this Corporate Cupid within his midst and, while acknowledging my holiday fervor, he was a bit concerned about me plying my romantic endeavors on his time! To show what a good sport he was through it all, he liked my drawing well enough that I was given several special projects over the next few months! It was a memorable day filled with laughter and smiles, kisses and hugs, and isn't that what it's all about?

A few paragraphs back, I spoke of likening Valentine's Day to that of Christmas. At Christmas we appeal to all mankind to try to keep the spirit alive throughout the year, and if we are lucky, most of us keep it till about the first week in January. I wonder if we could promote keeping the love we feel and experience on Valentine's Day alive in our hearts throughout the year? Like Christmas, there is a religious aspect to the day.

A young priest, Valentinus, was imprisoned by the Roman Emperor Claudius for helping Christians escape persecution. Refusing to denounce Christianity, Valentinus was ordered to be executed. On the eve of his execution he wrote a note to his jailer's daughter, whose sight he had restored via a miracle, thanking her for all kind things she had done for him in his imprisonment. The next day, at the moment of his execution, a messenger delivered to her the note and a bouquet of violets. The note was signed "From your Valentine." The date was February 14th in 270 A.D.

If we could retain the feelings of love that we enjoy on this day, throughout the whole year, it could do wonderful, marvelous things for us all. It could add so much joy and happiness to family situations and the relationships we share with others, either out in public, or at school, or in the places where we work.

Love is a decision that we make or not make. Love is a choice that we can accept or reject. Loving another person is a conscious effort. Life seems filled with so much peace and sweetness when we try to spread a bit of love around. And, if we accept love wherever and whenever it is offered, then our days can be filled to overflowing with contentment and happiness.

A study once revealed that it takes many more facial muscles to frown then it does to smile. There must be a similar parallel to the emotional energy it takes to ignore and remain indifferent to someone, versus the sincere acceptance and appreciation of and for another human being.

As always, with all my heart, I believe that the lifestyle and values all of you have established in this county, will allow love, to exist and flourish, in wonderful and magical ways. We just need to accept that decision to allow love to be a choice in our lives.

To all of you wonderful, real-life Valentines – young, old, male, female – that are a part of my journey . . . I love you all!

Today's Sunbeam, Salem, N.J., Sunday, February 24, 1991

Even in the Computer Age, One's Mind Still Matters

Part of the fun and magic and mystique of being an artist is the wonderful materials that you get to work with.

Paints, brushes, pencils, and crayons are all marvelous tools that most people leave behind in childhood; and I get to work with them forever, perhaps that is one reason why it is so easy to find the child within the artist.

There are wonderful sights, sounds, and smells that are part of the artist's creative process. The heavy, rich fragrance of oil paint and linseed oil, coupled with the pungent smell of turpentine create one of the headiest of all perfumes!

How beautiful is the soft, velvet dustiness of pastels, and the deep, red-brown creaminess of Conte crayon. What could be any more fragile and ethereal than the delicate glazes of a watercolor painting.

And paper. While most of the world looks at paper as just a white sheet that you write on, artists choose and select papers as one would choose wine, or medicinal compounds, or gemstones. D'Arches watercolor paper has been made by hand for the last five centuries.

Paper this exquisite almost guarantees success! Canson and Fabriano paper, respectively, are akin to the softness of peach skin and the texture of Irish linen. The Japanese make beautiful papers for woodcuts and watercolor.

There are special and unique sounds. The clean, crisp "ssshick" as a pen point creates a beautiful, flowing, undulating black line across a paper's surface.

The slapping sounds that a brush makes on a wooden palette as it hurriedly gathers paint and mixes colors, are followed by a delicious quiet, gentle sound as the colors are laid upon the canvas.

Caress and kiss are two words that would not be out of place in describing the attitude of brush to canvas. Now that I am writing a column, I find that I have carried over into this new area of expression the same sense of sensitivity to materials that I have when I draw and paint.

I love to think out my writing on yellow legal pads. I buy certain felt-tip pens by the handfuls because of the flow they allow when I am writing. A different pen, or change my paper, and the effect is just not the same, something becomes disrupted.

The flow from the heart, via the brain, to the hand becomes slightly fuzzy or blurred – disoriented.

I love the intimacy of writing by a small lamp in a dark room. In nice weather I like writing at night on the back porch by the light of a candle.

I have definite feelings about my surroundings and my materials when I am working.

When I draw, or when I write, I am part of a creative endeavor that is centuries old and I get very excited over this relationship with the past.

That was until . . . One quiet and pensive eve as I sat by dim light's glow, chewing the end of my felt-tip pen and flipping the corner of my yellow legal pad, strange sounds began to creep from the outer circle of darkness that surrounded my writing table.

I stumbled and searched through the darkened house until attracted by a glow from another room. Suddenly, I was confronted by a brightly lit rectangular face, aglow in ever changing colors, sometimes blue, other times green on black!

It made strange, warbling, electronic noises! Flashing little red lights surrounded the mere slots that sufficed for a mouth!

Its glowing face appeared to be drawing my wife and son closer to it! Fearing more for their safety than of my own, I hurtled my body between "it" and my loved ones! As I commenced to smack at it with a yellow legal pad and poke and jab with pencil and felt-tip pen, my family pulled me away in angry protest.

My arms outspread, my back flat to the wall, my eyes darting in frantic and frightened glances from "it" to them, and from them to "it," I realized that life would never be the same again. While I had selfishly been locking myself into dark rooms beating out newspaper columns on yellow pads and typewriters, my dear wife and sweet, sweet son had been horribly and irrevocably **COMPUTERIZED!!!**

It suddenly became all too clear to me. My family had been under the spell of this high-tech world for months! Its arrival in our house was just the beginning of their attempts to see me buckle under the influence of its cold and impersonal ways!

How experienced they were in the ways of "disks" (that is what computers eat), "hard drives" (that's where they get their strength and power), and "monitors" (sort of like a TV set except it displays what you are thinking!!!) There are many other terms to discover and use when you converse with other humans who have succumbed to this siren song of bytes, bits, circuits and chips!

At first I resisted all attempts of falling under the mind-warping, creativity-stifling influences of this horrid piece of electronics. My family clutched my knees and begged that I not let my resistance to "it" doom me to go through life cast into the "outer-darkness" of computer illiteracy.

I grumblingly and groaningly consented to try taking a class, if only to save my marriage and my family.

Salem Community College offered what seemed to be a very basic course on understanding the computer. The course was taught on the premise that you did not know how to turn your computer on, boy, was this class just right for me! I think it's called "being led by the hand."

It was interesting to note that about ninety-percent of the class were about my age and couldn't figure out how to turn their computers on either! Six classes later I graduated Computer Cum Comfortable and I was now part of the real world!

I love working on and with the computer. I say "with" because it can be such a wonderful tool to augment and enhance any writing I may do. Certain programs will allow you to discover misspelled words, some even will identify punctuation and grammatical errors.

Sentences and paragraphs can be relocated within your text simply by hitting a few keys! The ease and convenience of storing information and copies makes a computer and its accompanying disks worth their weight in gold and file folders.

Coming of age artistically, during the same period of tremendous growth in the computer world, has always posed the question of whether an artist could, or would, ever be replaced by a computer. I never really believed it could happen but I thought it was an interesting question to think about nonetheless.

Now that I have learned a bit more about computers, I am all the more convinced that my artistic and journalistic lot in life is safe and secure! The computer can, in certain instances, enhance artistic capabilities and allow for some really neat effects, but, someone still has to sit there with the creative wherewithal to be expressive.

A technician punching a million keys and access to a carload of programs, yet without a sense of expression, ends up with all technique and no content. It is a plate full of icing without a cake underneath; it is life and love based only on the material and the physical.

Nowhere, on any keyboards that I have seen, have I ever found any keys labeled, *Imagination, Emotion,* or *Spirit.*

It has been said that art is an image carved out of the mists and I guess this is the way it shall always be.

Today's Sunbeam, Salem, N.J., Sunday, March 10, 1991

Spring Comes to the Salem County Countryside

Last year as I wrote about the arrival of spring in Salem County, the weather turned cold and it snowed the weekend that my column appeared!

With half-hearted belief that lightning never strikes the same place twice, I am willing to try again.

For several years now I have heard a friend talk about the planting and growth process of early green peas. He emphasizes that they must be planted as close to St. Patrick's Day as possible or as soon as the ground can be worked.

Once the seeds have been sown you watched every day for some sign of growth. Sam equates this watching period to an act of faith. These peas, for my friend, fulfills a need to believe in something unseen. He goes on by saying, "you have to *want* to see them!" And sure enough one day small green leaves will have emerged forth into the light!

Last Tuesday while on an early morning trip to Woodstown, without it being an act of faith, I saw evidence that spring was gently and lovingly swirling about the countryside of Salem County.

As my car looped along the "S" curve on the causeway that is part of the Salem-Woodstown Road, a most wonderful and welcoming sight caught my eye. The willow trees that grow along the roadside and meadows that border this patch of the Salem River were adorned in yellow-green branches!

As a young boy I would always be looking for the willows in my neighborhood to turn a slight yellowish color as a herald of spring. Those willows of my childhood worked for me in much the same way that Sam's peas work for him.

I had been to Woodstown that day talking to a breakfast assembly of honor-roll students in the middle school. I remembered how last year, on the first day that I really sensed spring had arrived, I had been with the kids over in Daretown School. I wonder if there must be some spiritual connection between my enjoyment of school kids and a yearning for spring?

Driving back home to Salem on this sparkling and gorgeous day I realized that certain heavy and ponderous decisions had to be faced.

I could go home, change clothes, make lunch, and work in the studio for the rest of the day; or, I could go home, change clothes, have lunch out, and spend an hour or two investigating and verifying the evidence of whether spring was, or was not, on her way to Salem County.

As I walked across my front yard a bit of amber and purple flashed up from out of the dry, brown, crinkly leaves that had collected in the flower beds over the winter.

Kneeling down I discovered two beautiful crocuses, and with a bit of pushing and scattering of leaves I discovered several more! As I lay on my back thrashing about in ecstasy I knew the destiny of my day was settled! "It was going to be a tough job but somebody . . ."

The day was just exquisite! The air was still a bit cool and breezy, but the sun was bright and warm. The sky was pearly white along the horizon and deep, cobalt blue at its zenith; and the atmosphere was as crisp and clear as a newly washed window.

Clad in my best set of "nature investigating grubbies" I set off. Knowing this sort of work to be hard and demanding, I stopped by the Salem McDonald's for a bit of caloric fortification. After getting my lunch I decided that it would be fun to find a place to sit in the playground area out front.

It was so nice to be able to sit outside on one of the benches in the warm sunshine, and be sheltered a bit from the breeze by a gigantic, pre-fab, plastic cheeseburger!

As I sat there enjoying and sensing the beauty of the moment, and being surrounded by the trappings of one of America's best corporate success stories, I got to thinking about this particular McDonald's. If ever a fast-food restaurant generated a real hometown flavor about it, this McDonald's was it!

When you walk through the dining area you always see lots of familiar, local faces. The folks who work the counter all seem to love to joke and laugh with the customers and with each other.

Today at lunchtime the whole place seemed to be filled to overflowing with lots of smiling, happy, and laughing people and it only served to intensify the content I was feeling for my lot in life that day!

By sitting outside I tended to draw fun comments from people using the drive-in window. Some I knew and some I didn't. Who cares? All seemed so very right with the world that noontime. Even the painted, plastic smile on the statue of Ronald McDonald seemed happier than usual!

As I headed on down Salem-Quinton Road it didn't take long to get into the "you have to want to see it" frame of mind. Between Quinton and Penton you could let yours eyes wander out over the fields and then so very quietly you would realize that all the maple trees were casting a faint, almost imperceptible, reddish glow across the landscape. This delicate, soft tinge of color was the result of maples' red-tipped flower buds.

The radio announcer kept exclaiming about the beauty of the day and how she hoped we, her audience, were all enjoying it. As a delightful background for my visual and sensual revery, she played Copeland's "Appalachian Spring" and the spring concerto of Vivaldi's "The Four Seasons."

Sunlight playing on the lake surface and through the still, bare, woodsy sections along Water Works Road, created shimmering pinpoints of light as it touched the glossy leaves of holly and laurel and ivy, and reflected off the ripples at water's edge.

Out among the more open fields of the county you would see acres of lush, bright green vegetation intensified by the contrast of the surrounding gray-brown fields and brilliant blue skies. I have it on very good, if not modest, authority that I was seeing a winter grain crop that was starting to fill out due to the warmer weather. I was told that I may have been seeing either oats, wheat or rye.

In the peace and quiet of the countryside and woods on this early afternoon you could hear the killdeer repeating its name as a call. A friend of mine later remarked that on that same Tuesday she had seen her first robin of the season in her yard in Salem.

As I stopped in Quinton to listen to the wind blow through the foxtails, the merry sound of an obviously happy group caused me to turn around to see what the fun was all about.

There stood, jumped, flapped, quacked, and splashed, a marvelous group of geese playing along the shore line of Alloway's Creek as it lazed its way towards Quinton Bridge and the meadows beyond. They were having the best time just being together and enjoying the sunshine!

It was such a wonderful hour that God and Mother Nature gave to me. An hour of feeling and renewing a deep, deep love; and an hour of being visually and spiritually embraced by the beauty of the land that we call home.

I would like to share with you why today's wanderings took on a deeper and sweeter meaning. Right before I left Salem to take my drive, a friend told me a story that I have heard all too often in the years since I moved back to Salem County. I was told about a person whose family ties go back in the area many generations. This person owns a business in the county. It was in the course of doing business that this person greeted a newly arrived family with the uplifting words of "Why in the world would you want to move here!"

It is this kind of person, who, for a while, makes me feel a certain kind of sadness. As I go through life trying to view it with rose colored bifocals, it is this brand of person who causes me to remember, that indeed, there are a few real "mental-midgets" out there in the bushes. An old friend of mine who was a real character and two-bit philosopher used to say, "if you can't help, don't hinder!"

Well friends, in spite of a few blooming idiots in our midst, there are other far more delightful and wonderful things a bloomin' and I can guarantee you, that as surely as Quintonian geese love Alloway's "Crick" and the county fair remains the highlight of the social season, and our mosquitoes outweigh our muskrats . . . spring is right on schedule!

• • •

If you remember, my last column dealt with my problems as an artist who has been forced to deal with a computer. Fifteen minutes after that column was processed onto a disk, the power source in my hard drive burnt out, blew up, whatever!?!

We were reduced to having to use paper and pencils for three days. It was horrible!!!

Today's Sunbeam, Salem, N.J., Sunday, March 24, 1991

People, Places of Days Long Past Leave Their Mark

I always enjoyed, as a young boy growing up in this area, to sit around and hear the old-timers talk about the things that went on well before I was born.

They were not any great, exciting, adventuresome tales, but just common, everyday occurrences that had happened to common, everyday people.

Many of the names of those who were mentioned had since passed on or were far too old for me to have easily believed that they could have ever once been young.

In my mind's eye it was so easy to see these stories: Men going off to war, marching from the armory through the streets of Salem to gather at the railroad station amid the hoopla of bands, and families, and friends.

How many times would I hear of the carnival-like atmosphere of Salem on a Saturday night when the farmer-folk and a least six bizillion other people came to town! And every last one of them ate peanuts that were sold from in front of Hurley's candy store and luncheonette.

The stories were told how on Sunday mornings there would be a residue of peanut shells, on the sidewalks of Salem, that was ankle deep! I can remember my Dad and I getting peanuts on a Saturday night walk uptown, but by that time, in the early 1950s, the crowds were no more.

I would hear my friends' parents and grandparents share their memories of the various restaurants in town and who had served the best food! This restaurant had raisins in their rice pudding; this one didn't! A bag full of weenies with onions and sauce from the Texas Restaurant was worth a king's ransom!

Whatever the stories related; whatever their content, I could always see them set against the scenario of the streets and countryside of the area as I knew it to be. The buildings and sidewalks and trees and roads became for me "silent witnesses" to the validity of all these stories.

The thought of what tales these silent witnesses could tell held me spellbound and in awe as a young boy. And now, as a man, the feeling has only intensified; perhaps mellowed and rounded a bit by my fancy for the romantic.

What wondrous images of human drama must be contained amid the limbs and boughs of those huge and beautiful buttonwood trees that stand by the Friends Meeting House in Hancocks Bridge. These same bricks—that my hand touches right now, in this wall—watched as 300 British soldiers stole silently about in the pre-dawn hours of March 21, 1778 as they prepared to massacre the sleeping patriots in the Hancock House.

As long as Pennsville keeps the latticework gate to Riverview Beach Park, a few thousand of us locals will always have a very visual childhood memory. We shall always be able to lean against it, close our eyes, hear carousel music and smell popcorn and cotton candy!

I have a straw "boater" hat with a wonderfully ornate label inside that marks it as having come from Leap's Clothing Store in Penns Grove. For me it shall always be symbolic of long ago summer days when all men looked like the "Arrow Shirt" man, and all young ladies had eyes like Greta Garbo!

My friend Dan Harris, who just celebrated his 90th birthday, was mentioning how he can still traverse the streets of Salem and see all of the old stores and restaurants and the social clubs that have all since given way to time and change and modernization.

Dan can remember the Ford's Hotel on Market Street before it became what is still commonly referred to as the "old hospital" building. Kudos to our freeholders, by the way, for the wonderful job they did in giving this building a new sense of dignity and pride!

It is so easy to get goose-bumps when you talk of times past with the likes of a Dan Harris, Evan Hitchner, Tom Bowen, Jim Endres or even youngsters like Vic Robinson or Mike Dwyer. The histories that they can relate from their own lives, as well as what they recall hearing from the generations before them, tend to take you back into time and the past real quick!

The fate of the Wheeler Building is a real issue right now in Salem. As much as I think it will be hard to find a developer for it, its demolition will leave a huge hole in our cityscape.

This paper, a couple of weeks ago, ran an old photo of the Wheeler Building from a much earlier day. In the photo there were several men leisurely standing around out in front and both they and the building gave one the feeling that on that day, those many, many years ago, they felt they were at the center of the world.

Those men are gone now. The beautiful ironwork and clock are gone now. And the building is in its death throes. What will become of our histories after we have torn down everything in our towns, and plowed under and leveled our landscape into tracts of condos and the like?

It will be so hard to stand, with our children and grandchildren, in front of empty spaces and try to convey to them a sense of "what had been" and its effect on our lives.

I have spent quiet times standing amid the cars in the parking lot behind the county jail and courthouse, and through half-closed eyes tried to "see" my old grammar school and the little park that stood behind it.

The park had lost its former glory even before my time, yet, I remember how beautiful it looked on autumn afternoons with dusty shafts of sunlight streaming down through the huge, old trees.

There were low, wooden rails that marked out the walkways. Time and use and weather had worn them silky smooth. They held the warmth of the afternoon sunshine and felt so good to sit on when the air was chilly.

I was sorry to discover that the large, white structure which was part of the old ferryboat "slip" in Pennsville had been torn down. As long as I could see it I was able to feel the throb of the boat's engines and the creaking sounds of the pilings as the boat docked.

As long as it was there I could hear the echoing sounds of the cars as they entered or exited the hollow interiors of the boats. I fear most I will forget the crispy, slightly burned taste of hotdogs with mustard I seemed to eat on every trip I remember making.

My bones shall always retain a bit of cold that came from always wanting to stand on the upper decks to watch the river and the other passing ferryboats regardless of the season! What high adventure and fantastic opportunity for a seven-year-old!

These things I remember are very special to me and I am sure that each of you have your own treasure trove of memories that are very special to you. We live in such fast-paced times that it appears that even 10 years difference in one's age tends to create varying memories of time, place and values.

As most of you have surmised by now, I do not always deal well with the practical side of life. I just feel that so much of our surroundings, be they a patch of trees, or a building, a marsh, a meadow, a street scene; each of these could have the potential of recalling a very significant memory in the life of anyone of us.

I think that perhaps we need to lead with our hearts a bit before we go tearing down buildings or selling off land and leaving the world with one more parking lot.

I feel that my life is greatly enriched because I can take a drive through the neighborhood I grew up in.

I can sit on a committee with a former teacher of mine. From my drawing board I can look out of my studio and see the windows, a block away, of the art room in my former high school building, now the Salem Middle School.

On a good day in the studio this is heart achingly poignant; hence on a bad day, well, would you believe that in certain light a building can look like it's laughing at you!

I think most of us would be all the poorer or lessened should we totally cast aside our roots, our sense of belonging or our familiarity with the things that surrounded and nurtured us as we grew up.

Part of my life was spent living in cities away from this area. I am fortunate that my career will allow me to live anywhere that there is a post office. I chose to return home. I returned to an area where the towns, the land, and the people, all had made a lasting impression on me.

It was a lasting impression because the area gave to me, selflessly and generously, those things that do so truly last—faith and hope and love.

Today's Sunbeam, Salem, N.J., Sunday, April 7, 1991

Well-deserved Salute to
Some of Area's Top Women

In Henrik Ibesen's play *A Doll's House* we find this piece of dialogue between a husband and wife: Helmer, the husband, says to his wife Nora, "Remember, before all else you are a wife and a mother."

Nora's response is, "I don't believe that anymore. I am a human being, just as you are."

The days of a woman's role being primarily that of wife and mother have since gone by the wayside. Gone, for better or for worse, is the Blondie and Dagwood scenario of another era.

A time when, for the most part, father rushed off to work while mother stayed behind to deal with getting the kids off to school. Then she devoted the rest of her day to cleaning, shopping, laundry, and cooking.

Today we live in a new world where in many cases both parents share in the responsibilities of earning an income. A woman today might also find herself being the head of a single-parent household. Women's entry into the job market and the workplace in so many cases has allowed women to grow and expand far beyond their traditional boundaries and roles.

A woman in the workplace who has children is referred to as a "working mother!" This causes me to believe that society still has her trapped somewhere between the standards of two worlds. On the one hand, she is expected to be the doting wife and mother who binds all wounds, handles every crisis with aplomb, creates gourmet meals, shops, launders, and cleans and does all of this while spending a minimum of 40 hours a week outside the home and on the job!

Yesterday our county had a wonderful opportunity to gather and identify some of the women in our midst who have distinguished themselves by their intellect, talents, spirit, and just plain hard work.

The social gathering yesterday at the Salem Country Club was the Third Annual Women of Achievement Awards Luncheon sponsored by the Salem County Commission On Women which is a relatively new county organization. Set amidst an atmosphere that is colored by everyone's happiness and excitement over the awards recipients, the luncheon takes on the feeling and thrill of a joy-filled celebration.

I take great delight in using the word "celebrate" here in this instance. Women, in my opinion, should be celebrated. In all of Creation could there be anything any more wonderful than Woman? I truly admire them for the wonderfully complex creatures that they are.

The Bible informs us that God created Man first. It is my contention that after God had fiddled about and knocked around a bit on Adam, he figured out what he was doing—then he made Woman. Perhaps this is poor theology but it serves to illustrate my value and regard for womanhood.

Will Rogers had said, "I never met a man I didn't like." I would like to be remembered for saying the same about women. What wondrous gifts of the soul and spirit women have brought to this world. It is but few times that I have been disappointed in my judgment and perception of them. Endearing and enduring abilities to care; to be compassionate; to minister to others, all seem to be innate qualities in women. Emotions and sensitivity being what they are to the artist, I am in awe of the broad emotional range and seemingly unlimited sensitivities to the world around them that most women seem to possess.

Yesterday's luncheon was a wonderful testament to all of the attributes that I find so admirable in women. The awards were often the results of these women being able to do the delicate balancing act of duality between home and career. Their many attributes were illustrated and symbolized by words that spoke of the special contributions that each had brought to Salem County.

Everyone at the luncheon was so excited that this one or that one would be receiving an award. It's like 250 people are really and truly happy for the success of the ten winners whether they know them or not. The commission's luncheon is fast becoming a very popular event and draws its nominees and winners from all areas of the county. Out of 10 winners it's possible to know at least one or two and sometimes more and that brings such a special delight to the afternoon's fun and merriment.

This year I not only knew several of the honorees, but I am wondrously in love with at least two of them!!

Doris Bryant, my former art teacher from high school, received an award for her work on the Salem County Cultural and Heritage Commission. Doris gently, sweetly, and lovingly sent me off to art school long years ago—I owe her my life and career— that's all.

I got to see Callie Davis get her award for the wonderful job she does as Patient Activities Director at the Salem County Nursing Home. Callie's sense of love and kindness and devotion to the home's residents far transcend the boundaries of a job description and the amount written on a paycheck.

If every artist tried to do as much good with their artwork as Aleasa Hogate strives to do with hers, we'd all have a better reputation!

Ann Gardiner, Business Award winner, combines good sense, great humor, love, care, and the tested eye of a wife and mother combined when it comes to the retailing of clothes.

Humanitarian winner Gertrude Evans, with her sense of love for everyone combined with sheer spunk, spirit, and attitude, could have only lost this award to a cross between Gandhi, St. Francis, and Joan of Arc!

All of these women and Jean Hepner Jack, Mary Saletra, Willetta Mulhorn, Mary Davis, and Gilda Gill should make us so proud that they and their work and their efforts are part of our existence here in Salem County. Each and every one makes a difference in the quality of our lives in some way or another.

If we were to read about these women in a newspaper coming out of Philadelphia or Wilmington, we would be rightfully impressed. We would think, "Boy! That area should really be proud of those women!"

These individuals would be an attribute and an asset to any area that they were a part of. Well, they belong to us. They are ours. And we should feel blessed and thrilled and privileged at this realization.

It has been said, "The position of women in a society provides an exact measure of the development of that society." If yesterday's awards and recipients are used as a measure, I would say that Salem County society is doing just fine!

Congratulations to each and every one of you. Thank you for making life in the county all the finer and all the sweeter for your contributions, your example, and your existence.

Today's Sunbeam, Salem, N.J., Sunday, April 21, 1991

Traveling Back in Time to the Days of Private Rail Cars

If I had *only* just spent last Sunday afternoon with C. Emerson Urion of Woodstown, and Sally Collins of Elsinboro, it would have been one of the better Sunday afternoons of my life.

Not only did I get to spend the afternoon with these two marvelous people but they came surrounded by, and encased within, the Mexican mahogany walls of a beautiful and charming 75-year-old private railroad car simply called "The One Hundred."

"The One Hundred" is the loving restoration project of Sally and Porter Collins of Elsinboro. Where does one park a railroad car while restoring it to the original beauty and grandeur it once had in the early 1900s? Why, on a railroad track of course!

Porter Collins is the maintenance supervisor for the West Jersey Railroad. Every day Porter and General Manager Harry Githens get to experience and fulfill the best fantasy of every small boy, that of working on the railroad—"all the live-long day!"

The West Jersey R.R. is headquartered in the former Conrail property on Grant Street in Salem. The West Jersey R.R., a relatively young venture in the annals of Salem County railroading, provides rail transportation service to several local industries.

Running mainly between Salem and Swedesboro, the W.J.R.R. may deliver fertilizer to the Farmer's Exchange in Woodstown; carloads of soda ash to Anchor Glass; magnesium oxide to Alu-Chem, and frozen beef to CPS Distribution Center of Woodstown.

As proof of the effectiveness and efficiency of linking local businesses to Port Salem, the West Jersey transports bulk paper for Budd Chemical of Carneys Point to Salem Marine Terminal.

It's possible to hear, all over Salem, the long, low sound of the air-horn on the West Jersey's huge yellow engine as it announces its approach at the various crossings here in town. The horn's blast is a wonderfully industrious kind of sound. It is a sound that gives a feeling that things are happening and being done as we each go about our own labors and leisures throughout the course of the day.

Harry and Porter share in all the varied roles of engineer, conductor, brakeman, and a hundred other less glamorous jobs. They speak with hopeful expectation of the West Jersey's future here in Salem County. They are excited about the part the railroad could potentially play in future industrial growth.

The occasion last Sunday afternoon that "stirred up the cinders in my blood" (a term used by C. Emerson Urion to describe a railroading man) was an open house on the semi-restored "The One Hundred." This private railroad car was built by the Pullman Company in 1916 especially for Solomon Guggenheim of Anaconda Copper fame. Daddy Solomon parlayed his money in copper mining and his daughter Peggy made hers by investing in paintings. One of the family's legacies is the wonderful Guggenheim Museum of Art in New York.

This wonderful Grand Dame of the Rails fell from grace and onto hard times until three years ago when it was saved, literally from the cutters torch, by Sally and Porter Collins. Oddly enough, it was saved from a restoration committee who had bought it from the Long Island Railroad. Just goes to show the power and strength a married couple can elicit when confronted by a committee!

This car is so very beautiful to look upon as you approach it from any distance away. Its proportion of length to its height (82 ft. x 15 ft.) gives a wonderful long, low, graceful sweep of design, elegance, and style. It is hard to believe that something so eloquent in its design would weigh 79 tons!

The car would have originally been painted the deep, dark, rich green of the Pullman Company, but Sally and Porter have an abiding love for the old Reading Railroad and therefore painted their car Tuscan Red in tribute to the Reading Company's color.

As opposed to the classic beauty of this coach when viewed in profile, when you look upon the rear of the car you see a view that is almost dollhouse-like in its charming lines and shapes. The whiteness of simple tie-back window curtains is in contrast to the seemingly dark window glass. The crispness of this black/white contrast only serves to intensify the rich, warm, red-orange glow of the Tuscan Red color.

After having stepped up and onto the rear platform, it is a very inviting and welcoming feeling you perceive as you see the white wicker furniture and large windows of the observation parlor within. Resisting the urge to sit for awhile and observe the rest of the world, I let the sound of merriment and laughter draw me deeper into the car.

A long narrow hallway or walkway leads you past some small, little compartments that served as sitting rooms or sleeping quarters. The closeness of the area is relieved as you round a turn and find yourself in a large room mid-train.

This must have been the main dining and social area. Beyond this area one returns to another narrow passageway that leads you past additional small rooms. This area served as kitchen space and quarters for the car's staff.

On this Sunday it was a crowded, merry lot of folks who, with drawn-in elbows, gingerly worked their way through and around each other! Bill and Marge Brown, of Brown's Bed and Breakfast on Market Street, added a historic flavor by showing up in period costumes: top hat, vest, and all!

The happy and excited voice of Sally Collins swept over and rose above the general din of everyone else as she would greet newly arrived guests with delightful amounts of excitement and enthusiasm for her restoration project.

It is a very fitting and wonderful paradox that such a happy, up-beat, gracious person as Sally should serve as the mistress of this lovely, old railroad car; this piece out of the past that reflected a time of grace, elegance, and opulence.

Sally and Porter are quick to point out that while it was the resources of a millionaire that originally built the car, it is certainly not millionaires who are restoring it! This labor of love will, like most restoration work, take a long time to complete, but what a wonderful gem they will have when it is finished!

Speaking of gems. No two strangers, unless they be a sadist and a masochist, ever hit it off as quickly as two artists when they meet! C. Emerson Urion and I met one another amidst everyone jockeying for refreshments and the delicious buffet luncheon served at this wonderful open house! Open car? Open coach?!?

Mr. Urion of Woodstown, former railroader, spent his artistic career as a technical illustrator for Mobil Oil Corporation. This afternoon he had presented the Collinses with a wonderful drawing he had made of a steam locomotive. He is now retired and spends his time keeping up with his collection of railroad memorabilia.

We discovered that we had both commuted to art school in Philadelphia. I rode a bus, he rode a train! On snowy wintry days my bus would slip and slide and get stuck, his train would derail!

Mr. Urion's self-proclaimed first love is that of the railroad. While getting his artistic career under way, he worked as a conductor and brakeman for the Pennsylvania Reading Seashore Line. Emerson is the last Salem Countain to have worked on a steam-powered railroad!

Carrying just a mere sampling of his railroad memorabilia collection with him, Mr. Urion showed wonderful photos of several old steam locomotives that traveled the various rail lines here in the county.

Along with the stories of some of the local men who were engineers, he showed neat photos of some of the old train depots in Woodstown and Alloway. Just sitting with this man and hearing his great stories and seeing his pictures added a wonderful and rare kind of historic dimension to being aboard this car.

Among many fun moments of the afternoon, one of my favorites came with Sue Githens, wife of the general manager, pouring a bottle of champagne over the coupler of "The One Hundred." This was done to celebrate the inauguration of the car into service on the West Jersey. Also, this year marks the 75th birthday of this lovely old car.

One of the more well known services provided by the West Jersey is its twice weekly dinner excursions to La Vita Restaurant in Woodstown. They also run trips for private parties, groups, and clubs.

"Mo" Githens, Harry's father and the head of Passenger Service, owns the lines one passenger coach which is vintage 1929. Both the coach and the "The One Hundred" will be featured on this season's schedule. A ticket for "The One Hundred" will be higher, but will include some special features during the roundtrip to Woodstown.

Any mode of transportation that gets you to the great food at La Vita's is fine but the train trip makes it all the better! You can experience an all new point of view on the landscape of the area and see parts of Salem County that you will only be able to see via the train!

We have taken the Wednesday night "Moonlight Excursion" and had a ball! Everybody is all excited and caught up in an anxiety that makes everyone feel like they are a little kid again taking their first trip on a train!

The 1991 season starts Sunday, May 5, at 1:30 p.m. Trains will run on Sunday afternoons at 1:30 and on Wednesday evenings at 6 o'clock. All trains start from the Salem Depot.

"The One Hundred" will be part of the Fenwick's Colony Open House Tour on Saturday, May 11. It has to be a first of sorts to have a railroad coach as part of our tour! Isn't that great? Only in Salem!

Salem's Presbyterian minister, Jim Brown, gave a small blessing for the occasion that went something like: "We give thanks and praise to our Lord who made such a beautiful world that includes railroad cars."

To that brief but appropriate blessing I would most heartily add my "Amen!"

Perhaps, "All Aboard!"

Today's Sunbeam, Salem, N.J., Sunday, May 5, 1991

A Columnist Marks Two Years, Heads Into the Third

For any of you out there keeping score, this Tuesday, May 7, marks the second anniversary of this column! Today's column is the fifty-second one that I have done since I started in 1989.

When I first started I remembered wondering about how much experience I would need before I could say I was a writer.

I had decided that I would wait and see if I could keep the column going for a year and if I could, then I might call myself a writer. Well, I expressed this idea to a friend and editor who makes her living writing and this was her answer: "Honey, from the minute you start trading the written word for money, you are as much of a professional writer as you are ever going to be!"

For some dumb, inane, masochistic reason, I love doing this column. I still say the only reason I was asked to do it was that the *Sunbeam* got tired of printing my "Letters to the Editor!"

This column brings large doses of grief, worry, anxiety, stress, arguments, heartbreak, and indigestion. And it is one of the things that I do where I make even less money than from my artwork!

For two years, I have been sharing with you a lot of my feelings and hopes and dreams, so what is one more among old friends, eh?

The opportunity to do this column fulfilled something that I used to joke about, but never quite believed would ever really happen.

I used to say how wonderful it would be if I could spend the first half of my life as an artist, and the second half as a writer.

Today's Sunbeam sure has had a part and a stake in my creative career. With about the same casual air that Managing Editor John Schoonejongen offered me this column in 1989, former owner and Publisher Emeritus Tom Bowen offered me my first paying job as an artist back in 1966. Come to think about it, Tom didn't pay me any better than John. What price opportunity!

Every creative person, regardless of his or her form of expression needs an audience. And if the truth be known, most of them want approval. Show me 10 creative people who say they can continue on without benefit of an audience or approval, and I'll show you eight liars and two idiots!

And this, my friend, is where you play a role in bringing about so many of the blessings that I have in my life. I do not come easily to doing this column.

So many times its deadline conflicts with those deadlines imposed on me by publishers for whom I do artwork. It is so much easier making pictures using paints then it is using words. I know every other Sunday is a span of fourteen days; but most times it feels more like three.

But then I have you. And for this, I am so grateful. It is your response, to my expression, that makes my life feel as beautiful and sweet as a shiny red apple. You do wonderful things to me and for me whenever and however you respond to this column.

So many of you will come up to me and tell me what you thought of a particular column; or how you felt about my approach to a certain theme. I want to, and sometimes I do, hug you when I know you laughed in all the right places, and also when I know you cried in all the right places too.

What a wonderful and special feeling it is when you send me notes from several states away saying how someone at "home" cuts out the columns and sends them to you. Thank you for telling me that the columns, for a few moments, allow you a feeling of being "home" once again.

How interesting to discover what columns seemed to have appealed to you, versus, what I thought would have really sparked your interest. During the Christmas season in 1989 I wrote a poem about "writer's block" that was set to the meter of "The Night Before Christmas." Not only did I write it, I think I was the only one to have read it! I am still waiting for a response from somebody . . . anybody? . . . to that one!

Many of you seem to regard the column in the manner of a "good ol' days" type of writing. While I do like to reflect on an earlier time occasionally, most of us know that we in the county share in a wonderfully rich Americana type of heritage; but I am more interested in showing all the wonderful qualities that life in Salem County has to offer now, at this moment in time.

And so, on any given subject, should I find that the same values and virtues of an earlier day still exist, then they shall always be a part of my writings.

While I have no desire to wear the mantle of a county historian, I do hope that I could be considered somewhat a "keeper of the faith" in regards to the beauty of the land and the goodness of the people which is so much a part of our county, and is its greatest attribute.

Thank you all for so many tokens and gestures of love and faith that you have given so generously to me over the last two years. They are beyond measure . . . touching notes; phone calls; a beautiful and sensitive piece of artwork; 150 pounds of the Wheeler Building; invitations; a coupon book to McDonald's; molasses cakes, and lemon butter, and venison baloney, and handshakes and hugs and tender, loving words . . . only in Salem County.

Free-lance artists live lives that are great balancing acts in disguise. We stand on one leg upon life's tightrope, blindfolded, and juggle feathers and lead weights together, all the time trying to reach the other side. I worry, not so much about falling, but that of standing still.

And so dear friend, let us try for another year . . . I sure don't know where we're going but we're on our way!

Today's Sunbeam, Salem, N.J., Sunday, May 19, 1991

Along with Spring Comes the Magic of Prom Night

Spring gives to our winter-weary souls soft, sweet days filled with flowers; intensified in hue by their play against bright, new, green grasses. Warm, longed for and prayed for sunlight; softly blown breezes seem to meld all of a season's beauty into one lovely hymn to our senses.

As the days are lovely, so too the nights are magical, poetic, star-filled . . . just such stuff as dreams are made of. All of my life, it seems, some of my sweetest, happiest moments were set among the twilight hours of a spring evening. Each season colors our memories in its own way, but what season creates for us memories as delightful and delicious as spring?

Each spring, long years ago, one special night would arrive that seemed to be the culmination of all the sweetness, beauty, and grace that a season could offer. This wonderful and special night of magic, romance, and fantasy was "prom night."

The junior-senior prom was always the reserved and sacred territory of big brothers or the older guys down the street. It was a night where the pretty, young, baby-sitter in the next block was crowned queen of the prom!

It was a night where the soft swish of prom gowns could be heard coming down front porch steps all over town. It was a night where young men desperately tried to remember everything their mothers had ever told them about how a lady wants to be treated. It was a night where boys in rented tuxedos, timidly and gently, ushered girls down the front walks as if they were as fragile and delicate as they were beautiful.

It was a night of all winners and no losers; every girl who wore a gown that twilight evening was as beautiful as any queen could ever hope to be.

And one spring season came along and a young boy had grown a bit and now it was his time and his turn. His time to have a mother straighten the bow tie of the rented tuxedo one last time. It was his time to enter into a soft twilight spring night carrying a corsage. The smooth, white florist box still chilled from the refrigerator where it had rested for most of the afternoon, except for the thousand times the boy looked at its delicate beauty.

All the neighbors, as tradition dictated, were sitting around outside to await his return with the girl and to give their approval. And the boy knew that he would be bringing to them the prettiest girl that they would have ever seen.

As the boy drove across town in the ten-times washed, waxed, vacuumed, sterilized car that he borrowed from his Dad, the boy pondered, yet reveled, in how life had brought him to this moment. A time when being nervously ill and being frantically joyous and thrilled were but half a heartbeat apart.

How did it happen that the boy, whose whole life thus far was spent mastering the art of shooting basketballs in back alleys and pool balls down at Frank's, could and would end up in such a sweet dilemma as this?

The "man" on the outside told the "boy" on the inside that tonight he was 18 going on a very suave, dashing, bon vivant 36-year-old man-about-town!

The boy remembered just how "suave" he had been a month ago when he spent three nights trying to get the courage to make the call to the girl. After a hundred false starts, it was no debonair, dashing Cary Grant who finally got his nerve up!

Wit, spit, and aplomb abandoned him as he heard the phone ring on her end! Please Lord, let her not be home! Maybe they moved? Please let it be a wrong number, please? Maybe God would grant him a small heart attack (just a little one) and he could pass out for a while!

The phone was answered by the girl's mother, a bit of respite at any rate. In answer to the boy's request the mother replied: "Yes! My simply gorgeous and beautiful daughter, the one with all the poise, charm, and intellect of a goddess, the one that every guy in the world would love to date and die for, is home, and miracle of miracles, I am sure she will grant unto you a few brief seconds of light banter, but please, be brief as she gets a thousand calls a night from other more important people!" Or so I imagined she said.

The silence was six hours long. The girl picked up the phone, the boy in one huge explosion of air and words exclaimed: "Hi how are you and I know every guy in the world has begged and asked you to the prom and I'm sure you really wouldn't wanna go with me and I just know some great-lookin' football hero has asked you and besides I wear glasses and have a big nose and six ears and warts and listen it's been great talking to ya and this is just a joke and I did it on a dare ha! ha! and you really wouldn't wanna go to some dumb stupid ol' prom with me wouldja!?!?" Whew!

Way deep in the boy's heart there will always be the memory of the sweet laughter to her voice as she said "yes!" and the boy found out, in one brief moment, the arid desert of the senses he had dwelt in all these years.

He was the frog-prince kissed by the princess. Her answer "yes" told the boy that Christmas, the Fourth of July, and his birthday would all be coming twice that year and it was only April!

The days that followed were days of bliss, delight, and dragging hours of sweet anticipation.

The girl told the boy that her gown would be blue. Did he like blue? Did he *like* blue? At that moment the boy thought blue was the most wonderful color in the world and surely God had ordained that only those akin to angels could wear it!

The boy went to order the corsage with a sense of purpose that the florist never quite forgot nor forgave the boy for.

The boy assumed that he would be able to see the corsage selections beforehand, not the day he picked it up! The florist saw it differently. The boy reminded the florist, that when it came to corsages, that his was not the only game in town! And when it came to choosing the flowers for the wrist of the girl in the blue prom gown, one needed to be very careful.

The disgruntled, but beaten florist, took the boy into the back room. There together they designed, in approximation, the corsage the boy would be placing, as gently as ten thumbs would allow, on the wrist of the girl in the blue prom gown.

And the night finally arrived.

The boy sat with the girl's father for long nervous minutes trying to act as man-to-man as possible. The father knew and was very kind to this Cary Grant in the rented tuxedo who was gracious enough to adorn his living room couch.

The mother, with sweetness and pride and tears in her eyes, and with mock flourish, presented the girl in the blue prom gown.

But where was she? This was not the girl! This was a beautiful young woman with coiffured hair; this was a sweet smile and laughing eyes made heart achingly beautiful with eye shadow and lipstick; she was as sparkling and crystalline as her earrings and necklace; and a young girl's hands were made elegant and lady-like in long, blue, evening gloves.

The boy was dazzled and spellbound—and for one brief moment the world had stood still and the sweetness of that moment would stay with him forever.

If this is what growing up and leaving boyhood behind was all about; if this was a rite of passage, he knew he had truly passed over; it was to be "so long" to the guys at the pool hall, good-bye back alley basketball!

It was a beautiful night for the boy. It was a night that would change him forever.

It was a night of knowing and sensing a whole new kind of relationship with another person. In his naivete, the boy had chosen so well, so wisely. He spent a magical night held in awe by her sweetness of spirit; an intellect tempered by charm and grace and humor. Armed with all of her attributes, the girl made the boy confident and secure and feeling ten feet tall. What a wonderful gift the boy was given by the girl in the blue prom gown.

The boy has now grown. Oft times the boy in him is more in evidence than the man. He lives in a world where he creates new worlds out of this one. It is important that he remember and retain all those things that have had an impact on his life, that caused him to view his world in wonderful new ways and emotions than he had ever done before.

The other night the man stood in a school parking lot and watched as several "stretch limos" unloaded groups of boys and girls, all laughing and giggling in make-believe attempts to appear gown-up.

Not many of them succeeded. How could you stand by and watch as a chauffeur touched the gloved hand of your prom date and it was he, and not you, who presented her to the world!

Across the lot a car pulled in, not as flashy as a limo; and the boy almost fell as he quickly ran around and helped the young girl out of the car. They looked over and waved as they walked through the shadows of trees and parked cars.

Once into the light, the man saw that the girl wore a soft blue prom gown. Unlike the movies, she never turned to look back, they became lost in the crowd.

For a magical night all their own, for endearing memories, and for growing up, the man whispered "good-luck" and blew a kiss to the ebbing twilight, for the boy, and the girl in the blue prom gown.

Today's Sunbeam, Salem, N.J., Sunday, June 2, 1991

Whatever Happened to the Old-fashioned Cookout?

With the Memorial Day weekend behind us, we now find ourselves in the first week of the unofficial beginning of the summer season. And one of the glories of the summer season, in my book, has always been cookouts! Ah, yes! Time to dust off the old charcoal grill!

Memorial Day mornings, as a kid growing up, were always observed with solemnity and respect, but come the afternoon, we always gathered with the neighbors for a cookout!

Lug out the bag of charcoal, ice up the washtubs full of sodas, beer, whatever you will! It's picnic time!! Hot dogs! Hamburgers! Chicken right off the grill! Spread out the lawn chairs in the shade of the willow or maple trees!

Adults collect on this side of the grill, kids on the other side. Our neighborhood chef looks like a bad joke in his floppy chef's hat and apron emblazoned with some silly phrase. He wields his long-handled fork and spatula with the finesse of Jack the Ripper.

Everyone laughs and coughs and sputters and flails away at the air as this happy scene of leisure is obliterated by huge clouds of smoke that smells of burnt meat and charcoal starter fluid!

Kids run devilishly about putting ice cubes from the soda tubs down each other's back while mothers try, in vain, to keep them under control, and dads will be gathered around a transistor radio listening to the ball game.

How happy and joy-filled were these pleasant and relaxed "day off work" afternoon cookouts I remember so well from childhood.

Boy! Are traditional cookouts fast becoming a fading memory in our collective culinary conscience.

A few days ago the ringing phone delivered to us an invitation to a friend's home for a cookout. Was I excited or what!?! I love being around the food and the conversations, and just hangin' round the old grill swapping horror stories of past incendiary exploits; discussing the how-to's and how-not's concerning the cooking and subsequent charring of everything from ribs, burgers, fingers, beards, and the family cat!

Off I headed with the obligatory folding aluminum chair, a big straw hat, shorts, sandals, Hawaiian shirt, everything you could want to make yourself comfortable for at least eight hours of food, drink, and conversation all to take place amid the dappled shade of a great maple tree.

I envision myself but a few brief moments away from sipping ice tea garnished with a fresh mint sprig; sitting midst charming friends engaged in splendid dialogue and still be able to observe my host's techniques at the barbecue grill. If this isn't heaven, it has to be pretty close!

Here I am!!! I rush around the corner of Dave's house expecting and prepared to wave and shout "hi" and "hello" to at least a dozen folks who I know are invited—the yard is empty! Not one person or folding chair in sight.

No croquet mallets strewn about. No badminton nets strung across the yard. No sign that a cookout is to take place here. No sign that this beautifully shaded patch of grass will witness the public engorgement of at least ten pounds of hot dogs and hamburgers and possibly five gallons each of ice tea and pink lemonade.

Maybe I'm too early. Am I too late? Do I have the right day? House? Street?

Stunned to an uneasy stillness, my eyes shift upwards to Dave's deck where my eye is attracted by sunlight's gleam on metal.

I see something that is reminiscent of a grill, yet appears to be a cross between a heart-lung machine and a smelting furnace at

Bethlehem Steel. It is omitting a pallid bit of whispy smoke that vaguely smells like a hamburger.

Suddenly, there is a rapping at the window above me and I see ol' Dave yelling at me through the window, "Put your chair by the gate! Come on in! Everyone's in here!"

As I cross the deck, I give dubious glances and wide berth to "the grill" as I pass by. The Wanamaker Organ is smaller then Dave's grill.

Once inside I notice that I'm the only one arrayed in straw hat, sunglasses, and my favorite picnic shirt that, despite numerous washings, will eternally smell like Cutter's Mosquito Repellent.

As I mention about eating outside, it is as if with one collective gasp and groan from all present, that I am informed we ain't moving outside 'till the temperature drops to a mild, balmy 72 degrees which isn't going to happen till sometime next fall!

Besides, I am told, if God wanted people to eat in the open air, why did he imbue man with the intellect to invent air-conditioners!

Since folks were shying away from my bug repellent Hawaiian shirt, meaningful conversation was becoming a bit difficult, so I thought I'd amble out to the deck and swap tales with Dave.

At least Dave was into the spirit of things as he stood there flipping burgers and hot dogs. I was surprised to notice that his "grill mobile" didn't have some sort of captain's chair or recliner as part of its gimmickry.

Dave asked me to watch over things while he ran back inside for something cold to drink. In response to his offer, I said I'd like an ice tea. In a flash he was back outside again ripping the flip-top off a "can" of ice tea for me and a "can" of lemonade for himself!

I made the comment that I noticed that his burgers weren't dripping any grease onto the hot coals. It is the flare-ups that help give a "cook out" taste to your foods.

Dave's response was, "Yeah, that's the beauty of these babies, no grease, no mess, no flare-ups."

He then went on to explain that the "burgers" were made from a mixture of ground turkey and tofu! For the uninitiated, tofu is an opaque, jello-like food product made from soybeans. No taste, but high in protein. No fat content, no flare-ups!

Dave gave them a real out-doorsy taste by brushing them with bottled "liquid smoke." The hot dogs were made from turkey also, but if you used enough real old-fashioned yellow mustard and honest-to-goodness pickle relish they tasted pretty good!

For dessert we all had boysenberry yogurt sprinkled with wheat germ. It was a teeny bit of a departure from the deep-dish apple pie or the triple layer chocolate cake I usually feel rounds out a cookout nicely.

All the kids and me felt ridiculous trying to toast marshmallows over a piece of equipment that looked like something a space shuttle puts into lunar orbit, so we just sat out on the deck eating them raw and counting stars.

On the way home I made a pit stop at Hudock's just to reacquaint my system to the fat content of a real hamburger. As I sat there munching away I kept thinking about all those poor turkeys and what a cruel trick Fate has played on them.

If these turkey burgers and hot dogs catch on for the cookout season, well . . . If they thought they had it rough during Thanksgiving and Christmas, wait till they see how long it is between Memorial Day and Labor Day!

Today's Sunbeam, Salem, N.J., Sunday, June 16, 1991

Adjusting the County's Calm after Visiting New York

The meadow reeds, and the hedgerows, and the flat expanse of plowed fields appear in softened dark silhouette against the ebbing colors of the twilight sky.

Here and there amid the blue-brown darkness of marsh and field are small little patches of water that mirror the fading light and colors of the sky. The horizon is pastel-rose evolving to pale yellow-orange to green, and then to the deep, lush, jewel-like blue that becomes the darker hues of the nighttime sky. And like an old, old friend, I am happy to see the Evening Star glowing from out of this soft, delicately colored sky.

The broad and open expanse of the landscape around me is so lovely, so calming, so serene, and so therapeutic to my city-weary soul. I really need this after-dinner-at-the-diner ride through the Hancocks Bridge-Elsinboro area to let my body reacclimate itself to peace, quietude, and a semblance of South Jersey sanity.

Earlier, in the afternoon of this now sweetly dying day, I was having a nervous breakdown on the back seat of a cab stuck in bumper-to-bumper traffic on Seventh Avenue in New York City!

Need I say more? Should I just cut the column short and let you go on to other parts of the paper?

A New York City cab ride is the moral equivalent of being self-flagellated by your own nerve endings. I love that neat gasping for breath sensation that happens with the G-forces when your driver decides, that from a standing still position, he can lunge five car lengths and hit 70 mph before having to slam on his brakes! The G-force causes the corners of your mouth to touch your ear lobes, and your glasses slam against your already flattened eyeballs! Neat!

It always seems that brakes, attention to red lights, and pedestrians are optional to New York cabbies. Someone once said that in New York City, traffic lights were only meant to serve as rough guidelines. Boy! Could I believe that! Gads! Let me out! I'll take my chances among the robbers, muggers, and rapists and any other deranged denizens of these steel and concrete canyons!

Several weeks ago I had accepted an invitation to speak to an association of educational publishers meeting in New York. I couldn't wait for the date to get here! Two days in the Big Apple! Wow! Move over Donald Trump!

To coin the old cliché, I LOVE NEW YORK! For me, New York has always possessed magical ways of making all things and experiences wonderful. All things, whatever you may want and wish them to be, become so special in this rarefied ambiance New York City seems to exude over and around everything that falls under its spell!

There are so many wonderful things about New York: to stand on the top of the Empire State Building at night and hear the "hum" of the city rise up to you from the streets below; to gaze in awe of the fairyland of lights spread out all around you for as far as you can see! The cultural Mecca that is Lincoln Center with its theater, operas, and symphony orchestras. Great restaurants, museums galore, wondrous and inspiring churches, and just the feeling you get knowing that you are truly in a world capital like Paris or London or Rome.

I have always loved winters in New York. In my art student days, my friends and I would go to New York at least once a year to see the annual exhibit at the Society of Illustrators. A winter visit to New York makes for a special kind of romance to an ordinary day. It makes one feel that everything and anything is possible and attainable regardless of the goal. As we trekked about the museums and galleries we never doubted for a moment that we would not be a part of it all someday.

Many of those dreams and hopes of several years ago came true for me as I started my career. The various publishing houses of New York still make up a large part of my work load.

I have always left this city with a yearning and a longing and a promise to myself to return as soon as possible. I have been able to believe that I could really live right in the middle of it all.

And yet, this time it was all different. Perhaps it was the season. Any extended stays I have had have usually been during the days of the late autumn through early spring. The hot, summer-like days of last week seemed to bring out a whole different look and feel to the city.

After my talk on the final day of the conference I could have stayed around town for at least another six hours had I wanted to, but all I could think about was going home.

I use to defend New York when people accused it of being dirty and unfriendly. This trip it seemed as if litter was everywhere you looked. The streets appeared so crowded, so disheveled, noisy, odorous. New York needed to comb its hair, wash its face, buff its shoes.

Famed Fifth Avenue had at least five men per block standing against the buildings with open attaché cases selling gold jewelry, chains, and watches. On the curb side were folding tables with vendors hawking cheap, crass-looking clothing. I saw how this form of low overhead, no-tax retailing drove some fine stores out of Center City Philadelphia, and I'm sure it could happen in New York too.

Every third person seemed to be pan-handling using a Styrofoam cup to collect money in. I had to give credit to one girl at Pennsylvania Station who kept up a steady flow of directions to the various subway concourses. She at least was providing some sort of service in return for trying to make a few bucks. She probably makes sixty thousand a year and commutes from Long Island!

A piece of welcome relief to the seedier signs of life about the streets were the various groups of street musicians and mimes. The latter who juggled and performed magic tricks in hopes of attracting a few paying customers. One could choose from a brass ensemble by the Metropolitan Museum of Art, to Bluegrass fiddlers around the edges of Central Park, and some very cool, funky jazz in front of St. Patrick's Cathedral on Fifth Avenue!

The thought of joining the street artists who made huge chalk drawings on the sidewalks occurred to me more than once or twice! Maybe someday I'll decorate Star Hall Corner's sidewalk in pastels and see if I can make more money working outside my studio than I can inside! Some days this wouldn't be hard to do at all!

The train ride home, a good book, and pleasant conversation with my seatmate acted as a nice sort of buffered transition from The Big Apple to Fenwick's Colony.

On the way back from the Wilmington, Del., train station we stopped at the Oak Diner for dinner.

The Oak Diner has its own special brand of noise and sounds. People at one end of the diner tend to hold conversations with folks at the other end without anyone moving closer. The same happens from one side to the other. But these are the sounds of friendship, and of care, and of concern, and of sharing good news. Before I sat down I had to stop and chat a while at two booths and as many tables and it was wonderful!

It filled me with great happiness that all this noise, and chatter, and clatter and merriment meant that once more I was home.

As backdrop to these conversations, I could see the beautiful old oak tree across the street that gave this diner its name. How so very peaceful and serene it appeared as long, low rays of sunlight sweep over and flood it with a golden glow.

The melody of the siren song is never far from me, always there, always beckoning, always I feel the yearning and it always leads me here again.

And it is here, at home, that I can and have found all the sense of hope, acceptance, and dream fulfillment that I could ever wish for, or desire.

And I guess I am one of the lucky ones, that for me at least, I know wherein my treasure lies.

Today's Sunbeam, Salem, N.J., Sunday, June 30, 1991

Celebrating Precious Freedoms Found Only in America

Once again it is that time of the summer season when the Bridgeton Symphony presents its annual concert in celebration of America's Independence Day. Last night's performance was a great collection of American music: Victor Herbert, Cole Porter, Aaron Copland. The finale, set amid a bomblast of fireworks, bells, and cannon fire, was the traditional Tchaikovsky's "1812 Overture." Marvelous!

This outdoor concert was performed along the shoreline of Sunset Lake in Bridgeton Park. The audience sat on a lovely wooded hillside, in amphitheater fashion, to hear this wonderful orchestra and the great musical sketchbook of Americana that they played last evening.

After a picnic supper, it's fun to stake out your spot and people-watch for a while in the dusky light of mid-evening. Ah, but sweeter still is to watch the woods and sky and the lake ready themselves for another night of gentle slumber.

The lake and shoreline lose themselves in each other as the twilight atmosphere creates soft passages of blues, and violets, and of lavenders and rose. The evening mists rise slowly upward from the water's surface, to merge and mingle the trees and lake into one lovely, lacey edged shape set against a fragile blue sky streaked through with fingers of crimson clouds edged in gold.

How can it be, how is it possible, that one such small piece of creation can bring to a soul such a sense of peace and rest and comfort. This lake. These trees. This sky. To open your heart to this scene is to see prayer made visible.

Lost as I am in a revery of spirit and heart, the beauty and expression of the music serves to push me deeper into a sense of appreciation of all that is around me this night. All of these musical expressions were created and inspired by composers trying to give form and substance to the love they felt for America.

My fingers unmindfully press against the grass and earth beside me; and I see the lake, the trees, the stage, the people gathered on this hillside; all and everything that is around me this night is in the greatest country in the world . . . America. Thank God, thank God.

As I let my eyes and mind wander and wonder through and about the gathered audience, I can feel their happiness and contentment in response to the beauty of the night and the magic of the music. I find that I am prayerfully and thoughtfully giving thanks for all of the freedoms, and liberties, and peace seeing these people and hearing this music seems to excite within me.

Our greatest blessing, as Americans, may be that most of us never had to experience the anguish and horror of being denied and deprived of our freedom.

Lulled by and lost to the music, other faces come into my mind's embrace. How happy I am to see them again. What gratitude I feel for their having passed through my life, whether it was for many years or a few brief moments.

I see the sweet, endearing smile of my art school friend Dora. Dora was eleven when the Russians invaded Hungary in 1956. She lost most of her family during the revolution. In 1961, on their fourth escape attempt, and dragging a drugged younger sister through a minefield, Dora and her mother and sister made it to freedom.

A visage of love and kindness stirs my heart as I see John Hussian before me. Hussian was the founder and president of the art school I attended. When he was ten years old the Turks invaded his village in Armenia. The entire male population of the town was herded into a barn and slaughtered by the Turkish soldiers standing at the doors and windows firing their guns. Hussian lay for three days under the bodies of his father and uncle before he felt it safe to come out. He was the sole survivor of over 300 men and boys.

I recall a Saturday afternoon spent with Federico, a Cuban journalist in exile. In exile now, but not before he spent eight years in the sewers that Castro called a prison. I will always remember how he talked of seeing Cuban women on their knees in the streets, eyes and arms lifted upward, begging God to send the American bombers to reduce Cuba to ashes so that at least they could all start over again.

Never far away, at any time, is the look on an old woman's face when she was told that I was an artist. I was just finishing art school and at the beginning of my life; she was near the end of hers. She had been a sculptor in Russia until the Communists took over and refused to let her work on anything unless it was for the Communist Party. She was denied a life of artistic freedom. It was in a tearful embrace that she asked of me to live a little piece of my career for her. I only met her this one night. From 20-some years ago I've forgotten her name, but not her face, nor the request, nor the promise given.

The memory of these people and the stories they have shared are very important to me. They become bittersweet fragments of reality in this rose-colored, idealistic world that I live in. Hearing these stories from those who lived them is to know the uglier, darker side of mankind in a very real way. I thank God that this is all the further I have had to travel down these darkened roads.

By this time the long, low, sad tones of "The 1812 Overture" have given way to the exuberant and joyous pealing of bells and cannons roar that mark the glorious finale of this great piece of music.

Fireworks light up the sky all around us. The lake reflects the colors and patterns of the aerial display. The man sitting next to me pulls me into a discussion on the great Russian composers. We swap stories on our favorite Russian music and copy titles and composers down on various scraps of paper that we find tucked inside our wallets. It has been a wonderful evening. My soul and my senses have been touched and caressed by the bow of my emotions, as surely, and as passionately, as any violinist has done on stage. I have gone great distances, visited special people, laughed, loved, talked, and brushed away a tear or two, and all accompanied by a symphony orchestra!

What a wonderful celebration we have had this night. A celebration of the spirit of our country, a celebration of the genius of its composers, and the talented musicians on stage who loved and played this music into existence. Our presence here tonight becomes its own celebration of the freedoms that each of us is privileged to have.

It is a privilege granted by the Grace of God; the sacrifice of others; and the blessing of living in America.

Two years ago on a July 4th newscast, the commentator, Jim Gardner, closed with this thought, "Tonight, all over the world, people are turning their countries into democracies and they are looking to America as the example. This should make us both proud and humble."

Today's Sunbeam, Salem, N.J., Sunday, July 14, 1991

The Horrors and Joys of a Summer Job with Heinz

The characters: A heart-wrenched mother, teary-eyed son, disgusted father. The time: Summer of 1964. The location: The main gate of a factory.

Mother: "Oh no! My son, my poor, delicate, sensitive, creative, artsy little boy, I can not bear to send you in there! No! No! No!"

Son: "Oh! No! Mamma, don't send me in there! Won't you please scrub floors all night, and take in washing and ironing all day, so I won't have to go in there?!?"

Father: (As he struggles to pry apart hysterical mother and weeping, clinging son) "Will you both shut up!" (to mother) "You! Get back inside the car!" (To boy) "Get on inside and get to work before someone has the two of you committed!"

At this juncture in today's column, dear and gentle reader, you may be asking: Was the boy going to work in the deep and dangerous bowels of the earth as a coal miner? Could he be working within the fiery man-made hell of a steel mill? Ah, then surely he must be breathing the air of the doomed and the damned at a concrete plant.

This scenario of pathos and tears was enacted nightly by my mother and me at the main gate of the H.J. Heinz plant in Salem during my summer vacation in 1964.

I tend to think of that summer as the "Summer of the Tomatoes from Hell."

I worked a 12 hour shift from 6 p.m. to 6 a.m. with no days off for almost 3 months. Since I slept from dawn to dusk, I never saw the full light of day that whole summer. I returned to art school that fall looking like I had spent the summer living under a rock.

My chosen career has had wonderful blessings showered on it in terms of accolades, awards, respect and many other wonderful things, but the memory of that summer will always keep me humble, always reduce me to blubbering, and never, never, let me forget from whence I came!

At the Heinz plant, usually college students were assigned to rather clean, office-like positions where they wore nice white uniforms. Well, I guess the personnel department figured that anyone whacky enough to want to be an artist wasn't going to cut it in an office.

I had this really gross and grungy job. To refer to it as "a job" was to elevate it to a stature it hardly deserved. I was taught that suffering built character and substance in the work of an artist, but this was ridiculous.

See if you can get the picture.

Huge flatbed tractor-trailers and other large farm trucks would pull along side of a narrow walkway that was as high as the truck body. Teams of guys would commence to unload the trucks by tossing baskets of tomatoes to each other, which in turn, were dumped into a water-filled trough that carried the tomatoes into the plant.

As was bound to happen, tomatoes would fall down below and either squash, squish, or roll around underneath the trucks or elsewhere about the area. With several trucks being unloaded at any one time all of this made for quite a mess. It was my role, in the modern miracle of turning a sun-ripened tomato into a bottle of ketchup for your table, to clean up this mess and try to salvage any usable tomatoes.

In order to do this task it was necessary to scoot and duck-walk underneath of truck bodies all night long. I also had to drag a shovel and basket around with me to gather up those tomatoes which did not survive the fall!

Spending 12 hours in a semi-crouch while tomatoes fell and squashed around you, near you, and on you was bad enough without the extra thrill of trying to escape being run over by a truck.

The building had a small crawl space about two feet high so that if I was under a truck when it started to pull away I could duck into that space to avoid being run over. I felt like some sort of gnome with bifocals who lived under the Heinz plant and only came out at night.

About an hour into my shift I'd be soaking wet with water from the trough or flume above, covered in various layers of seeds, skins, and tomato pulp, and trying desperately not to have this coating marred by a tire tread!

If you ever saw how adorable Dick Van Dyke looked as the soot-covered chimney sweep in the movie "Mary Poppins," I was sort of the Heinz 57 Varieties version, only not quite as cute and lovable. Other workers would let me have lunch with them, but, only if I sat at the next table. Not only did I have a disgusting and dangerous job but I had the heartbreak of having to talk to people 10 feet away.

From my position under the trucks I would truly admire the almost ballet-like movements of the guys who unloaded the baskets. As a team, one guy would climb high up on top of the trucks and toss or throw baskets down to his partner who then dumped them into the flume of water.

One night, one of the guys didn't show up for work, so I was elected to take his place! These rather rough guys had more muscles than my art school anatomy book ever even suggested that the human body had. It was determined rather quickly that I would "catch" rather than "toss." Well, I soon learned that you didn't try to catch a basket of tomatoes thrown at you from 10 feet above. You sort of flipped the basket in mid-air and in the same motion you stacked it on top of other empty baskets.

If you didn't do it quite right, you tended to crush your fingers between the basket and the edge of the water flume. I decided that if I ever wanted to paint again, I better get into the rhythm real quick. I got to be really good at it and so every night thereafter I'd trade off with one of the guys up above for an hour or so of slinging baskets while he did my job below. They all thought I was crazy, but figured that's what happens when you spend your shifts dodging truck bumpers.

With any luck, about three-thirty in the morning the trucks would have quit coming and everyone else would be sent home. I was left alone to hose down and sweep the entire front area of the plant. This was a wonderful time to me, a time to get reflective and think about things. If I had the time, I'd run to the far side of the plant and watch the sunrise over Salem Creek for a few moments. That was always my treat to myself for working so hard for the company.

The night-shift plant supervisor, a wonderful man who would tease me every time he saw me, would come and he and I would have a smoke break together. He was a perfect double for Jim Bacus, the actor who played the millionaire on the TV show Gilligan's Island. Now in the early hours, instead of teasing, he would conduct wonderful advice-filled fatherly talks with me, and I loved him for it.

He was by the gate one night as my mother dropped me off for work. He rushed over, bowed low to the ground, and opened the door for me. He then told my mother that I was the only one who really knew what was going on around the company at night and surely the Heinz Corporation would collapse if it wasn't for me keeping everything so neat and tidy! Naturally, my mother believed him and ate it up!!! Two things I learned at my mother's knee: sensitivity and gullibility.

Every morning at 6 a.m., my mother would pick me up at the main gate. With me sitting on an old blanket to protect the car seats, she and I would take a ride out and around the countryside because she felt that I needed a piece of beauty and serenity in my life after 12 hours of slogging through tomatoes. After sleeping all day, and getting up just in time to have dinner, it would be time to return to the Land of the Tomato Gnomes once again.

In 1977, amid a storm of protest, upheaval, and ill feelings, the Heinz plant closed its gate after being here for 70 years.

Often, in the normal course of doing errands, I end up driving by the old plant. I still can see the ghostly and ghastly image of my former self clutching the chain-link fence and waving to carloads of my friends (?) who would ride by on beautiful summer nights to taunt and tease me!

The plant is missed by many people for many reasons. There are of course those reasons that focus on tax rateables and the plant as a source of local employment. It served as a close and ready market for Salem County farmers.

Other folk will talk of how they miss seeing the tomato-filled farm trucks stretching the entire length of Griffith and Grant streets waiting in line to be unloaded. Others will tell of the lifelong friendships that were made when they worked at the plant season after season after season.

If you were born in Salem, and are a bit over 20 years old, then you and I know what we miss the very most from Heinz's, don't we?

Will July, August, and September ever be quite the same without the sweet, warm smell of ketchup being made? How can kids truly feel that school has started without smelling ketchup cooking on their way home on warm, hazy September afternoons?

My son just started his first paying job. He works part-time at the Salem McDonald's. He goes to work smiling and looking very nice and clean in his company uniform; and he returns home smiling and looking just as clean as when he left.

Well kid, you really got it made. Why, when I had my first job . . .

Today's Sunbeam, Salem, N.J., Sunday, July 28, 1991

A Lush Field of Corn Is a Field That's Filled with Magic

Driving about the county, be it on main thoroughfare or quiet little back road, how delightful it is to see all the various crops of vegetables that are growing; and the special look and quality that they bring to our countryside.

To see this tangible, green, growing evidence of a man's labor makes a person realize that if anyone in our society should be held up as a hero, it should be the farmer.

Of all the rambling acres of wonderful things that are growing right now, the fields I most love to see are the cornfields. For me at least, the words "cornfield" denotes many things and causes my thoughts to run afar.

There is a line from a 16th century version of the 65th Psalm that reads, ". . . the valleys also shall stand so thick with corn that they shall laugh and sing." Two thousand years or more might separate me from the psalmist who first wrote these words, but we are together in a spirit and a sentiment that transcends any mere span of time.

Gazing out over a field of corn, I am caught up in sensing some sort of aura about these endless rows and stands of strong, tall, green plants with wispy tasseled tops. There is a sense of stability and nobility about them. A very visual and spiritual affirmation that if we will take care of, and preserve our land, this can be earth's bounteous reward to all of us.

To walk through a field of tall, tasseled corn and lose yourself among shiny, rubbery green leaves is to enter an almost surrealistic world all its own.

Especially exciting is to be able to view the sky and surrounding landscape through the topmost delicate green leaves and the gossamer-like tassels. To recall the swirling and swaying motions they make in a breeze-blown dance, is to remember a very melodic French term used in painting.

The word is "repousser" and means to push something back. In this case, viewing the world through these lacy patterns creates a marvelous sense of depth and distance. For an artist, the study of Nature is to study with an almost perfect teacher.

A hot, humid, August summer evening, a few seasons back, I was treated to two special viewpoints and all within the same field of corn.

In the fading daylight, and looking through the corn at the deepening blue of the eastern sky, you saw the field awash in the yellow-orange glow of the lowering sun. Every edge of every leaf appeared to be gilded in gold; and every tasseled top appeared to shimmer in varying light effects from silver to orange-red sienna.

When you turned to see the source of light that created this incredible scene, the sun had become a round red disk overpowered by a vast amount of hazy, yellow sky.

The bejeweled cornfield of one direction now became for this new direction, a dark green, almost black, webbed silhouette of pointed leaves against the intense light of the fiery sun.

To lose yourself to this kind of world for a few moments is to realize how seemly it is that writers and film-makers will often use cornfields as magical, fantastical and moody, mysterious settings for their stories.

Cornfields make me think of American history. I think of the pioneers, the Indians, and of the Pilgrims. I see the work of the Midwestern painters of the 1920s and 1930s, called the Regionalists, who painted many wonderful genre scenes of life in Iowa, Missouri, and Kansas all seemingly set amid the cornfields of those regions.

Indians, with their intense spirituality for all things that were on and of the earth, had a special reverence for corn. Corn, to the Indians of the South West and those here in the Northeast, was as important to their survival as the buffalo were to the Indians on the Western Plains.

The biggest mistake the Indians probably made was to help the white man, in the guise of Pilgrims, to survive by teaching him how to grow corn.

The tribes of New England believed that corn was given to them through the sacrifice of the life of First Mother, a deity figure for the Indians. In response to the cries of her starving children she allowed herself to be slain. As she had instructed, her dead body was dragged over the bare earth until her flesh mingled with the soil.

After seven moons had passed, her children, the Indians, discovered that her flesh had manifested itself into another form, her goodness had become substance. We call it corn.

This was her flesh, given out of love, and it would nourish and strengthen her children always. By saving some of the kernels and replanting them, every seven moons her flesh, her spirit, and her love would be renewed for generation after generation.

The early settlers and sodbusters relied almost exclusively on corn meal, as wheat flour was hard to come by. An early Nebraska newspaper listed 35 ways to use corn. What johnnycake was to covered wagon trains heading westward, so too are hush puppies to southern tradition.

Current food trends seem to be emphasizing what has to come to be called "comfort food." With Yuppies being on the wane, we say good-bye to sun-dried tomatoes, mineral water, and designer vegetables.

Comfort food is homemade vegetable soup on a wintry day. It is "soul food" regardless of your racial background. It is the type of food that will soothe the soul and spirit as well as nourish the body. To me anything made with corn seems to fit just nicely into this line of thinking.

The taste of food has always held wonderful associations for me. I love cornbread, and its aroma and taste can take me to any of several places. I can close my eyes and sense a taste that a Civil War soldier might have sampled around a camp fire.

I can be on an Oregon Trail wagon train. Quaker friends of mine serve thick bean soup over a hunk of cornbread placed in a deep tin plate. They call it their Depression Dinner. I love eating this dish and I can, if I choose to, feel a real sadness for people of that era, or any time where people are hungry.

By using my imagination, it was the only way, as a kid, that I could play with my food and get away with it!

I never close my eyes and fantasize when plundering a table laden with the corn products found in Mexican food! I am too busy devouring corn tortillas and cornmeal tamales wrapped and steamed in a cornhusk. Occasionally, I glance upward and offer praise and thanks for the Mexican people who discovered that anything was fair game, food-wise, just as long as you wrapped it in a corn tortilla!

Lester Richie's home and produce stand on South Tilbury Road in Elsinboro must sit on the only high ground in Salem County. As I stood in his front yard the other evening buying sweet corn, I could look across the way and actually see sort of a valley and hillside with corn growing on it! It was a wonderful bit of a view going from young corn close by, to tall, tasseled acres basking on a sunlit hillside in the hazy distance. At Lester's, not only do you get a great view, but his corn and cantaloupes are super!

Speaking of great views, I love coming down Pennsville Road and seeing that great old red barn on the Griscom Farm rising right up out of the corn fields. Early morning, a few days ago, coming down Route 49, that whole rural scene was sparkling crisp blue sky, great puffy white clouds, red barn, and lush, green stalks of corn. "Gee, Toto! We must be back in Kansas."

The next time you pass a cornfield, I hope you'll remember my column, but most of all, I hope you remember the words of Garrison Keillor, host of the radio program "Prairie Home Companion" who said, "Kissin' is great, but not quite as great as an ear of fresh sweet corn."

I'll tell you what's as great as an ear of fresh sweet corn: the 1992 season of Oakwood Summer Theatre!

Do you know what's worse than a wormy, rotten ear of fresh sweet corn? The wormy, rotten idea of building a Wal-Mart store and parking lot in back of Richman's on Route 49! If that bright idea becomes reality, maybe an earthen mound could be built around the stores and the 800-space parking lot. Then you could plant corn to hide the dumb thing! If they use plastic artificial corn stalks, sort of Astro-Stalks, why it'll even look good in the winter.

Question: Do you know what a buccaneer is?

Answer: A terrible price for corn! Pretty corny, eh?

Today's Sunbeam, Salem, N.J., Sunday, August 11, 1991

Shore Visit Provides a Break From Hectic Life at Home

Dear friend,
Ahhhh . . . this is the life! Surrounded by books, sipping coffee, swooning in a wondrously cool morning breeze, and watching the morning sun glint off the ocean.

You may be asking yourself, "how can he see the ocean from Salem?" A vivid imagination has never been a problem, but, in this case, I am writing my column whilst I lounge in placid splendor on the upper porch of a rented vacation home in Ocean City, New Jersey!

You may now be asking yourself, "why in the world does someone who sits around all day and draws, colors, and writes screwball columns, need a vacation? This guy needs a *real* job, not a vacation!"

Look at it this way: Do you remember how much fun you had using your crayons and paints and coloring books when you were a child? Well, I have about that much fun most of the time when I work, except sometimes people yell at me because I didn't finish my coloring book fast enough. Sometimes people give me several different books to color and they all want them done at the same time, or they needed them finished last week! Besides, people give me books with blank pages and not only do I have to color, I have to draw a picture first so that I can have some lines to stay in! You folks who live and work in the real world call this stress, so do I, except, mine comes in various assorted colors.

At any rate, it is just great to be here. It's so neat to hear sea gulls and know you're really at the shore and not the parking lot of the Salem Acme or the Ames Shopping Center in Pennsville!

Speaking of home, I just glanced up in time to see a Waddington Dairy truck going by!

I've been here about two days and have already run into six or seven people from home who have been out riding bikes, or shopping on the boardwalk or sunning on the beach.

Speaking of bikes and boardwalks, here at the shore they have this incredible, early morning ritual. Between 6 a.m. and 11 a.m., folks are allowed to ride their bikes on the boardwalk. A seemingly nice, quaint bit of vacation by-the-sea nostalgia, right? Wrong!!

My first morning here I ambled out to buy a Sunday paper and some doughnuts. As I headed back I decided that I would cut across to the boardwalk and do the return three blocks in a nice, slow, early morning walk by the ocean.

Between joggers and bicyclists, you couldn't even find the boardwalk! The gentle wafting breeze was heavily perfumed (?) by at least 27 different scents of sun lotions ranging from Tropical Coconut to Old Sweat Band. As hard as it was to breathe, had it not been for all the suntan oil, this teeming mass of biking, hiking humanity would never have been able to slide by one another! The tide was up, and although a bit precarious, I found it safer to hang off the railing on the ocean side and edge my way along the outer four inches of the boardwalk! Do you know how incredibly long it takes to inch your way three blocks while hanging on with one hand and using your newspaper in the other to beat off sea gulls who are attacking your bag of doughnuts!

Sea gulls must have lookouts who hang around the bakeries and signal the others when some unsuspecting vacationer walks out with a bag of doughnuts. They all tend to hover and circle over you hoping that you'll stumble and fall and then . . .!

Alfred Hitchcock must have been inspired to make the movie "The Birds" after vacationing at the Jersey Shore.

I found it a bit unnerving to awake in the early dawn and see, perched high above the still, quiet streets, sea gulls lining the roof peaks silently awaiting the doughnut shops to open.

Well, once past 11 a.m. it's fairly safe to head on up to the beach for a few hours of basking in the sunshine and soaking up some natural vitamin D via the sun.

So we spend about an hour getting into our bathing suits and coating ourselves in suntan lotion. More time is devoted to figuring out the best way to carry beach chairs, books, flip-flops, umbrellas and other sundry items needed for beach time.

Once at the beach we stake-out a place in the sand to call our own. As we begin to set up, every one around us has to move over a foot or so. This in turn then makes the people next to them move a bit and you now have this ripple effect that extends from 16th Street beach for at least 10 blocks in both directions!

We set up the umbrella, spread out the beach blanket, open our books, twitch the sand with our toes, read five lines of our beach novel, and then someone suggests that we should head back to the house for lunch.

Convinced as we are that at least 90 percent of the populace on the beach would love to get their hands on our faded, taped-together, tattered umbrella, our (circa 1968) Lone Ranger beach blanket, and our two and a half rusty, bent aluminum chairs, we gather it all up and head back to the house for lunch.

After lunch, we gather it all up again, head for the beach and the staking-out ritual begins again. Why is it, I wonder, that I feel like a Bedouin nomad with an Ocean City beach tag and flip-flops!?!

It is now mid-afternoon and we are finally ready to lay back, soak up some sun and fight off the bathers and the jellyfish for a square foot of surf to get wet in! Wow! Is this fun!!! Say kids, aren't we havin' a blast!!!

As I lay back in the miniscule shade of the beach umbrella, trying to avoid skin cancer and sea gull droppings, and trying to brush away the sand that has gotten inside every fold and crevice of my body, it is through the shimmering heat waves rising off the sand's broiling surface that I see a wonderful sight . . . could it be a mirage?

As I glanced down the length of the boardwalk my eyes beheld some sort of small, pavilion-like structure. Its white railings and roof posts gleamed in white brilliance against the deep blue sky. Beneath its roof was the promise of copious amounts of cool, breezy shadows. The few people sitting or standing about its shady deck appeared to have had at least ten feet of space between them and the next person.

With tears making rivulets down my sun-lotioned cheeks, book bag clutched against my thumping heart, it was with stumbling, faltering steps and flailing arms that I made my way across the burning sands, maddened and crazed in my pursuit of some shade, no sand, no sun worshipers, and no sea gulls!

I stood upon its cool, shady deck, raised my arms in thanksgiving, and offered a bidding prayer to the beach and its suntanned, lotion-soaked inhabitants. I was here for the duration!

I spent the remaining days of my vacation in wondrous afternoon bliss high above the beaches. Just me, my beach chair, 43 pounds of books, huge container of ice-water, and a box of molasses-mint salt water taffy. Am I mistaken? Is this real? Or did God move Heaven to Ocean City for the season?

Because you are higher up, and extended out over the beach, you get a wonderful sense of the ocean. You can see the waves rolling in from far out and watch the distant patterns they make as they spread out over the shoreline. As you glance up from your book, you get a feeling of being on the stern of a ship, because all you can see is railing, sea, and sky.

So delightful! Calm, joy, peace; created by the sight and sound of the sea, and the feel of its breath making cooling, swirling, arabesque movements around you.

One early afternoon as I glanced up from my book, I got to see the sun reflect, seemingly, off of every ripple of water for as far as you could see. The sun's position must have been just right because the entire ocean seemed to sparkle and glitter like diamonds. I have seen small patches of sunlight and water create this effect, but never this vast an expanse of brilliant glittering light.

On my last morning I watched the ocean through breaks in the morning's mist. I love to sense the ocean as a power, and as a force, and as a wonder of nature. I love to look out across it to the horizon and think of all those souls, those riders of the tides, whose destinies, for better or worse were linked to its lure.

I ponder all the distant shores these waters sweep across, and the wonderful creatures that live in its deep, silent world.
Byron wrote these words to describe the mystery of the ocean: Dark-heaving—boundless, endless, and sublime, the image of eternity.

As you read today's column, alas, I will have been home for several days. Regarding, if you will, today's writing as one long postcard, I am duty bound by the code and creed of all good vacationers to say, "Having a great time! Wish you were here!"

Today's Sunbeam, Salem, N.J., Sunday August 25, 1991

A Loving Tribute to a Special Woman, 'Alloway Mae'

Mae Allen, retired Salem High School English teacher, has been quoted as saying, "I have always believed the teacher's more important than the subject."

Last Saturday, a couple hundred of her former students came to Alloway to prove her correct. We were attending a semi-surprise 80th birthday party held in her honor.

Mae Allen is the unofficial associate editor of all the rantings and ramblings that go on in this column. With just about every column, I have called her in anguish and despair over what to do with commas, prepositions, and dangling participles!

It is a privilege to still have her as part of my life, and I can assure all her former students that she is as kind and patient and gentle a teacher as you remember her being.

I wouldn't wish me and this column on anyone, yet she sweetly assures me, "my child, you are never a bother." Such is the loving approach she brings to all of life's dealings.

Mae Allen, Former Salem High School teacher

It takes a lot of nerve to publicly write about your high school English teacher, let alone compose a poem, so it is with loving apologies to Miss Allen, and to Edgar Allen Poe's poem, Annabel Lee, that I offer the following:

ALLOWAY MAE

It was many and many
A year ago,
How many I dare not say,
That a teacher did teach
Whom you may know,
let us call her Alloway Mae.
Now this teacher she taught
With no other thought,
Than to help me understand
Of sonnets and poems
By Shelly and Keats,
And Shakespeare, a most
Talented man.
I was a devil, she was a dear,
I made her earn her pay,
Yet, she taught with a love
That was more than a love,
What a blessing was Alloway Mae.
And this was the reason
That long ago,
In a high school down the way,
Not only did I love
Old Byron and Burns, but,
Fell in love with Alloway Mae.
She was gentle and sweet,
So good and so kind,
A harsh word n'ere heard her say.
Devoted to others,
No thought for herself –

Selfless was Alloway Mae.
No student so lacking,
No student so smart,
That some bit of knowledge
She couldn't impart.
With eyes so expressive,
With a smile that spoke love,
For many a student
She was sent from above.
She brought to a classroom
Gifts of care and concern,
They were fuel for your fire
If you wanted to learn.
I've met lots of people
Very established in life,
Great jobs, home, and money,
Children, a husband or wife.
If voting for someone
Who helped on Life's way,
Without hesitation –
It'd be Alloway Mae.
We tried to learn our English
Of pronouns and of verbs,
Everyday we had a test
On our vocabulary words.
The very best of lessons
To take upon our way,
Were lessons of love
And of caring,
Lived out by Alloway Mae.
We live in a world
Oft times cruel and unfair,
We seem surrounded by others
Who are too selfish to care.
And here in our midst,
Amid all of this strife,
Is this example of love

As shown by her life.
A teacher n'ere to busy
To spend some time with you,
You never were a bother "child,"
She was there to see
You through.
From sentence structure Run amuck,
To some trauma in your day,
Always there with love and faith,
Devoted Alloway Mae.
Each student she has ever taught
In her heart has had a place,
It matters not how far
They've gone,
Or how they ended up the race.
She loves them just as
Dearly now,
As she did way back then,
And scrapbooks of her "children"
Help reflect it all again.
. . . And the moon never beams
Without bringing me dreams
Of her classroom long ago,
and the stars never rise
But I see the kind eyes
Of caring Alloway Mae.
. And now as I go
I just want you to know
What this poem has tried to say,
You are a gift, a treasure,
A joy . . .
We all love you Alloway Mae.

Today's Sunbeam, Salem, N.J., Sunday, September 8, 1991

Choosing Friends: Narrow-minded Guidelines Don't Work

The other day while in Woodstown, I was privy to, or rather eavesdropping on, a conversation being held amongst a group of teenagers at a local eatery.

After they joined in a collective moan and groan over the fact that school was to start soon, they commenced to discuss all the old friends they hoped to see again; the various students, both male and female, that they hoped to befriend; and then there were those who would be avoided like Lymes disease.

It seemed that this group picked their friends based on how cute or how sexy they were, if they were athletic with nice eyes, if they dressed well based on currents trends, if they were popular, and most of all, if they were "cool."

Any others who fell outside these guidelines, while acknowledged as being nice or intelligent, were nonetheless destined to be placed on the "geeky" side of the high school social spectrum.

As I listened to them I couldn't help but think back on my own days of trying to be a social survivor as a 16-year-old kid.

When I was in high school, the only thing that saved me from being cast into the outer darkness of the social netherland was a sense of humor.

I had no sexy smile, wore bifocals, was in a remedial gym class, and dressed to the beat of a different drummer. All in all, I didn't even come close to having any of the requirements for basic high school stardom.

For one reason or another it was ordained by some "higher being of popularity" that if I could manage to arrive at school everyday for four years with at least eight new jokes, then I would be allowed into the inner circles of social acceptance.

Bruce Willis apparently had the same gimmick going at Penns Grove High School. How is it that he is making $8 million for a picture in Hollywood, and I'm still selling portraits for five bucks apiece at Market Street Day!?!

Based on these kids' conversation, I was sorry to discover that despite all the consciousness-raising social upheavals between 1963 and 1991, teens still paired up and off along the same narrow-minded guidelines now as when I was in school.

I wanted so very much to jump into their discussions with my voice of experience, but then I remembered that when I was sixteen I'd have just ignored and laughed at any advice that was more than 20 years old, let alone 46!

I wanted to tell them that the fancy clothes, good looks, and attitudes built on being "cool and with it" are fleeting and fragile.

One of the great truths I've discovered along life's path is that a lot of "geeky, nerdy, non-cool" teens grow up to be exciting, interesting adults and real winners in society.

I've seen it happen so many times, and I love it! What wonderful retribution for the years of hurt and heartache they may have experienced at the whims and wiles of others.

I know of five or six situations that just make my heart thrill to see both how far these people have come, and the contributions they have made to life either in this area or elsewhere.

The friendships that we establish in high school can become lifelong. I am blessed with having wonderful relationships with many of the "kids" I grew up with and or attended school with, and I value these friendships so very much. My very best friend from high school is still my very best friend.

Many of my friends have become like family. They are a part of the roots for the life I now live. They have provided form, color, and fabric to my memories of growing up.

They create for me a beautiful and warm sense of love, peace, and assurance I find very fulfilling and meaningful during the times when life and career aren't going along as smoothly as I'd like.

Growing up in the small towns that dot our rural county can provide us with wonderful opportunities to learn about the importance and meaning of having friends and creating friendships.

I see my teenage son not only having relationships with people his own age, but as he goes about various errands here in town he is forced to deal with an adult world at the bank, the supermarket, and many other places of business.

He will come home and relate to us how much fun he had at this store or that because of a conversation he may have had with the owner or a customer.

He has discovered that teasing from an adult at the post office or at the market can many times be a sincere form of affection. He takes real delight in discovering just how nice people can be.

After I left Salem for college and the start of my career, I set off into the world with the naïve notion that every place else was just a bigger version of Salem. I tended to treat people in Philadelphia, Kansas City, and New York the same as I would if I were in Salem, and it worked!

In spite of well-intended warnings, I found that people did not stand in line to kick my teeth in or to take advantage of me.

Someone recalled for me the other day the old adage, "a stranger is just a friend you haven't met yet."

Well, to my teenage lunch partners, I wish you well in your coming school year. I will never be so old as not to be able to remember being a teenager.

It had some wonderful times and a few not so wonderful times, but I was lucky enough to have had good, true friends through it all.

I just ask of you to be careful in deciding who you will accept and who you will reject. As someone once said, "Paybacks can be tough." One of the frustrations of being your age is that there are no real certainties as to what life will deal to you or to your friends, and therein lies a wonderful kind of mystical beauty. Life at this point is fair game for all, only you just don't realize it now.

It is fair game for the "out group" just as much as it is for the "in group," and you may be shocked someday to see who is to be "in" and who is to be "out."

To this group of very normal teenagers, I wish for you good things and a bit of luck, but more so, I wish for you the courage to share with others an open heart and an open mind.

Friendship is its own best reward.

To the non-reader of this column who so bitterly told me I

was an idiot for my love affair with life in Salem County, along with "raspberry" I offer this counter: a few minutes after we were talking I ended up at Smick's lumberyard in Quinton. I dealt with four men and a woman who treated me like my $12 purchase and my presence were the only reason they came to work that day.

To Kathy, John B., Russ, John H., and Paul, thank you for being the kind of people that this column is all about.

Dear Harold . . . If it's true that at Smick's the customer is always boss . . . please give the above mentioned folks a 300-percent raise. Thanks!

Today's Sunbeam, Salem, N.J., Sunday, September 22, 1991

Scenes of the Local Store Through a Candied Haze

Often I have mentioned my fondness for cruising and perusing the wide, well-lit aisles of the local Acme or Super-Fresh market. I love the vast selection of products available to us. I love speaking with folks over the frozen food cabinets or while selecting canned goods.

I don't even mind long checkout lines provided folks remain friendly, civil, and somewhat optimistic that they will be getting through sometime between now and the 11 p.m. news.

Standing in these lines, the thought will sometimes surface about what we have lost or traded in our demands for convenience and abundance of choice, quantity, and product.

Time was when every town in the county had several "neighborhood" grocery stores. Practically all are gone now, and only a few remain: Ashley's Market in Pennsville, Santucci's in Penns Grove, Dodge's in Elmer, Bud's and Remster's in Alloway.

In talking with various friends, we have come up with at least twenty stores that were in business just here in Salem, and all at the same time! Some operated for years practically next door to each other.

This was a time when the store owner knew all his customers. Tabs were kept, people were trusted till pay-day rolled around. Kids showed up with notes from their mothers. And you never shopped but what you didn't know everyone there.

The American Store, run by Russ Downs, and located in what is now Mike Gayner's Beverage Mart, holds the only memory I have of a "wheel" of cheese and a large, foul-looking barrel of kosher pickles.

While I remember so many of these stores, the one that is most meaningful to me was a wonderful place named Harris's Market. Any kid, in the last four decades, growing up on the East Broadway end of town knew that its "real" name was "Torbie's." It was located right next door to the Washington fire house.

"Torbie" was the nickname for Clinton Torbert Harris, Jr. whose father bought the house in 1910. In 1948 a small store was added onto the east side of the house. The store was built in that by-gone tradition of combining home and business.

Mr. Harris, Sr., a house painter by trade, maintained a greenhouse where he raised plants for sale. A widower, he had four children, Oscar, Torbie, Martha Counsellor, and Caroline Bennett.

Oscar, built and ran the store from 1948 until 1953 when his brother Torbie took over and Oscar went into house painting.

Harris's, while it did sell some groceries and meat items, always seemed to be more of a candy, soda and ice cream kind of place.

On long ago summer days, how I loved making trips "up" to Torbie's. It was a very special sort of place to visit. It was fun to go there not only because of penny candy, or Popsicles, or creamy root beer soda in dark brown bottles, but for many other reasons.

It was sort of like visiting "The Waltons," if you remember that wonderful TV program of a few years ago. It always seemed like one or more of the family members and their spouses were running around doing something or other, and they all treated me like a member of the family.

In front of the house and store stretched a wonderfully huge and high awning. It was as wide as the house and store and ran across the broad sidewalk to the curb's edge. What a wonderful patch of cool shade it created, especially pleasant on a hot summer's day.

Beneath this canopy, Mr. Harris, Sr. had tiers of planks and cinder blocks upon which set flats of pansies, marigolds, and geraniums making glowing patches of color in the cool shade. Later on, these same tiers held baskets of summer vegetables.

I would sit on the front steps of the house and drink root beer and devour my bag of penny candy and pretzel sticks, very content to just watch the world go by. I was six going on 80 in those days, and just another of the characters that shady spot and front steps seemed to attract.

Old Mr. Harris once offered me the job of sweeping the front walk for a nickel. After about three days of sweeping I decided I wanted the nickel plus a candy bar. Well, I was fired on-the-spot but in my terms of release I was still allowed to sit on the front steps.

I really loved all the family members very much because they were always so good to me. I especially loved Oscar's wife Lou. She had beautiful red hair and I thought she was as pretty as Lucille Ball. If she happened to be in the store I would be able to flirt with her through the glass front of the candy counter. No bag of penny candy was ever as sweet or plentiful as the one she would make up for me.

Summer would be officially over when Mr. Harris took down the canvas awning and set out pumpkins and baskets of fall apples and squash.

The bare pipe framework would be a reminder to me all winter long of the special beauty that would return to this patch of sidewalk come the spring and summer.

The bare structure also served as a reminder that soon my mother and I would be coming here with the wagon or sled to pick out a Christmas tree!

The old Washington firehouse was about 30 feet away from the Harris house, and so Mr. Harris would lean trees against the sides of both structures and festoon the whole area with strings of naked light bulbs.

We lived a block or so in back of the store and firehouse. When December arrived, the firemen put up colored lights on the siren tower atop the firehouse. At night, I could lay at the foot of my bed and see the firehouse decorations as well as the glow from Mr. Harris's tree lot. This caused me to go to sleep each December night in a sort of Yuletide "feeding frenzy."

On Sunday nights I'd watch the Gene Autry show on TV. Good ol' Gene would end the show sitting astride his horse Champion extolling the benefits of "clean, refreshing Doublemint gum" for getting the trail dust out of a cowboy's throat. He would then invite you to join with him in chewing a stick of the cowboys' favorite gum.

The minute the show ended I'd grab my cowboy hat, my double six-shooters, mount my make-believe horse, and gallop "hell-bent for leather" to Torbie's for Doublemint gum.

I couldn't read yet and for some reason I never trusted him to sell me the real thing. I'd get a suspicious, accusatory tone to my voice, and Torbie would get an exasperated tone to his as he tried to assure me this was Gene Autry gum!

I'd finally leave, but not before warning Torbie that I was gonna show the pack to my Dad and it better be the right stuff! We played this game every Sunday evening for the better part of a year until I finally learned to spell Doublemint.

Among other memories is the feel of ice cold water and clinking soda bottles as I rooted around in the soda cabinet inspecting each kind only to end up with the same brand of root beer I always bought. And, of course, returning bottles for the two cents deposit!

I never liked ice cream very well but I loved the dark, crunchy sugar cones. So all the kids would go to Torbie's for ice cream and I'd buy an empty sugar cone. Strange child!

When you bought penny candy, Torbie had the knack of holding the bag in one hand and tossing candy with the other. The candy sailed through about three feet of space, and he hardly ever missed!

Some of my favorite candy were the black licorice pipes with red "jimmies" to look like they were lit. Do you remember tiny little pie tins filled with fudge that you ate with a little tin spoon?

White nougat squares with gummy colored candy mixed in were wonderful. Mary Janes in yellow waxed wrappers, midgy Tootsie Rolls, was there ever really a time when we could buy a candy bar for a nickel?

I loved the chewy, red candies called "red-hot dollars" which I liked to hold up to my eyes because they made everything turn red. After you tired of this game they were soft and sticky and easier to chew! I guess they were my first pair of rose-colored glasses.

I disliked the little wax bottles filled with sweet liquid and the strips of paper filled with candy pills! I would get goose-bumps as my teeth scraped across the paper . . . aaaggghh!!!

"Torbie's" or Harris's Market was the last of its kind in Salem. Torbie ran the store up until last September when illness forced him to close. He passed away this past spring. I attended his funeral and took part in the Masonic Service conducted for him.

I was there as an adult doing adult-like things, but in spirit I was very much the little boy saying good-bye, for awhile, to a marvelous part of my childhood.

The candy store is gone now, there are new owners for the house. I see painters, and roofers, and electricians climbing all over it these days.

The handiwork of the renovator's hammers and pry-bars, nor a hundred coats of paint, or siding will ever hide the look of "Torbie's" to my mind's eye, or my heart's desire.

Some summer's day, I think I'll park across the street, and thru the magic of a couple of red, chewy candies held up to my eyes as I look across Broadway, perhaps for a little while, I will see it all once again.

Other than two special friends of mine, do any of you remember a candy called "Squirrel Nut Zippers?" They were toffee candy with nuts and came in a yellow wrapper and sold for a penny. I never heard of them, but love the name!

Today's Sunbeam, Salem, N.J., Sunday, October 6, 1991

Time to Savor the Aromas, Taste Sensations of Autumn

It is autumn. The evening skies of the vesper hour are as orange as a box of ginger-snaps, and long ribbons and tendrils of dusky gray, and rose, and buff colored clouds reach in descending lengths across deepening blue skies.

The crisp, cool light morning gives way to the poetic, suffused golden glow of the afternoon sun.

In painting, this soft, golden feeling would be referred to as "Venetian glow," a term that describes the soft light created by the water that surrounds, and affects the atmosphere of, this Renaissance city. The low lands of Holland gave this same effect to the Dutch painters of a later century.

The meadows and waterways of Salem County create a special kind of atmospheric light for this area, and at no other season is it ever as beautiful as it is in autumn.

There are so many kinds of beauty to autumn—digging in the earth to plant bulbs; trees aglow with color; roadside stands that are beautiful still-lifes of pumpkins, brightly colored mums, and Indian corn; and hanging herbs to dry in attic eaves.

It is the season of the romantics. It is a settling back, reflective kind of time. It is a time that gives me cause to recall sweet memories of old friends and family, of other times and other places.

The cool, crisp chill of autumn days are one of my favorite times to gather together and bask in the warmth and blessings of good food and good friends.

A few Sundays ago I mentioned "comfort food" in my column. I referred to it as any food that gives you the same cozy feeling that you get with homemade vegetable soup on a blustery, rainy day. Sound wonderful? Makes you close your eyes and smile? Conjures up warm, loving feelings of coming home from school and finding Mom in the kitchen, doesn't it?

Comfort food just seems so right for this time of year. The flavorings, spices, and other ingredients seem to reflect the mood of the season. They are subtle and delicate, with the good earthy taste of potatoes, carrots, parsnips, and onions. The aroma of fall leaves released by rake or shuffling, schoolboy feet can be as deep and heady and delicious as the first pungent whiff of a sauerbraten.

Soups, stews, goulashes, and ragouts that seem too heavy for other seasons seem to fit in so well with fall. The casseroles and one-pot dinners that I love so much originated because of the demands that cold weather made of people in terms of vitamins and protein. They were dishes that were both sustaining and restorative in keeping body and soul together.

Roots vegetables, dried beans and peas, fruits, and grains were all easy to store and keep over the cold months, therefore through the centuries they formed the basis for many dishes when fresh vegetables were not in season.

The wonderful dishes of Central Europe, with their dependency on cabbage and potatoes, are due to the fact that the long cold climate of this region is favorable to the growing of these two favorites.

I find and feel a wondrous sense of romance in good food. It is this same sense that I carry over to my preferences in wine. I love an almost bitter wine called Retsina because it is the wine that Greek shepherds drink. German May wine, flavored with woodruff blossoms, is a bottle of springtime and wildflowers. And all Rhine wines elicit my German-Austrian ancestry in delightful ways.

Food can become a marvelous link to other times and people and settings.

When we gaze upon the moon and stars, we are seeing those same heavenly bodies that guided a long-ship of the Norsemen; this same light illuminated the snowbound encampments of Valley Forge.

The taste and fragrance of a dish that has remained unchanged for a few hundred years can, for a magical few moments, transport us to another time.

Our sense of taste and smell can stimulate our emotions and memories just as effectively as the other senses. Knowing that someone else, somewhere back in time, was experiencing this same taste sensation connects me quickly and inextricably with the past.

One of my favorite dishes is Chicken Marengo. This is a dish that was "thrown" together by Napoleon's chef as a celebration dinner after the battle of Marengo in Italy. It became Napoleon's favorite dish and sort of a good-luck symbol to him. It is made with chicken, tomatoes, mushrooms and onions and is a delicious blend of French and Italian influences.

Coq au vin, chicken and wine, was first a creation of the Romans. Caesar and his Legions introduced it to the Gauls. The French, being great lovers of food even way back then, decided that any people who had native dishes this good couldn't be all bad, and so they surrendered and submitted to Roman rule, swiped the recipe, perfected it, and became the gastronomic center of the world!

It is the dishes that evolve from out of a peasant tradition that are so special to me. Stews of any variety and form can evoke a delightful sense of poignancy within, and I find a kind of hominess in them that reflects a simpler kind of life-style of the people and products of a land and a region.

One of my favorite stew recipes, while fairly traditional in its ingredients calls for yams and peaches. It is wonderful! It's gorgeous! It is the culinary embodiment of all that is autumn.

The addition of fruit, both fresh and dried, to many dishes is centuries old. Many chicken concoctions call for grapes, or plums, or prunes. Dried apples and raisins make a perfect marriage with ham or pork. The mellowed sweetness of dried fruit gives a warming touch to the other ingredients.

When I make Chicken Marengo, I always add Mandarin oranges as their sweetness is a nice bit of contrast to the tart tomato base of the recipe, as well as a nice touch of color. At my house the on-going joke is that I'll cook anything and everything in orange juice! Not true!

Oft times I find that the romance and enjoyment of cooking can be heightened by the cooking vessel itself. I have several cast-iron skillets that came down to me from my grandfather who owned a restaurant in Ohio. I never knew him but cooking with these heavy, iron skillets allows for some sort of bond that connects me to the old photos and the stories I have heard of him.

Several of my favorite stoneware casserole dishes were handcrafted by Linda Hutchinson of the Sly Cat Studio in Woodstown. There is a special feeling about using something that is not only beautiful and utilitarian, but that has been created by a friend.

In Spain, nearly everyone, in spite of their position in life, owns a paellero. Since paella is practically the national dish of Spain, it is considered almost high-treason not to have the proper vessel to prepare this delicious one-dish meal. A paellero is a large, flat dish with sides about three inches high. Onto this culinary altar you place saffroned rice, chicken, sausages, shell-fish, shrimps and a variety of vegetables and seasonings.

Hemingway, in any of his novels based on the civil war in Spain, always finds a way to mention paella. Whenever I eat paella I feel that I am keeping the faith with Roberto and Maria, characters in "For Whom the Bell Tolls."

I recently bought a huge nine quart cast-iron Dutch Oven. It weighs a ton but it is a wonderful looking affair. Because it is dark gray, when you cook in it, you can see the steam rise in delightful flowing and entwining swirls that only seem to intensify the aroma of your soup or stew.

On the plains that lie between the Danube and the Carpathian Mountains, Hungarian herdsmen use a "bograc" which is a cooking pot very much like mine in which they cook their evening meal of "gulyas" or goulash as we call it.

What could be any lovelier than the beautiful red sauce, flecked through with amber highlights, of the goulash ladled over a bed of egg noodles dotted here and there with small mushroom caps; and all the romance and history of a country assembled in one marvelous creation of beef, onions, mushrooms, and paprika!

Talleyrand once said, "show me another pleasure like dinner that comes every day and lasts an hour."

Food is so indeed a pleasure. And I find that its enjoyment becomes wonderfully intensified when I can blend it to my moods and feelings, and the twilight world of the artist that I live in.

To surround myself with aromas and taste sensations that reflect the mood of a season, or a day long since gone; to gather good, loving friends and family together—this is when I can close my eyes and my soul hears a lovely music, and never am I quite so happy and content.

In my last column I mentioned a candy called Squirrel Nut Zippers. You can buy them at, of all places, the Beverage Mart on East Broadway in Salem.

Today's Sunbeam, Salem, N.J., Sunday, October 20, 1991

Mean-spirited Have Stolen Some Magic from Halloween

Halloween, like many things, is surely not the same as it use to be. Oh! What a magical time in childhood this day created. What delicious delight it was to live on the misty, blurred edge of the real world and the never-never land of ghosts, goblins, and witches.

Were there truly such things? What if they really did exist for one special night and the grown-ups were wrong? A child had to weigh the dangers of running costumed through leaf strewn streets begging for candy and caramel-covered apples, against the chance of being snatched up by cackling witches, shrieking demons, or skeletal figures in long, black robes!

For many reasons, this most ancient of all holidays has seen a real demise in the past 20 years.

Certain, sick, selfish, or just plain greedy people in our society have caused October 31st to be turned truly into a "fright-night." Most people have shut their doors in the face of this most magical time in childhood.

As any basic study of human nature will prove, deny or take away something from folks and they will compensate for, and create, new approaches to make up for that which has been lost.

For the past two or three Halloween seasons I have noticed a perfect case in point that excites and delights me no end—people are really getting into decorating their homes for the Halloween season, and it's terrific!

For many years Halloween decorations were, for the most part, just large flat cut-outs of ghosts, witches, and pumpkins, etc. that were taped to windows and doors. Jack-o'-lanterns usually sat on kitchen or dining room tables, or occasionally in a window.

There appears to be a whole new approach to decorating for this spooky ol' season. I think people want to try to recapture some of the "spell" and "spirit" of this fun holiday, bless their little hobgoblin hearts.

Since the beginning of October I've been seeing some wonderful Halloween decorations all around the area. It's a lot of fun to experience the charm and humor that they bring, not only to streets and neighborhoods, but to the viewer's day.

While flat cut-outs of ghost, black cats, and pumpkins still are taped to windows, front porches and steps are being transformed into exciting tableaus of bed-sheet ghosts and cotton twine spiderwebs. Myriad assortments of stuffed figures lounge about a porch swing or front steps. Huge, leaf filled, orange lawn bags create instant pumpkin patches!

Several of the homes that I've seen are decorated along the lines of autumn or harvest themes. Doorways are flanked with dried cornstalks and pumpkins, with Indian corn or grapevine wreaths centered in between. An old, weathered, wooden wheelbarrow holds a gorgeous grouping of various hued chrysanthemums. Lamp posts become cornshocks held in place with autumn colored ribbons.

In this season of frightful happenings, if you dare go out at night, you will see that some folks have strings of lights that are alternating pumpkins and ghosts! If you get close enough to see the lights, you'd probably discover that hidden behind the shrubs would be an outdoor speaker emitting eerie music and haunted house sounds!

I hope that I am right about what appears to be a reincarnation of the spirit of this frightfully good holiday. For all the kids coming along, I would hope that they have a lifetime of knowing the special thrill, mood, and magic of an All Hallow's Eve.

Place me alone in a darkened, chilly, wind-blown scenario, where dry leaves rustle and swirl on the ground below, while high above, bare tree limbs creak and groan and seemingly claw at the surface of a cloud enshrouded moon.

It is in such a setting that I will conjure up wild and spooky notions of witches and warlocks with hissing black cats in tow. Between the dried-up cornstalks and the dead plants of a once lush summer garden, surely I will see roaming, wailing banshees intertwined with the ebb and flow of a swirling ground mist.

Tickling and teasing your own nerve endings with the brush of imagination is almost as much fun as the real thing!

Back when I was a boy in those wonderful believe anything and everything years of childhood, we had three special nights that made for a Halloween trilogy of fun.

To awaken on the morning of the first of these days was to begin to feel the magic and anticipation of the three special evenings that lay ahead.

This first evening was called "Chalk Night." It was a night of lurking about neighborhood sidewalks and writing or drawing various messages and images upon the familiar pavement. They might have been spooky messages, or perhaps, outlandish statements such as "Susie loves Billy" when indeed Susie would rather eat a slug than share her affections with him!

I tended to stake out a well lit street corner and spend the evening drawing a haunted mural of skeletons, hobgoblins and other assorted demons of the season. I loved having a drawing surface a block long! Chalk Night was a gentle form of neighborhood harassment that warmed you up for the second night.

And then came "Mischief Night" or as some call it, "Tic-Tac Night."

Ah! Beware and behold those shadowy small figures who dash from tree to bush and gatepost to porch steps, with weapons of destruction and devilment clutched in their hands!

One heinous urchin carries a bulging shopping bag brimming over with hard, orange kernels of horse corn. A handful of this stuff, when deftly thrown across a front porch, made a wonderful racket!

Others would clutch a bar of Ivory soap for marking up car windows. The understood code of the evening said that you did not mark up the car's windshield.

The very best of the night's dastardly deeds were deigned for those who carried rolls of toilet paper!

Till that time when I spend Halloween in spirit form sitting atop my tombstone, I shall always thrill to the memory of the visual delight of a well tossed roll of toilet paper.

To watch it streaking and streaming its yards-long tail of whiteness against an inky night sky as it arched, up, up, and over the telephone wires was just fantastic! And to catch it on its descent, and in one fluid, ballet-like motion heave it aloft for a second looping of decoration, this was to know wild abandon at its utmost!

When you ran out of corn, toilet paper, and soap, you rang a few doorbells for good measure. Tradition ruled that you had to keep your finger on the bell till you heard the door start to open, and only then were you allowed to run. How brazen you were was in direct proportion to the width of the porch and the amount of steps you had to leap in your flight to escape!

All of the above were rather tame in comparison to others, but certainly fiendish and diabolical enough for our group.

The morning of Trick or Treat Night found you walking to school through some of the very streets you had "terrorized" the evening before.

Streamers of toilet paper fluttered in the early morning light; and you passed by cars whose owners had yet to discover the skull and crossbones drawn on the side window. If you were lucky, you'd wave a greeting to someone sweeping horse corn off their porch!

The morning session of school was seemingly endless. After lunch came the long awaited costume party. One feasted on glazed donuts and delicious, sweet cider from Lounsbury's in Quinton. Sugary orange marshmallow jack-o'-lanterns and little cups of candy corn rounded out the fare.

My mother always made stew for our Halloween supper. In between stirring the stew she managed to drape orange and black crepe paper all over the house. This was the same lady who ran rampant at Christmas with spray cans of artificial snow!

Our ceiling light would be swathed in orange paper napkins so as to create an orange glow throughout our small kitchen. How she ever kept from burning down the house is still one of the great mysteries of Halloween for me. God truly must look after his merrymakers.

Dinner would be interrupted about every other forkful by trick or treaters. This only served to heighten my anxiety to hit the streets before all the goodies were gone!!

Leaving the safety of my crepe paper enshrouded home, I would join the creepy hordes of masqueraders that went running to and fro about the normally placid streets, adding my voice to choruses of "trick or treat!!" that echoed from all the doorsteps.

Dragging homeward hours later, the streets would be all but deserted. Across the way, a sheet-draped ghost would be slowly shuffling furrows through the collected leaves at sidewalk's edge. Snow White or Cinderella would wave good-night from her castle's front porch.

The final act of my Halloween Trilogy was to cast nervous, sidelong glances towards the weedy, over-grown cemetery that was catty-corner to our house. Always, there would be a bright moon whose light was caught by the tops of old gravestones poking up, here and there, from out of the underbrush!

My eyes would dart from gravestone to moon and back again, daring myself to believe that I just might see eerie specters swirling upward, caught in the swishing wake of a witch's broom.

I'd walk a bit faster as I shot nervous glances backward at the moonlit cemetery and by the time I got up the front walk I would be scrambling up the porch steps two at a time!

Slamming the door shut behind me, expelling a long sigh of relief, I would head for the kitchen to examine my "take" for the evening.

In the orange half-light of the kitchen, with pieces of costume draped everywhere, and with greedy abandon and the skill of an accountant, I would take stock of my night's work.

Lastly, before falling asleep, and with one last All Hallow's Eve glance at the old graveyard across the way, I would total up my scores for the three nights' efforts.

There was a perfect 10.0 for the Chalk Night drawing that went halfway around the block on Johnson Street.

Another 10.0 for the Mischief Night obliteration of Craven Avenue with toilet paper, and even though my trick or treat bag had a bruised apple and not one Hershey bar with almonds, this night too was good enough to be a ten!

May all your Halloweens be happy, spirit-filled, and boo-tiful!

Today's Sunbeam, Salem, N.J., Sunday, November 3, 1991

One Small Gesture Can Be Answer to Another's Prayer

The other day, after offering advice to a friend concerning his daughter's options for an art career, he referred to me as "an answer to a prayer."

My friend was so earnest and sincere that although while a bit embarrassed, I walked away feeling good about being able to help someone who needed it.

He was very grateful that I would share my "special knowledge" with him. I simply regarded this information as part of my career and background, something picked up along the way.

Here was something that I just thought of as second nature, yet, to another, it was a valuable piece of information that became, for my friend, the answer to a prayer.

Later, while still basking in the glow of my friend's kind words, I thought of the times when, with great sincerity, I, too, had expressed to others that they indeed were an answer to my prayers.

Answers to prayers can come in many shapes, sizes, and colors; therein lies the beauty and sweetness of the deed. The answer need not always be monumental in scope or effect. For often, it is the little thing . . . the minor, seemingly insignificant thing that arrives with the most meaning and love from another.

Each one of us need to realize that we all possess special resources to help out each other. We all have it within us to be, for another, an answer to a prayer . . .

The history of this great country shows that one result of the pioneer spirit and the quest for spiritual freedom was the willingness of people to pitch in, pull together, and help each other. Our memories are charmed with the tales of barn raisings and corn shuckings and the sense of community spirit that these social events nurtured.

In our young country, as this sense of helping and volunteerism developed, imagine the prayers that were answered by the Underground Railroad, Red Cross, Salvation Army, and the United Way, just to touch on some of the more well known.

We need not be a Mother Teresa, a Father Damian, William Booth or Levi Coffin, we just need to keep, with them, the faith and the spirit that will allow us to reach out and help one another.

Most of us seem to have in our makeup a gene mutation that will not allow us to see and sense our own worth and value. We tend to fail to discover just how important we can be in helping out the rest of us. We will not allow ourselves to believe that we could have an impact on the life around us. We will not believe that we could be the answer to a prayer . . .

"Look at me," we say, "I am too old, too young, too short, too thin, too tall, too fat, can't write, can't sing, no money, who am I? What am I? I am chewing gum on the sole of humanity and how in God's name could I ever be of help? How could I ever be the answer to a prayer . . . ."

In a local doctor's office the other day I had a wonderful conversation with a very sweet, elderly lady. That morning her ride to the doctor's was detained and she was worried about not being able to keep her appointment. When she called in to say she couldn't make it, one of the office staff drove across town to pick her up. If this lady mentioned the kindness of this act once, she said it ten times in the few minutes we were together in the waiting room.

A special friend of mine asked at a local nursing home if there wasn't some patient who needed a friend or companion. She was assigned a completely bed-ridden resident with whom she visited several times a week. The love and light that they brought to each other was truly an answer to both their prayers . . .

We just celebrated All Saints Day at our church on Thursday. It is a day to recall and honor all of those who have labored to do

God's work here on earth through the ages. We are talking about some very ordinary, everyday type of folk. God has set them among us to be answers to our prayers . . .

Whenever I am awakened by the sound of a fire siren in the dead of the night, and hear the cars of the volunteer firemen rushing down the streets, I figure the least I can do is to say a prayer for their safety and protection.

Through friends, I know of the intense emotional drain that handling a suicide call at Contact "HELP" can be, and the feeling of elation when you know you have made a difference.

There are those who reach out and offer friendship and care to the terminally ill in the Hospice program. There are the saints who minister to others via hammers, saws, and nails in the Habitat for Humanity programs.

Salem County, I believe, has a population of about sixty thousand people. I bet you'd be hard pressed to find another area of sixty thousand people who have as many volunteers as this county.

The United Way of Salem County has six hundred volunteer workers who work on raising funds for United Way. United Way then helps to support the volunteer agencies such as Meals on Wheels, Boy Scouts, Girl Scouts, Women's Services, Big Brothers/Big Sisters, and on and on. There are literally thousands of volunteers here in the county.

The Memorial Hospital of Salem County has five hundred volunteers, Elmer Community Hospital has over a hundred. Think of how many fire companies there are in all the municipalities and each one is manned by volunteers. There are all the folks who show up to offer help and hugs in the Special Olympics.

Think of all the people who participate in the various "walks" to raise money for the fight against birth defects, hunger, and so many other things. School kids doing bike-a-thons, rock-a-thons; Tall Cedar Clowns fighting for crippled children with silly antics and lots of love.

There are all of those who are sort of freelance volunteers sans benefit of an organized group. They go about unnoticed and unrecognized quietly doing their own thing to make this world a bit sweeter and kinder for someone else.

They are looking after their neighbors; sending notes that congratulate or console, or just letting someone know that they are being thought of; they give music recitals at nursing homes; they help keep our libraries functioning; they give up their own holidays to create a holiday for those who have nowhere to go. They do this, or that, or some other loving and caring gesture, and I think they make God very happy.

Our world is filled with those who just need a kind word, a bit of encouragement at the right moment. A smile; a "Hi! How are ya!" can be a real gift to someone.

The other day at an office downtown, I was offered a cup of coffee and a warm, sweet smile. It made a lovely day all the lovelier. For those twenty minutes or so, I wouldn't have wanted to be anywhere else in this world.

The main thing about helping and reaching out to others boils down to one main fact: you don't have to do it, but you do. You had a choice and you made it. And with all my heart I know that we are all better off because of you. You who have given so unselfishly of your time and your caring for what happens to others.

John Denver sings this refrain in one of his songs:

> *My heart to yours,*
> *Your heart to mine,*
> *Love is the light that shines –*
> *From heart to heart.*

A nice set of words to help express the feelings we can experience when we reach out to others.

So, whether you man a fire hose, or a crisis-center phone line; whether you deliver lunches to shut-ins, or smiles and fruit juice to hospital patients; if you hammer nails for Habitat, or offer peace and solace to the terminally ill; whatever your service is to others, I believe that truly, you are an answer to someone's prayer . . .

• • •

Donald G. Smith, writes in the current issue of *The Reader's Digest:* "The professional criminal is a volunteer. All that society asks of him is that he stop doing what he is doing, and this doesn't seem to be an unreasonable request. It isn't a great exaggeration to say that every man, woman and child in the United States is capable of *not* stripping a car, *not* selling drugs, *not* vandalizing property and *not* robbing a store. No one is asking the lawbreaker to run a four-minute mile, to translate the Dead Sea Scrolls, or to play a fugue on the harpsichord. Obeying the law requires no talent and no training. Anyone can do it."

Today's Sunbeam, Salem, N.J., Sunday, November 17, 1991

Fascinating Alloway Store Recaptures a Bygone Era

It is the discovery and the experiencing of all the gems and treasures that are part and parcel of Salem County life, that makes it so much fun to live here.

The people, and their activities and traditions; the land, and its ever-changing beauty; these are all blessings for the soul and gifts to the spirit for each one of us to enjoy and cherish—available to us if we wish to make the effort.

An exciting case in point would be last Sunday morning. A good friend and I spent three hours at the pancake breakfast sponsored by the Salem Rotary Club. We had a great time just sitting around talking to everyone. My friend Jim is a past president of the Salem club and moved away from Salem about 12 years ago. Every year he returns to attend this breakfast and to renew old friendships.

Jim's annual arrival in town on the first weekend in November is akin to that grand tradition in nature of the clock-like return of swallows, lemmings, groundhogs, and spawning salmon. Jim is attracted back to Salem County by the fulfilling promise of friendship and Niblock's sausage. The invitation for dinner at Travaglini's the night before doesn't hurt either!

Where but at a Salem County food-fest could you have, along with your breakfast, a mini lecture about floating shad cabins by Salem's Jim Waddington; a gentle, poetic, and loving discourse on growing roses by Quinton's top horticulturist, Ben Rainear; and the pleasure of listening to sage advice and inspiring thoughts from Elsinboro's Bill Waddington. Hugs from at least five women added wondrously to my total enjoyment of the morning.

I offer the following for an "only-in-Salem County" type of experience: The day after the breakfast, a fellow caught up with me in the canned goods aisle of the Acme. He shared with me how he discovered, in an old family trunk, what he believes to be a rough draft of the surrender papers, signed by Generals Lee and Grant, ending the Civil War! What a marvelous and heady discussion to have take place between the wax beans and the creamed corn! For the time being, he opted for a bank safety-deposit box versus the offer of my studio as a safe place to leave his papers. Drats!

Later in the week, I spent all too brief, yet enchanting, moments with a special friend who gave to me some carefully chosen books from her own library. She wanted me to have them, not only for reference, but as inspiration for my writing. We spent part of a lovely autumn afternoon in her small, cozy kitchen discussing the beauty and gentleness of Emily Dickinson's poetry, which I had just recently started to read.

This visit was a lovely little piece of time that held special quality for me; and I shall tuck it away and remember and treasure it sweetly.

Good friends, and good books, and autumn afternoons just seem to be a perfect and loving combination.

I live two blocks from the Acme market in Salem. When, I drive there, I like, sometimes, to take the-long-way-around to get there. It was while on such a jaunt, the other afternoon, that I discovered an ideal place to while away a bit of time and be charmed and delighted all in the same motion.

My discovery was the Old Alloway Merchandise Store. It is located right on a corner of the main intersection in downtown Alloway.

What an exciting experience! I urge everyone in the county to visit this neat store just so you can rediscover the fun and fine art of browsing, which the modern mall had bludgeoned out of most of us.

A visit to this store is like a step back into time . . . it is a time warp of delightful proportions and charming dimensions.

The building has always been a general store since at least 1838 if not longer. Bob and Sandy Dorrell have owned and operated the store since 1984. Previous owners had been the Ewens, an old and familiar Alloway name.

Bob Dorrell is a member of the well-known Alloway family of craftsmen, antique restorers, cabinet makers, musicians, and artists. The Dorrells are to Alloway what the Wyeths are to Chadds Ford. By way of a personal comment, (it's my column!) I like the contributions of the Dorrells a lot better than the Wyeths.

The only personage at the store who refuses to talk with you is the female mannequin who sits outside on the porch and watches the world passing through Alloway. You will notice, they tell me, that her attire will change depending on the season. One of her duties is to inform folks, by her presence, or absence, whether the store is open or closed. The store is open, by the way, from 10 a.m. 'til 5:30 p.m. daily, and closed Sundays and Wednesdays.

Once inside you are faced with a difficult decision: Where do you look first! You are surrounded by a marvelous array of items. It is a bit like walking through your grandmother's attic only a lot more organized, but every bit as visually exciting and captivating.

Just about the time when the brass bell on the door has finished tinkling your presence, a friendly voice will arise from out of somewhere and bid you welcome. You will also be requested to browse around and enjoy yourself. Boy! What an easy request to abide by!

The store is part museum, part retail, and all fascination. Most of the store's items are high quality, modern reproductions of books, cards, curio items and just a wonderful potpourri of delightful gifts.

When I walked in, they were starting to set out their newly arrived Christmas inventory. I found myself surrounded by beautiful antique Santas, imported hand-blown glass tree ornaments, various wooden toys, feather trees, antique gift wraps and limited edition dolls. Only a visit to Santa's workshop could rival the yuletide flavor of this place!

The store's philosophy is against the modern "chrome, plastic, and glass" type of merchandise. The various items on display have an allure of uniqueness and one-of-a-kind type of quality.

The store physically has retained much, if not all, the character and ambiance of the general store it has been for the last 150 years.

The Dorrells maintain, in one part of the store, what they refer to as the "old-fashion candy counter," and it contains some wonderful sweet delights. I was treated to one of the licorice pipes that I mentioned in my column a few weeks ago.

While you are standing there, rather child-like, trying to make up your mind, your attention is drawn to the wooden cabinets and shelves behind the candy counter.

Here, is a fascinating collection of old boxes, tins, bottles, and crocks whose contents would have been commonplace to the households of long ago. Several of the containers are original to this particular store. Inventory lists that Bob Dorrell has from the 1800s show that this store once sold beaver hats, salt mackerel, and opium among other things.

A stairway, right in the middle of this delightful adventure, leads you upstairs to what had originally been the store's linen and dry goods department. The second floor is light and airy with a wonderfully homey quality to it. Draped over the stair railing and on a few antique chairs are reproductions of old-fashion coverlets, each with a lovely design motif.

One coverlet has a special design created by the Dorrells. It is referred to as the Salem County coverlet as it features, on its borders, a wide variety of old, well known homes and buildings from throughout the county. If I ever saw an heirloom just waiting to happen, this particular coverlet is it.

Another line of things with a local flavor are the pretty, gray stoneware crocks embellished with an individual town name from Salem County finished in a deep, blue glaze.

Part of the store's charm is created by a very engaging salesperson whose name is Anna. Anna gets as excited over a sales item as does the customer who is buying it! Her love for the store and the folks who shop there is infectious, and her spirit creates a real warmth and glow to the surroundings.

The Dorrells also get very caught-up in their customers and it is by their example that the store reflects an atmosphere of relaxed friendliness. People usually tend to run into someone they know while shopping there, and this can lead to all sorts of happy dealings and doings.

On many occasions, someone has come in who had grown up in Alloway, and has since moved away, but remembered the store from their youth. Anecdotes and stories are traded and a bit more is added to the collective history of this special old landmark.

The store has a comfortable, gentle, sienna-colored patina about its interior that is broken up, here and there, with little islands of afternoon light that stream through the windows.

Elsewhere, small lamps provide a soft, warm glow. Sunlight, lamplight, deep varnished wood, all merge and mingle to maintain a magical feel of a bygone era that you have stumbled across for a few brief moments.

The warmth and charm and hominess of this little piece of long ago makes it hard for one to enter the outside world again.

Once outside, I enjoy and love just standing here, for a moment or two, on the corner in the middle of Alloway. The marbled, autumn afternoon sky casts a soft, suffused light all around this lovely little town. The huge sycamore trees, over by the old Alloway Hotel, thrill me with their majestic beauty. My eyes trace the intricate patterns of a gorgeous wrought iron railing across the way.

How lucky we are to live in an area so bountiful with good things, good people, and great beauty; where only doors with tinkly, little brass bells separate us from one treasure to another.

In my column about small, neighborhood grocery stores, I forgot to say that Marie's Market, formerly Woldoff's, on West Broadway in Salem, is still going strong!!!

Sincere sympathy to my dear friend Barbara who informed this columnist that because Canton hasn't any sidewalks, that, as a child, she was unable to celebrate "Chalk Night" during Halloween.

Today's Sunbeam, Salem, N.J., Sunday, December 1, 1991

Christmas Here Is Rich, Rewarding

On the masthead of today's paper you may have noticed that the countdown of shopping days till Christmas has begun. Ho! Ho! Ho! Not a nice way to start out a column is it?

How sad it was for me to realize that childhood fantasy had become adulthood frenzy when Christmastide rolled around. How depressing to think that just because I am now grown-up (a debatable point among friends) age and responsibility seemed to ordain that I am not allowed to enjoy this most magical, mystical, and beautiful time of the year.

Always, starting about mid-July, I would begin to anticipate the arrival of Christmas. On a frosty-cold winter's morning I would awake and discover that it was now . . . JANUARY!!! Who stole Christmas!?! Where was it!?! Once more I had been hassled and hustled through the entire season. What an awful, sinking feeling this discovery leaves upon the spirit.

To spend the Christmas season in Salem County is a delightfully rich, rewarding experience. There is a stocking full of yuletide treats and treasures awaiting all who will just avail themselves of the opportunities.

This afternoon, at 3 p.m., in the Old Courthouse in Salem there will be the annual holiday choral concert, performed by the Salem City Singers, under the direction of Hazel Davis. In concert along with this talented group, is the Johannes Brass ensemble.

As the beautiful sound of the music swirls around you, allow your gaze to wander a bit and be visually enthralled as well. Notice the delightful contrast between the delicate tracery of a brass chandelier to the beauty and strength of an 18th century window, whose panes of glass are glazed with a wintry sunset's glow.

You may see a yuletide kaleidoscope of garlands, red ribbons, and Christmas tress reflected on the shiny brass surface of a beautiful French horn. Hear the sweet, angel-beauty of a soloist singing a favorite carol; how long-ago into your Christmas memories does she lead you.

What an endearing tradition of sights and sounds and setting; thanks to all the participants for their gift of Christmas beauty to our county.

What could ever weave the spell of Christmas more than strolling the streets of Woodstown, during the Woodstown by Candlelight tour. Every house aglow with tiny, crystal-like flecks of candlelight; a front porch becomes a concert stage for a brass ensemble; and the haunting quality of carolers heard sweetly singing in the distance.

Each home offers a myriad of little still-lifes to look at. The delicate, porcelain face of an antique doll sitting amid a tableau of pine boughs, lace trimmed velvet ribbons, and never once did her sweet smile falter the entire evening. Ground pine swags and oatmeal-colored hand dipped candles festoon an ornately carved oak mantle.

The charm and fun of the evening starts early if you choose to have a soup and sandwich supper at the Reliance fire house on Broad Street. Costumed hostesses and candlelight transforms the meeting hall into the coziness of a country inn. Their vegetable soup is a perfect start for a night of Christmas touring. The Woodstown by Candlelight tour is this Friday, Dec. 6, from 6 to 10 p.m.

After being inspired by everyone's decorations in Woodstown, you may be so inclined to rush home and start decorating your own place. Well, you can't start yet! First thing the next morning you have to be in Salem for the Magic of Christmas Parade.

Yep, it's official! The first place this side of the North Pole that Santa visits is Salem. He comes all this way just to make an appearance in our parade. What ghosts and goblins do for Alloway in October; elves, angels, and Christmas trees do for Salem in December. The atmosphere is charged with a feeling of magic and fantasy and all those special feelings created by children awaiting Santa's visit.

All the friendly, good folk that this column usually extols will be out that morning, so make sure you are there to add to everyone's enjoyment. See you on the morning of Dec. 7th! The parade starts at 10 a.m.

Right after the parade, the West Jersey Railroad is, once again, featuring their yearly "Santa Special" train rides. The train rides start at noon and 2 p.m. Santa shouting "all aboard" is a bit different than the usual "on Dasher, on Dancer . . ."

The following Saturday evening, Dec. 14th, is the 4th Annual Yuletide Tour on Market Street in Salem. There is an ambiance to the beauty of this centuries-old street that defies description. The atmosphere is as delicate and gossamer as an antique spun glass ornament. Last year, the tree branches and sidewalks were wet from an earlier rain, and the candlelight from the homes shimmered and sparkled and transformed the scene into a fairyland.

There is a rich, deep, serene kind of beauty to this tour that is most spellbinding. This special night, on this special street, the sense and romance of history abounds.

As Town Crier, I enjoy standing outside and peeking through the windows and doorways. You can see scenes that would have looked the very same way two hundred years ago.

One year, taking a rest from our tour duties, a group of us sat around the fire in the Swedish cabin at the foot of Market Street and sang Christmas carols. In this small little cabin the open fireplace is in the middle and all of us were in costume. Sitting there, softly singing "Silent Night," as you looked around you saw only costumed figures illumined by firelight's glow. This scene, if seen through the heart, afforded a beauty and timelessness that brought tears to your eyes. What a special Christmas memory those few moments shall always be for me.

New to the holiday scene this year will be several performances of Dickens' "A Christmas Carol" in the new arts building at Salem Community College. What would the holidays be without the wonderful story of Scrooge and Tiny Tim! What a nice way to inaugurate and show-off the college's new facility.

A few years ago, another popular seasonal tradition was started by the various Salem churches. It is called "Walk A Christmas Mile." This year it starts at 5:30 p.m. on Dec. 29th. In the past the only people who ever got to enjoy a church's Christmas decorations were its own members. Now by taking the tour everyone gets to "oooh and aaah" over the beauty of each church. At each stop a piece of Scripture is read and an appropriate carol is sung. The walk provides a wonderful spirit of fellowship and comradery to the various congregations. Hope to see you there!

There are so many other wonderful things that can help us catch the spirit. I especially love all the church Christmas bazaars with their soup and sandwich lunches. What a happy break in the middle of my day!

What a special feeling it is to be out walking in Salem when the bell carillon of the Presbyterian church is playing Christmas carols. Your eye is drawn towards the loveliness of the church's stately white steeple, so striking against a wintertime sky. The purity of the bells and the power of that steeple can preach a wonderful "silent sermon" to all who will listen . . .

I find that a visit to Costello's Christmas store in Deepwater is a really fun way to soak up a bit of atmosphere and to add an ornament or two to our collection.

On December nights I love to watch the stars from a favorite spot amid the fields of Elsinboro. Someday, I like to think, God is going to show me the Christmas Star for just a fleeting moment; or perhaps I will hear a sound and as I turn, I will see, just for an instant, a shepherd making his way across the fields . . .

Perhaps, I am like Linus sitting in the pumpkin patch looking for the Great Pumpkin . . . it's all a matter of believing.

Christmas is the sweetest time of the entire year. It comes down to us from a setting of peace, serenity, reverence and love. We seemingly have turned it against ourselves by creating a hectic, frantic, fast-paced circus. How sad to hear someone say, "Gads, I'll be so glad when it's over and done with!"

As long as memory and spirit allow, I will always be able to rekindle the magic and beauty that I felt, as a child, at Christmas. I refuse to subject and limit my adult memories only to shopping mall decorations and TV specials featuring Madonna and Michael Jackson "rapping" and writhing to "Frosty the Snowman."

A lot of planning, hard work, and love have gone into the various activities of this holiday season. Think of them as a little present just for yourself, a bit of a treat because you were so very good this year.

Each and every one is a perfect fit; it's just the right color: and the style is so "you!" The joy and the memories that they bring never, ever wears out, and therein lies their beauty.

Today's Sunbeam, Salem, N.J., Sunday, December 15, 1991

Sweet Holiday Memories: Church on Christmas Eve

As gently and as quietly as a late afternoon snowfall . . . that is the way Christmas memories retrace themselves on my heart and soul.

For me, there is no other time in the course of the year when the eye of the artist and the soul of the poet work in such delicious and delirious harmony as in those magical days leading us to Christmas.

Christmas memories seemingly come in various shapes, sizes, and colors, just like many other things in life. We have those memories that thrill our souls and raise our spirits to delightful heights of joy and happiness; and we have those that can so wistfully bring tears to our eyes and an ache to the heart. We need both the sweet and the bittersweet to help us appreciate each and every one for the special memory that it has become.

Oft times, if we are lucky, we may have a special place where we can go to be in touch with the dearest and best of our memories. It is in such a place that we can unlock that treasure trove within us and admire and take stock of our collection.

When I need and wish to revive some of the sweetest, most moving moments that Christmas has ever been for me . . . I know where I must be. For as long as I can remember Christmas, I can remember going to church on Christmas Eve. For as long as I can remember, our beautiful candlelit church at midnight was, for me, the very essence of all that was the embodiment of Christmas.

It was all the beauty, the glory, the magic, the pageantry and the poetry of a most wondrous night. It has never changed for me in all of these years. I will go to church on Christmas Eve this year filled with the very same sense of expectation and anticipation that I carried with me when I was just a young boy.

This was the magic hour, I knew it then, and I still sense it now. This just had to be the time when the Christ Child was born, it just *had* to be. To my young mind, the world was never this beautiful, never this holy, never at any other time but now, here, at this very moment. How could we kneel surrounded by all of this candlelight, softly singing lovely carols, and not believe that this miracle wasn't going on right now in a faraway land . . . in a town called Bethlehem.

The love and anticipation of this beautiful service only grew stronger with each passing year. When I think of the traditions and scenes of families gathering for Christmas, it is here, at St. John's, that I most lovingly remember all of my family being together.

In the years that were to be when our family could no longer be together, it was here, in our pew, that I found I could once again, feel their presence. At any time this is possible, but it is most especially on Christmas Eve, when I am once more with those who are long gone but much loved.

At home on Christmas Eve, as a young boy, in the hours before going off to church, I would find myself quite alone as other family members were secreted away doing last minute wrappings or preparing for church. This quiet time, by myself, became for me a very special part of Christmas.

My mother would transform our simple, half a double house into what appeared for me to be every bit as beautiful as a scene from a Christmas card. So what if we had a cardboard fireplace with plug-in firelight, cover it with enough greens and stockings and candles and what more could you ask for? There would be carols playing on the radio, the tree would be lit, and red candles were aglow everywhere. It was here that I learned to do my best and purest Christmas dreaming; here amid the beauty, the peace, and the sweetness of home.

My reverie of Christmas fantasies would end as the evening picked up in tempo. As my folks and kid brother would arrive via the stairs, my big brother, home on leave, and his wife would dash in the back door and one, two, six, before you knew what was going on, we'd all be piling into Dad's car for the ride to church.

As we all jostled and jockeyed around in the car, trying to get comfortable, my mind told my heart, that this was a most special moment and needed to be remembered for always.

How I can still feel the softness of Dad's wool top coat as it brushed against my hand, and how elegant this everyday tire salesman looked in his pearl-gray homburg hat. My mother's laughter and joy at just being together as a family, and the fragrance of her perfume will always be with me. And there was my big brother the soldier. Second only to the Christ Child, this night, in my terms of love and adoration. How heroic he looked in his uniform with shiny, black paratrooper boots and a green beret.

A short ride later, as we walked up the front walk toward the church, I would gaze about at the churchyard and feel great sympathy for all those buried there who would not be able to celebrate Christmas! What a tragedy this was to my young mind.

Climbing the solid, strong granite steps you would begin to catch small glimpses of the flickering candlelight from within. It was as if you were being teased by the beauty that you knew was soon to be. You knew what was coming, you remembered so well from last year, but, you soon learned that always, always, it was as if you were seeing it for the very first time.

The elegance and solemnity of candlelight was everywhere. At the end of every pew was a wrought iron candelabra holding tiers of candles. Wall sconces were trimmed in pine and holly and red silk bows. Burning tapers surrounded by masses of red and white poinsettias transformed our usually simple, wooden altar into a scene of majestic beauty. How could it be possible for one's senses to absorb this much beauty?

And it only grew lovelier and more dramatic as the night evolved. There were deep, rich, rounded tones of a pipe organ, and soprano solos of "O Holy Night" and "What Child Is This." Father Schultz would be wearing beautifully embroidered vestments whose golden threads caught the candles glow, and white robed altar boys in procession preparing for the Christmas Gospel to be read. And the wonderfully mysterious fragrance of Communion wine as it wafted throughout the church.

The ultimate moment of Christmas came as we knelt and sang "O Little Town of Bethlehem." We would sing " . . . how silently, how silently, the wondrous gift is given" and at these words I would always start to cry, my soldier-hero-brother would elbow me sharply and my mother would hug me to her fur coat and cry too! Yes, I learned my sensitivity at the knee of the master!

Christmas Eve at St. John's is the sweetest and best of all my Christmas memories and traditions. On this night, in this church, be I the little boy or the grown man, I sense with all my soul, that I have borne witness to all that is sacred, holy, and miraculous about a lowly birth in a stable in Bethlehem.

What better Christmas memory could I ever want?

To all of you who read this column so faithfully and have been so kind in showing your support, it is with a full heart that I wish for you all that which is good, and sweet, and pure this Christmas season. God bless you all.

Any words or images of Christmas that I may ever put on paper, I lovingly dedicate to the memory of my mother and my sweet friend Becky, both of whom were, and are, truly Christmas angels.

To all the folks of Salem's Magic of Christmas Parade Committee: to be picked as parade marshal was a wonderful honor and will always be a delightful and "magical" Christmas memory. Thank you so much!!

Today's Sunbeam, Salem, N.J., Sunday, December 29, 1991

True Meaning of Christmas Is Found in Salem County

What a wonderful, fairy tale time I have had this Christmas. My mind holds a montage of memories from the past few weeks that are, in themselves, the most wonderful gifts that anyone could ever want for Christmas. A lot of my Christmas memories were brought about by many of you and I am so appreciative and grateful for having you in my life.

In trying to balance a heavy work load with my desire to celebrate the season, I have been in my studio almost everyday well before dawn. While growing a bit tedious, it has made for some very special memories.

Have you seen any of the December sunrises? If red and green are the colors that herald the pageantry and traditions of Christmas, then it must be the sunrise colors of blue-violet and orange that are the heralding hues of nature. In the early, half-light of these December dawns the morning skies take on the depth and richness of stained glass. An hour or so later, the mists rising off frosty Elsinboro fields create a landscape as delicate and ethereal as a Chinese watercolor.

Those wonderful beginnings to another day of Christmastide evoked feelings of sweet carols and silent prayers for the true meaning of this season.

As the yuletide season unfolded, any celebrations or festivities were always tempered and mellowed, in special ways, because my days had started amid this sunrise revelry.

Any time I participate in the Woodstown by Candlelight Tour I can count on falling in love once again with many old, familiar friends, and as always there are a couple new ones. The comfortable, familiar ones are the Biernbaums, the Johnsons, "Fattie" and Marge Flitcraft; the new ones are an enchanting jewelry maker/pseudo fortune teller named Rae, and a lovely woman named Barbara who faithfully reads my column and then writes me letters "here," as she pats her heart.

Jim Tyson, shuttle bus "conductor," spent the entire evening extolling the virtues of practically every inch of Salem County and everyone in it to all the visitors on his bus. A young policeman over by the Friend's Meeting House shared with me his feelings on how much he likes living in Salem County, and how fortunate he thinks we are to live in such an open and rural area.

The morning after the Woodstown tour I had the honor of being the parade marshal for Salem's Magic of Christmas Parade! My family and I found it great fun riding down the parade route waving to everyone from an open convertible. I decided it would be fun to be a politician. I don't want to hold office, or even win, I just want to go campaigning!

The newly formed Friends of the Library held a book signing party the following Saturday. Orders had been taken for two of my latest books and I was there to autograph them. Well, it was like a stand-up viewing! It was a wonderful experience. All kinds of folks turn out to see you and say nice things about you. You get to hear it all and can even make appropriate responses. Best of all you get to go home when it's over!

At the signing I met a wonderfully sweet lady name Doris from Elmer. She came to buy books and to bring me a present. It was a little Christmas stocking tree ornament that she had made for me. It is just big enough to hold two chocolate kisses and a tiny candy cane. Along with it came a hug, a real kiss, and some kind and loving words for me and my column.

If Christmas had ended just then, with this heart-sent little gift, it would have been a lovely Christmas, but there were still about ten days to go.

The day of the book signing was also the day of the Market Street Yuletide Tour. It had been raining all day and I was worried about the night's event.

In mid-afternoon on my way to the dump, as if in answer to my prayer, the sun gushed out in a wondrously dramatic fashion. The entire landscape around Grieves Parkway started to brighten and glow. Huge, gray, billowy clouds parted to reveal gold tinged layers of lavender clouds that created at least eight or ten Hollywood-like sun beams. The shafts of light fell exactly on the Salem Convenience Center (dump) and it glowed as golden as the Seven Hills of Rome! Seeking some spiritual message, I decided it was God's way of saying He is all for recycling.

The rain ceased, a bit of wind kicked up, and the charm and beauty of candlelit Market Street enchanted hundreds of visitors that evening.

The following Saturday night I attended a performance of "Scrooge" at the Salem Community College's newly opened Davidow Theater. What a wonderful job the cast did in bringing Dickens' 19th century London to Salem County. Tom Mason was outstanding as Ebenezer Scrooge. The play began and ended with cast members singing Christmas carols and it created a nice mood for the opening and the finale.

A special friend, Kathleen O'Neil, played the Ghost of Christmas Present. Her costume was a visual delight. A metallic gold gown trimmed in flashy red tree garlands, red velvet bows and an assortment of plastic holly and mistletoe made a wonderful crown atop her red hair! This ghost has always been my favorite, and to see someone I know play the part was a real treat!

In cold, miserable February, the remembrance of Tom, Kathy, and the others will make me laugh, grow warm, and I'll be as happy then as I was the other night. Thanks.

Speaking of warm and happy feelings . . . about the friendliest Christmas spirit this side of old St. Nicholas is that of Mary Hogate. Mary, I just discovered, is the "customer greeter" at the Kmart store in Pennsville. She has a delightful smile and laughter in her voice, and it was a real treat to see her.

Another very special "Mary" is Mary Sampson who is the unofficial greeter at McCoubrie's Pharmacy in Salem. Mary had the most wonderful laugh you'd ever want to hear, and she couples it with love and a tender sensitivity to and for other people.

These ladies are but only two examples of all the "earthly angels" so abundant here in our county this Christmastide. Have hope, and keep the faith . . . Salem County abounds with those folks who are so expressive of the love and care for others that Christmas would ask of all of us.

In this very same spirit of love and care, I was invited to a wonderful luncheon and open-house at the United Way office. It allowed me to dress in my most resplendent red and green "Christmas partying" attire! Becky Purchase and Sue Dilks can turn any gathering into a very personal, heart warming affair and I appreciate that they think of me as "staff."

. . . And of parties! John Jones, the owner of Associated Printers on Hook Road, a rather rascally, curmudgeoned old Christmas spirit, like Ebenezer Scrooge before him, really knows how to "keep Christmas well."

Christmas Eve at St. John's (sound familiar?), was 10 times lovelier than my last column predicted. That evening at church I spoke for a while with Cyril Gibson . . . Peace on Earth needs to start within our own hearts, Cyril has a headstart on a lot of us.

Christmas at home was its own wonderful memory of fireplace and candlelight; and a simple dinner for three taken amid the suffusing glow of a late afternoon Christmas Day sunset. We are surrounded by green garlands and red velvet ribbons hung in graceful swags against white lacy curtains; our tree is decorated to look like a Thomas Nast illustration, and all around are the special momentos of Christmas collected over the years. Best of all—we are together.

Due to the harried and hurried nature of today's column, I know I've forgotten things that I had wished to share . . .

Yes! Do you know that in Woodstown on Christmas Eve Day Santa Claus stands on the traffic island in the middle of town waving and shouting greetings to motorists and other passers-by!! In my phone interview with Santa, he indicated that he has been doing it for several years. We both agreed that to give up on the magic and belief of Santa Claus is to lose out on the magic and fantasy of life. Hey! Is this guy my new found hero for the '90s or what?

On the Market Street tour I met up with two special friends, Sharon and Janet. We stood outside talking in the sparkling, candlelit glow from one of the homes. We talked of many things in those chilly few moments, but our thoughts kept returning to our belief and feelings in and for each other. It was with loving spontaneity that we sealed our pact with a group hug and kisses all around.

Fantastical, marvelous visions of a traffic island Santa Claus; and the sweetness, purity, and joy of friendship renewed on a wintry night on Market Street may be the very essence of all the magic, beauty, and happitness that color my memories of this Christmas season.

I wish you peace, joy, and fantasy in the coming year. God bless each one of you.

Love,
Ron LeHew

A
Gallery
of
Ron LeHew's
Illustrations

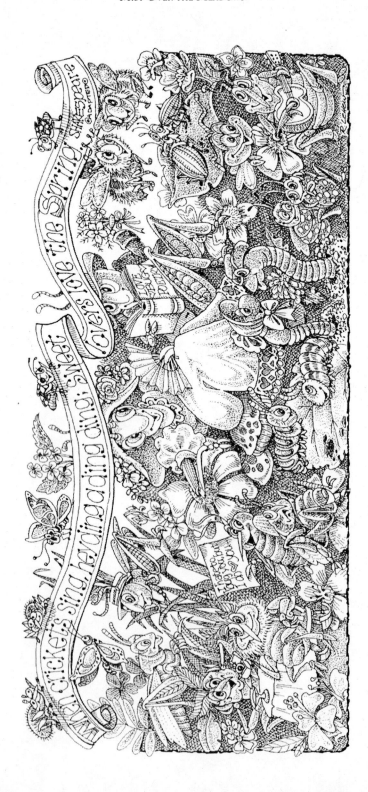

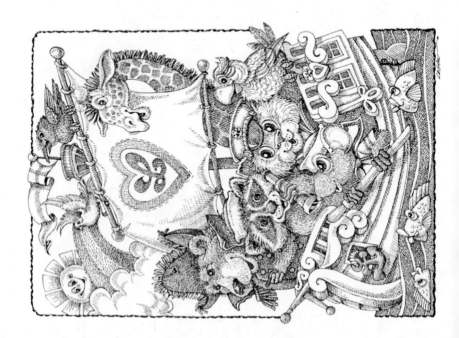